Empty Pocket Blues
The life and music
of Clive Palmer

Grahame Hood

'I wrote this song forty years ago. Nothing's changed.'
Clive, introducing Empty Pocket Blues in 2003

To Frank,

best wishes,

Grahame Hood

27/8/10

Empty Pocket Blues
First edition (UK) published in 2008 by Adrian Whittaker
    in association with Helter Skelter Publishing
Copyright © 2008 Grahame Hood
Cover design, Cornwall map, banjos and chapter title pages:
    Mychael Gerstenberger (www.malbuch-berlin.de)
Front cover photo © Shirley Palmer
Back cover painting by Elaine Warwick Simpson (www.ewsart.co.uk)
Typesetting and interior design: Caroline Walker
Editor: Adrian Whittaker
Printed by The Cromwell Press

A CIP record for this book is available from the British Library.

ISBN 978-1-905139-25-5

Contents

Foreword

*C*live is unquestionably the best banjo player I ever heard. He could frail as well as play bluegrass, and I loved his lifestyle and his exotic hippiness. He was, and still is, my banjo hero.

In the early Sixties Hamish Imlach told me about Clive, who had been wandering about the Edinburgh scene for a while and was the most amazing Edwardian Music Hall banjo player. I first saw him performing in a Paisley folk club with Robin Williamson. I couldn't believe how good they were.

One of the highlights of my life was teaching Clive a tune when we were performing at a folk club in Sheffield; it was an old frailing piece called The Old Man at the Mill and you can only imagine how it felt for me to play with him. He is truly a wonderful player.

Billy Connolly, January 2007

Introduction

*W*hen I began writing about Clive, nearly twenty years ago, not a lot was known about him. He was recognised as a fine musician and was known to have written a handful of quality songs. He had a reputation for leaving bands just before they became well-known, almost as if he was afraid of the success his talent would inevitably bring him. He had spent much of his career living in Cornwall, rarely playing outside of the county. Apart from the first Incredible String Band album, his record sales can rarely have reached more than four figures an album. If he was American he'd have been a veritable cult hero.

Born in 1943 in North London, Clive contracted polio as a baby, the legacy of which was a pronounced limp. At the age of ten he acquired a banjo and spent the next few years mastering the already near-obsolete Edwardian classical banjo style. As he grew older he also began to play skiffle and later mastered jazz and folk styles too. By his early teens he was regularly seen playing in the folkier coffee bars in London along with people like Wizz Jones, Long John Baldry, Davy Graham and even Rod Stewart and Ian Dury. After two years at Art College, he travelled to Paris and made a living as a busker, this period strengthening both his playing and singing. He was eventually asked to leave France by the Sécurité for visa irregularities.

In late 1962 he travelled up to Edinburgh. What had been intended to be a few weeks in Scotland turned into a few years, Clive fitting easily into the Edinburgh beatnik scene, at one point famously living in a tent erected inside a squat (a perfectly sensible idea, Edinburgh gets very cold in the winter). He made a name for himself on the thriving Scottish folk scene of the day, which was full of characters like the larger-than-life Hamish Imlach, Robin Williamson and Bert Jansch, and stars-to-be John Martyn and Billy Connolly. He joined up with Robin Williamson to form a fondly-remembered duo, Robin & Clive, adding guitarist Mike Heron, a renegade from the city's beat group scene, in late 1965 to form The Incredible String Band. 1966 was a very memorable year for Clive. He helped open the legendary (and surprisingly short-lived) all-night Clive's Incredible Folk Club in Glasgow, recorded the first Incredible String Band album and hitchhiked overland to Afghanistan, having many adventures on the way. He returned to Glasgow in time to spend the New Year in prison, being the first man in Scottish legal history to be charged with possession of LSD, made illegal only a few months before.

Back in London he formed a duo with Wizz Jones and recorded an LP of banjo music judged so uncommercial that it took forty years to be released. Eventually he moved down to Cornwall and formed The Famous Jug Band, recording a fine album before being asked to leave due to personality clashes. He then started The Stockroom Five to play the old-time music he loved so much, which the following year became The Temple Creatures, an intriguing acoustic band playing mainly original music with a host of exotic influences which perfectly suited the times.

This group evolved into Clive's Original Band (COB), whose two albums are now revered by a new generation of fans of acoustic music, both in the UK and the US. Despite the quality of the band's music and many gigs around the UK, including a long tour supporting Pentangle, they ultimately failed to break through. They split up in 1973, and Clive ceased to regard himself as a professional musician at that point. He spent a year studying instrument building and repair, getting particularly interested in the Northumbrian small-pipes, got married and moved down to Cornwall in 1975. Though he never stopped making music, playing in duos and bands and releasing an album and several cassettes, he hardly ever played outside Cornwall. In 1990 he moved to France with his new partner Gina.

By the end of the Nineties, CD re-issues and a fanzine had reawakened interest in The Incredible String Band and its offshoots and Clive recorded and toured with Robin Williamson in 1999. The next step was the reformation of The Incredible String Band itself, who, though latterly without Robin, continued to tour and issue recordings until 2006.

Clive returned to live in Cornwall in 2006 and continues to play low-key gigs there. He has never sought success (though there have been times he has come close to getting it), despises the falsity of show business, and has many interests besides music.

A few years ago I was privileged to see Clive play in a small London club, to an audience who, in the main, had absolutely no idea who he was. With just his banjo, he charmed everyone in the room for an hour. He is an immensely talented man, and I hope this book does him justice.

This book is largely based on recent original research conducted by the author. Thanks to all those I spoke to or corresponded with for this purpose:

Dave Arthur, the late 'Henry' Bartlett, Jenny Bartlett, Mick Bennett, Pete Berryman, John Bidwell, Steve Bonnett, Gavin & Ronnie Browne, Nick Burdett, Billy Connolly, Stephen Delft, Bob Devereux, Peter Eden, Ian Ferguson, Mike Heron, Bert Jansch, Sandy Jones, Wizz Jones, Bruce May, Gillie McPherson, Chris Newman, Sean O'Rourke, Clive Palmer, Shirley Palmer, Chrissy Quayle, Nick Saloman, Andy Scappaticcio, Ronnie Simpson, Pierre Tubbs, Demelza Val Baker, Genevieve Val Baker, Martin Val Baker, Jake Walton, Tim Wellard, Robin Williamson.

CHAPTER 1

Half-a-crown each lesson

1
Half-a-crown each lesson

'We only played one chord.
All the Lonnie Donegan stuff.'

Clive Harold Palmer was born in the North Middlesex Hospital on the 14th of May, 1943. The Second World War was in its fourth year and the tide was slowly starting to turn for the Allies. On the previous day it was announced that large numbers of German and Italian troops had surrendered in Tunisia, and the coming weekend would see the celebrated Dambuster bombing raids on the Ruhr take place. Clive was named after Clive of India, with his middle name taken from Field Marshall Harold Alexander. Alexander had led the British Expeditionary Force and been the last British soldier to leave the beaches at Dunkirk. Later he had fought Rommel alongside Montgomery in North Africa, and had recently been made deputy to President Eisenhower.

Clive was the fourth child of William and Violet Palmer (always known as Bill and Vi), joining their previous children, Michael, Frank, and Jean.

Before the war Bill had been a mechanic in the City of London for the firm of Bulmer's, which involved his visiting offices to repair and service typewriters and comptometers (mechanical adding machines) as required. As this skill was vital during wartime and also translated to servicing encoding equipment, he was excused military service and placed in a reserved occupation. In addition he voluntarily served as an air-raid warden.

The family lived in a 1930s-style semi-detached house in Elstree Gardens, Edmonton, London N9. One of Clive's earliest memories is of being hurriedly taken down into the Anderson shelter in the back garden during an air raid, though he can only have been a baby at the time. Fortunately there was never any serious bomb damage near the Palmer home.

At the age of around six months, Clive contracted polio. As he grew older he had to wear a leg calliper, the first of which his father made for him, and he had lots of regular appointments for sessions of physiotherapy. Another early memory is of being collected in a huge green Army ambulance with large red crosses on white squares painted on the sides to be taken to the North Middlesex Hospital for treatment.

From the age of about seven up to his mid teens he attended regular therapy sessions at Roehampton Hospital, in Barnes in South West London, to try to strengthen his leg. The hospital was well known as the major one in England for the fitting of artificial limbs, with Douglas Bader being one of their most famous patients. Clive used to have to travel there on a Green Line bus with his father. The sessions included a lot of swimming, which also built up his arms and shoulders. He was helped a lot by a therapist who had been a PT instructor in the Army, and who used to set him goals and reward him with Army badges and souvenirs (highly desirable to boys of the time) when he achieved them. Clive was always grateful for his help and attention.

When Clive went to school he could be naughty at times as lots of young boys are, but he always got caught. At one point he had a three-wheeler trike, because of his leg, so if anyone threw a stone or a football or did something like that, he was the one the victim always remembered. It was that boy with the tricycle! He was the only boy in the school who had one.

For a short while he went to a school for children with physical disabilities, but he was a boisterous child and did not regard his disability as a major problem. Clive's mother thought he had some potential as a singer and, when he was around seven or eight, arranged for him to have singing lessons with a lady who played piano. 'My mother pushed me quite hard. She was the instigator of it all, really. She was involved in amateur dramatics, and all that sort of thing.' He sang, as he put it, 'popular songs of the day.' This led to his being asked to do vocal spots between the dance acts with a local tap dancing outfit called The Foster-Miller Dance Troupe, who took part in church hall concerts and the like. He even got the occasional solo booking, singing material like Jerusalem.

There was a tradition of music in his family; his father's grandfather had come from Austria to live in England and play violin in an orchestra that often played at Covent Garden. Clive's mother, brothers and sister were also involved in local musical events, which usually took place at social evenings in church halls. Before most people had television, these events were always packed, and an important part of local community life. Clive regrets their passing to this day. Things did not always go to plan, though. One opening number was a jaunty naval routine called The Fleet's In Port Again which involved some girls (including Clive's sister Jean) in sailor suits doing a deck-swabbing dance with brooms. However, the caretaker had neglected to sweep the stage beforehand and the girls raised huge clouds of dust, which engulfed the first few rows of the audience.

Clive: 'When I was about nine or ten my brother gave me a guitar that he had picked up. My grandfather had been a French-polisher by trade and he taught my brother quite a lot. My brother eventually did an apprenticeship and became a sign-writer. Anyway, he'd French-polished this guitar and it was all very nice. A friend of mine had an old five-string banjo, what they call a Cammeyer banjo. It's different to the American style of banjo; it's covered in wood, and it hasn't got an open back. It had a lovely smell, in this old case; it was just a superb-looking thing.' Schoolboys in those days got very little pocket money, and what they did get was spent on sweets and comics. Barter was king, and Clive simply swapped his guitar for the banjo.

Clive's new pride and joy had been made by a company founded by Alfred D. Cammeyer, who had been born in Brooklyn in 1862 and moved to England in 1888, where he lived until his death in 1949. Cammeyer had invented what he called the zither banjo, featuring a smaller skin than normal (8–9 inches in diameter as opposed to 11–12 inches), which was held taut in a rim screwed onto the top edge of a deep closed resonator. Another odd feature of the Cammeyer design was that it had six tuner heads, even though it only had five strings. Instead of a peg halfway along the neck to tune the fifth string, it had the string disappearing into a tube buried in the neck and emerging at the tuners.

Cammeyer was also a prolific composer of music for the banjo, his compositions being regarded as generally more refined than some of the imitation minstrel-style tunes which were so popular at the time. His compositions also always featured well-thought-out piano accompaniments. His banjos were designed to be used with steel first, second and fifth strings, and gut third and fourths. He personally taught King Edward VII to play banjo, and there was quite a craze for the instrument during the late Victorian and early Edwardian period. It travelled throughout the empire, too: Kipling was moved to call the banjo 'the war-drum of the White Man round the world.' Oddly enough, just before the First World War, it was nearly usurped by a brief fad for Russian-style balalaika orchestras.

Clive bought *First Steps*, the standard banjo tutor book of the time (which, though a delightful anachronism, is still in print), but wasn't getting very far with it. He found out that the library had a list of all the local clubs, and through that he went along to a meeting of the local Banjo, Mandolin and Guitar club. The BMG held weekly meetings and its members gathered together to play arrangements of the popular songs of earlier days. The club had been at its height in the 1920s and 30s and was starting to fade in popularity by the early 1950s. Many of the members were by then in their fifties or sixties, and were genuinely pleased to have some enthusiastic new blood.

Clive: 'They knew this chap Alfred Lloyd, who had actually been a teacher at my brother's school and had taught him. He later went into teaching autistic and mentally retarded children, using music as a medium. He was recognised as being probably one of the greatest players of that style. He worked with Joe Morley, who was one of the most famous banjo players of that style ever [Morley was also the composer of over 200 pieces for banjo, including Banjoland, recorded by Clive in 1967]. He really was brilliant, it's a real tragedy there are no tapes of him playing, he was marvellous. He didn't normally take pupils, he only took people he wanted to take. I got an introduction to him and he said, "OK, it's half-a-crown* a lesson." I was there for three years.' (*See Appendix for pre-decimal currency equivalents)

Clive learned what is sometimes called classical-style banjo. In this style the banjo was played without thumb picks or finger picks, which were commonly used in folk styles, and exclusively in GCGBD tuning. It was all played from sheet music, which specified exactly which finger of either hand was used to play each note. He learned how to read music and practised a lot. Though he was naturally left-handed, he learned to play right-handed. In later years he recalled the pleasure he used to get from going to John Alvey Turner's music shop in New Oxford Street to buy new titles and rummage in musty drawers full of music that hardly anyone was interested in any more. Some of the sheet music John Alvey Turner published mentioned a monthly magazine they put out called *Keynotes*, inviting readers to send for a sample copy. Clive did just that, only to receive a polite letter in reply saying they hadn't published it for fifty years!

He eventually went to an ordinary secondary school, though he admits 'nobody did any work – we just mucked about all the time.' He injured himself badly when he fell down a flight of stairs at school, dislocating his kneecap. Later he fell down the stairs again and broke his right hand index finger. He eventually had to have four operations to fix it, during which his knuckle was removed. He still can't bend the finger fully. His therapist at the time was a delightful lady called Mrs Marcus, who was Jewish and had been smuggled out of Germany by her parents before the war. She really got him interested in crafts such as basket weaving.

Clive, outside his house in October 1956. Courtesy Jean Howe.

Clive later started a skiffle group (he doesn't think they had a name), with himself on banjo and two guitarists. 'We only played one chord. All the Lonnie Donegan stuff. We had never heard of Leadbelly or anyone like that. People liked us though; we were a bit of a novelty.' For all Clive's modesty, they were good enough to do reasonably well in Junior Discoveries, a talent show at the Finsbury Park Empire run by Carroll Levis.

Levis was a Canadian radio broadcaster whose various talent shows on radio and TV and in theatres were hugely popular in the late Fifties. Billing himself as Mr. Star-Maker (later Mr. TeLEVISion), he claimed to have discovered Benny Hill and Max Bygraves among many others, and many stars of the future appeared on his shows before they came famous. The Beatles-to-be appeared as The Quarrymen, though later, as Johnny & The Moondogs, they failed their audition. On his talent shows five or six acts would perform, the winner being judged by a clapometer, which supposedly measured the volume of audience applause. (This idea was later used by another Canadian, Hughie Green, in his Opportunity Knocks TV show.) The clapometer always assured full theatres, as every act would make sure as many friends and relations as possible were in the audience to clap for them.

In 1956, at the age of 49, Clive's mother died. She had always been asthmatic, and a massive attack proved fatal.

2
A totally different world

'An army of British beatniks has swarmed across the
Channel with guitars, banjos and gravelly voices.'

s well as music, Clive was always interested in art, and
had been attending classes on Saturday mornings at
the nearby Hornsey Art College since his early teens.
He was allowed to leave school at fifteen, common in
those days, though he admits that 'I was on my way to becoming a
black sheep and they really didn't know what to do with me.'

As the teachers at Hornsey were aware of his artistic abilities it was
agreed he could start there in the autumn of 1958, and he began a
three-year Fine Arts course. On top of this he took lessons in
illumination, lettering and silversmithing. 'Going to Art College,
straight from school, turned out to be crucial. If I'd just got a job at
the Gas Board or something it would have been a completely
different lifestyle. At Hornsey I was going to parties, it was a totally
different world.' As soon as he went to college he threw away his
calliper, and never wore one again..

As Clive was starting at Hornsey, his father was preparing to
remarry. Clive's future stepmother already had a home of her own
and Bill intended to move there. Her name was Hilda Byford, and she
had run a grocer's shop with her late husband. Clive remembers she
always had an apron full of small change for the customers, and when
he came into the shop she would always give him a handful. She had
a house near Oakwood in North London, out on the Piccadilly line
near Cockfosters. Bill intended to sell the Edmonton house and move
in with her. Clive was asked if he wanted to move with his father,
Frank and Jean, Michael having already left home, or live in digs
nearer the college. He chose the latter, and moved in with a lady from
Glasgow who often took in students as lodgers. She was rather
domineering with her own children, none of whom had managed to
leave home, even though they were all in their thirties by then. She
used to play the piano on Sundays and her family had to listen while
she played and sang. Her husband had written many poems in praise
of her (very much in the style of Robert Burns) of which she was

CHAPTER 2

A totally DIFFERENT WORLD

rather proud. Clive heard them so often he can still recite one of them by heart. She had a budgie, and she used to call out to it, 'Gie's a tune, Tony!' Clive quickly began to feel a little uncomfortable there, and when the chance of a flat-share with another student came up, he jumped at it.

From about the age of fourteen Clive had regularly cycled down to London at the weekend and one particular haunt was a basement jazz club called The Nucleus near Covent Garden. It had an excellent juke box and at night featured live music from a band led by pianist Tony Wainwright. Clive regularly used to sit in with them playing rhythm chords on banjo. He was also often seen playing in the folkier coffee houses such as the Gyre & Gimble (known as The Gs) in Villiers Street, off The Strand. The Gs was where people like Wizz Jones, Davy Graham, John Baldry, Rod Stewart and even Ian Dury (who was playing washboard in skiffle bands in Soho at the age of fourteen) regularly hung out. 'It was opposite the arches underneath Charing Cross station where all the old tramps used to sleep, the ones Flanagan and Allen sang about in Underneath The Arches.' Wizz: 'Clive used to sit in the corner of the coffee bar playing his banjo. He was very kind of... inscrutable; he always looked worldly-wise for his age. Like Davy, he maintained an aura of mysterious aloofness. But in fact, beneath it all, once you got to know him, he was quite ordinary. I think he was a bit shy, but he managed to put on a knowing front all the time – he was a man of mystery.'

One player who helped Clive a lot in the early days was Greg Potter, who played the four-string tenor banjo in the jazz style. He had taught Eddie Morris, who replaced Lonnie Donegan in the Chris Barber Band. Greg helped Clive with technical matters, showing him how to replace skins and improve the sound of his instrument. Even then Clive's banjo repertoire was unusual. Apart from an elderly busker called Banjo George who used to play Edwardian banjo tunes to cinema queues using a cardboard train ticket as a plectrum, it was very unusual to see anyone, especially as young as Clive, playing music-hall tunes. One of George's favourite composers was Ollie Oakley, a music hall banjo player from the 1930s. After he had finished busking, Banjo George could often be found playing in a chess players' cafe on the Strand called En Passant. Clive knew him well, and particularly recalls sitting in a coffee bar with him, playing alternate tunes, and being knocked out by George playing a complicated Cammeyer composition called Dancer's Dream. Clive later learned the tune himself and would dedicate it to 'dear old Banjo George' when he played it live. Wizz: 'Clive was quite unique, doing

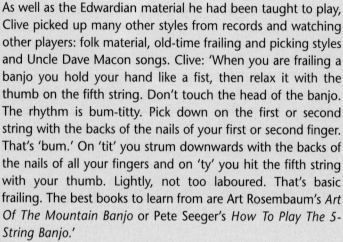

Frailing

As well as the Edwardian material he had been taught to play, Clive picked up many other styles from records and watching other players: folk material, old-time frailing and picking styles and Uncle Dave Macon songs. Clive: 'When you are frailing a banjo you hold your hand like a fist, then relax it with the thumb on the fifth string. Don't touch the head of the banjo. The rhythm is bum-titty. Pick down on the first or second string with the backs of the nails of your first or second finger. That's 'bum.' On 'tit' you strum downwards with the backs of the nails of all your fingers and on 'ty' you hit the fifth string with your thumb. Lightly, not too laboured. That's basic frailing. The best books to learn from are Art Rosembaum's *Art Of The Mountain Banjo* or Pete Seeger's *How To Play The 5-String Banjo*.'

all this weird banjo music you didn't hear any more.'

Many of the players of the time were influenced by Peggy Seeger, a young American from a family well-known in American folk circles (and married to Ewan MacColl) who taught many young players, including Wizz Jones's future musical partner, Pete Stanley. The legendary American banjo player Derroll Adams had also recently visited London and left a lasting impression. Another regular haunt for musicians was The Partisan coffee bar, in Carlisle Street, Soho, which had been opened as a forum for intellectual discussions, and was always full of people with left wing and communist leanings. Jimmy MacGregor used to play guitar there at lunchtimes. When, as half of a hugely popular duo with Robin Hall, he got too famous to do it any more, Wizz took over the slot, getting a bowl of soup and five shillings to play for an hour or so each lunchtime. The Partisan was famous for its shilling bowls of bread-and-butter pudding, and was also where Peggy Seeger gave her guitar and banjo lessons.

Clive: 'I was spending the weekends looning around with loads of people, that was part of it. As I got older I spent more and more time doing that sort of thing – some of that time I was at college too, so it was that young, growing up, period when you're going to loads of parties, and going to Brighton on the train. Basically hanging around Soho, meeting up with Wizz, people like that, old pals, going off on various things like busking down in Cornwall. It's hard to get dates right. After I went to Art College it's a sort of blur of parties, going off to places.'

Clive often stayed in London after nights out and found several reliable places to sleep rough around Soho. If the police found you they would wake you up and move you on. One place had a large dustbin outside, which was always clean, with a metal lid. You could climb into it and spend a reasonably comfortable night in a sleeping bag there. One of Clive's acquaintances of this period was called George, who came from a circus family and was an accomplished trapeze artist. 'He was quite fearless. He'd say, "Let's drive down to Brighton," and borrow a car. People would often leave cars open with the keys in and he'd borrow it and off we'd go. But he always brought them back and replaced the petrol.' There were also many bombed-out buildings they could sleep in, and one of George's favourites was an old hotel off the Charing Cross Road. 'If you climbed over the fence and through the rubble to the upper floors there were some good rooms and a sort of crow's nest with a good dry floor.' George and Clive were also involved in burgling a well-known jeweller's, and leaving the haul in a clean dustbin for the fence to collect. He paid them the next day. After a few months George disappeared from the scene and Clive never saw him again.

Princess Margaret married Anthony Armstrong-Jones in Westminster Abbey on the 6th of May 1960 and so London was packed with more tourists than it had seen for years. Clive, along with Dave Arthur and Mik Paris, spent much of the summer as pavement artists. Dave was seventeen at the time and was living what he hoped was a bohemian life in a garret off the King's Road in Chelsea, pursuing his dream of becoming a painter. His flatmate Mik played guitar and had taught Dave. He had first met Clive at the Soho Fair, an annual event celebrating the arts, when Soho was full of music, with jazz bands playing in carts and every doorway holding a busker. Long John Baldry, another regular at the Gyre and Gimble: 'They stopped the Soho Fair years ago; they were terrified of people having fun. It used to be with all kinds of buskers and a mixture of weird people. Redd Sullivan and Martin Winsor would be out there on the street singing, you'd get all kinds of Wally Whytons and Vipers and all that. I even saw Bert Lloyd. Ewan MacColl may even have been there. In the middle of it all Ken Collyer was singing Leadbelly songs.'

Clive and Dave used to busk under the arches in Villiers Street, Dave singing to Clive's banjo; they collected the money in a collapsible top hat, which was easier to conceal when the police came in sight. Dave remembers Clive's banjo playing as in a different class to anyone else's, using weird jazz chords that no one else knew or used. 'Clive taught me a 1920s song called The Blues My Naughty Sweetie Gave To Me which I played for years.'

The three pavement artists used to do their work around Trafalgar Square, by St Martin's-in-the-Fields and opposite the National Gallery. They occasionally did copies of the classical masterpieces, but mainly painted imaginary landscapes. Dave specialised in religious scenes, particularly Crucifixions, and Clive was a dab hand at drawing horses. They learned the tricks of the trade, seeking out the paving stones made of Welsh slate, which took the colours best. The other pavement artists, many of whom had been plying their trade for years, were surprisingly kind to the boys despite their bohemian appearance – long straggly hair by the standards of the day, as well as the obligatory bare feet and sandals. Dave particularly remembers the kindness of an artist called Jock, who was probably in his sixties then, and who had lived and worked in Paris. He was a genius with pastels and showed them how to use and blend their colours. Jock always claimed that he was an oil painter really and only did pavement work to buy oils for his real painting. Eventually he invited the boys to his flat in North London to see his oils. Dave: 'They were absolutely dreadful! It was really sad. But he was a brilliant pavement artist.'

They would stay on the streets until about 2 am, when the crowds died away. The street cleaners would come along soon afterwards to wash the pavements down. Drunks and gangs of youths were an occasional hazard. In the early morning the trio would often head over the river to the South Bank where the 1951 Festival of Britain had been held. Among the exhibits had been the Shot Tower, a well-known London landmark that had stood on the site since 1826 and had been restored for the event. It was about 200 feet high and was demolished in 1962. It was originally used to make lead balls for muskets. Lead was heated until molten in the high part of the tower then poured through a sieve. The globules of lead fell the full height of the tower and landed in a tank of cold water at the bottom. The water instantly solidified them into balls. Dave: 'It was like a lighthouse, you went about twenty feet up a ladder on the outside and climbed into the first floor. Lots of people used to sleep there, and the police used to visit it regularly looking for runaways and Army deserters. There were some strange people there sometimes; there was one guy who kept a revolver in his sleeping bag. He was on the run from somewhere. There was a circuit of places you would travel to in the summer, you'd spend a bit of time in London, then hitch down to the South of France for a few weeks and then maybe down to St Ives in Cornwall. You'd run into the same people in all those places.'

It seems Clive had visited Paris for the first time in the previous summer of 1959. Wizz: 'The first time I went to France everything went wrong because I was too shy to play on my own. I wound up hitchhiking from the South and ended up in Paris, where I was pleased to run into Clive. I walked into a bar and there he was. He told me he knew a great place to sleep. We went out to the Bois de Boulogne in the middle of the night, climbed over a fence and slept round the back of a puppet theatre. We had to get out early in the morning. We were both very naive in those days; later you learned to be more upfront. We were trying to follow in the footsteps of our busking heroes like the Bennett Brothers and even Alex Campbell, but somehow the first time you do it you're a bit too timid, you don't have the push you need. We were both in quite a sorry state. Neither of us had any money and we had to go off with our tails between our legs to the Consul to get our fares home. They kept your passport and you had to pay back the money you owed them in instalments before you could get it back. You used to be very embarrassed to admit it, but it seems everybody had to do it at one time, there's no shame in it. We all did it the first time. The next time you went you made damned sure you were prepared. The next year I was far more confident, and so indeed was Clive.'

Clive did not complete his three-year course at Art College: 'I did a couple of years and I wasn't intending to go into any further things, but it was a good start. At the time Wizz and I and a lot of others were staying with a Mr and Mrs Reiney, whose son I knew. They were Jewish, they came from Austria and they had been timber merchants and had been quite wealthy. They lived in a nice house in Barnes and they ran a hand-press laundry in Mayfair. Very high class, it did MP's shirts and stuff like that. They were nice people. They put up all these beatniks and the like.' Wizz's girlfriend Sandy had a little tape recorder at the house in Barnes and Wizz and Clive had a lot of fun making up and recording surrealistic scenarios very much in the style of the Goons, who were hugely influential and popular then. They also did parodies of contemporary adverts, and Clive had a thing where he would record a scratchy old 78rpm record with a long introduction. He would start the vocals a verse before the real vocalist came in and sing in a silly voice, then cough just before the real vocals came in, as if the vocalist on the record had had trouble with his voice. In 1960 Wizz and Sandy went to Paris and stayed in a scruffy hotel on the Left Bank. They made a living busking, with Sandy playing banjo. Wizz always tried to get his girlfriends to learn to play banjo, as it was a great asset when busking, both musically and visually, and therefore financially. Sandy was the only one who stuck at it. Clive followed them over a few weeks later. Clive travelled light, getting any clothes he needed second-hand from flea markets. As well as clothes he found the occasional curio that he could not resist buying, at one point taking to carrying a swordstick about with him. Wizz: 'There's a picture of Clive and me busking that year and he's wearing what look like sandals, but were actually my Italian winkle-picker shoes that someone had given me. He cut them down into sandals. In the same photo there is a hat to collect money; that was somebody else's hat that he'd cut the rim off. Once he cut his own hair and made such a mess of it that he kept the hood of his duffel coat up while he played.'

Another busker Wizz and Clive often played with over the months was Mick Softley, who was originally from St Albans and had been in Paris since 1959, staying for three years although he had originally been on his way to Spain. He too had been inspired by the pioneer buskers like Alex Campbell and Rambling Jack Elliott, who had given Paris its first

Wizz and Clive in Paris. Note Clive's 'sandals'.
Photo by Tommy Elder. Courtesy of Wizz Jones.

taste of British and American folk music. In the early days there was little competition; there were only Davy Graham, Alex Campbell and the Bennett Brothers doing the same circuit. Clive describes Alex at the time as being 'very much a Derroll Adams clone'. The only other problem was that drunken tramps with mouth organs would occasionally try and join in. Still, they did well, often making the equivalent of £25 a day, which was more than enough to pay for their cheap hotel rooms, food and drinks. Wizz and Clive had the dubious honour of having their picture published in the *Sunday Pictorial* in an article reporting the Parisian Gendarmerie clamping down on 'the army of British beatniks who have swarmed across the Channel with guitars, banjos and gravelly voices.' The Parisian police would arrest buskers as a matter of course.

Wizz: 'When we saw the police coming Sandy would be collecting the money – the procedure was she would hide the hat and melt into the crowd. We would get arrested and go back to our hotel in the morning when we got out of the jail.' Clive: 'Sometimes the police would only hold you in the cells for a couple of hours. They'd let you go if you promised not to do it again. I was in Paris for a couple of years; it did me a lot of good. You're really on the spot when you are playing in the street and your voice gets stronger and your playing gets stronger. I would say that was my formative period as a musician.' The police could be vicious, but oddly enough, once they had arrested you, they were usually very civil, as if they were just doing their job. Clive was once busking to a cinema queue when he saw how they dealt with demonstrators. 'I was picking up my money and I heard a growing roaring noise. Suddenly the lady who owned the cinema rushed out and brought down the steel shutters and all the other shopkeepers did the same. The demonstrators appeared and the police were all wearing cloaks. They used to sew lead bars into the seams of their cloaks and when they swung them they could cause real damage. They used to shoot people and throw them in the river.'

Sheila Rowbotham, then an eighteen-year-old student from Leeds studying at the Sorbonne before going to Oxford in the autumn, began frequenting the Monaco Cafe in Paris in April 1961:

'It was a tiny triangle of a place, near Danton's statue and overlooking the Carrefour de l'Odeon. It was cheap and served as a kind of beatnik social club. Two kindly folk singers were the first to befriend me. Wizz Jones, then a street performer, would twang a guitar on which he had written "Give me a guitar and I'll rock this old town, Archimedes". [Wizz: 'On my old La Foley guitar I painted this legend that I took from the frontispiece of an Alan Lomax book of folk songs: "Give me a lever and a place to stand and I will move the earth" – Archimedes. "Gimme a guitar and a place to play and I'll shake this old town!" – Old-time blues singer.'] Wizz, who had long curling brown hair, big square glasses and a cowboy hat, played with Clive, a gentle banjo player with pale red hair and a limp. Clive used to sit outside the Monaco and sing Blue Moon over and over again, and a mix of hope and melancholy would float towards Danton's statue to mingle with revolutionary ghosts and the noise of the traffic. Wizz and Clive helped restore my self-esteem by discovering that I possessed a practical economic skill – taking the hat round when they sang. This was based on experience gained through chapel collections at school and speaking French. I was chuffed, for I had quickly picked up that in the gossipy circles of the Monaco, where normal values were inverted, women who could get money were well esteemed.'

Later Sheila went hitching through France with a pavement artist called Mel, and ran into Wizz again in Nice, 'still with his hat and guitar but looking rather sheepish and subdued because he was with his mother, a middle-aged English woman with permed hair, a long pleated skirt and a Pacamac. The sight of Wizz's mother and her strange entourage striding along the Promenade des Anglais created a stir of astonishment in fashion-conscious Nice.'

During this period, Clive did not stay in France continuously ('you couldn't') but moved to and fro between the Continent and Britain. The law at the time was that you could only stay in France as a visitor for a maximum of three months in any year, though Wizz and Clive worked out you could extend this by taking the train to Brussels and re-entering France that way. One day he was helping Wizz fix a motorbike when 'a black shadow fell on me: it was two men from the Sécurité, the French secret police. They took me off and I was issued with a *Refuse de Séjour* which basically meant I had to leave the country at once for overstaying my visa. I called them fascists, which didn't go down too well. I took the *Refuse de Séjour* and stuck it to my hotel door in protest. Then a Mr Evans from the British Consulate came to see me and said that the French authorities were putting pressure on him, and that it was best if I left. He even offered to pay my fare if I didn't have enough money.' Clive left France, but the Sécurité had not forgotten him.

CHAPTER 3

TWO WEEKS IN SCOTLAND

3
Two weeks in Scotland

'Clive could play anything.'(Billy Connolly)

*I*n the autumn of 1962 Clive was staying in Shoreham-on-Sea, Sussex, with a friend called Robin Birch. Robin was a very interesting fellow, who had attended Gordonstoun School and been Private Secretary to The Duke of Westminster before becoming a beatnik. At one point he had gone out with either Christine Keeler or Mandy Rice-Davies (Clive can't remember which) before they became notorious. Clive had known Robin as part of the London scene in 1960. At Shoreham he was living on a barge moored in the River Adur, reached by planks laid over the mud. Robin had a passion for hunting and shooting and had just bought a shotgun, which in those days simply meant going to the Post Office and paying ten shillings for a licence. On one of the other barges lived a strange man who was an alcoholic. One evening Clive and Robin were on deck when they saw their eccentric neighbour running towards them over the planks waving an axe. Robin rushed for his shotgun and fired over his head, which fortunately drove him off.

One of Robin's friends from Gordonstoun was Rod Harbinson, whose family owned a whisky distillery in Scotland. They had a cottage on the island of Kerrera, just across the bay from Oban. Robin invited Clive up to Scotland with him to visit Rod in Edinburgh, and then go up to the cottage. The original intention was to be gone for a couple of weeks. 'In those days all the beatniks used to travel around and have houses, people they knew, where they could stay on the travels. We hitched up and arrived in Edinburgh. We'd forgotten to get the address but we knew the name, bumped into a guy who knew where it was, he directed us and we arrived at Society Buildings, at the top end of Chambers Street. At that point it was Rod Harbinson living there more or less on his own. And Robin, me and this other guy turned up, we stayed a night, we stayed a week or so, all very loose, nobody was particularly bothered. Rod wasn't bothered at all.'

Ian Ferguson was a regular visitor to Society Buildings at the time: 'It was basically one very large room, as big as a church hall. There was a raised area like a stage at one end where there was a table and chairs. The main hall would be full of sleeping bags and in the middle

Ian Ferguson 1962. Photo courtesy of Ian Ferguson

was a tent. Someone there, I don't remember who, had a pet monkey, a vicious, bad-tempered thing. You had to keep out of its way or it would bite you.' Clive: 'It used to steal things too. You'd be sitting having breakfast and it would suddenly grab the marmalade jar and run off up the curtains. The place had been a Quaker Meeting House. The police were always coming round to complain about the noise.' There was a huge gothic fireplace on one wall, in which everything flammable was burned in an attempt to keep warm. There was also the tent, big enough for about four people with a paraffin heater inside. The story of the tent erected indoors (actually a perfectly sensible way to help keep out the bitter cold of an Edinburgh winter) has passed into legend very much due to Billy Connolly, who would often mention Clive giving him banjo lessons inside it. Many years later Billy admitted that, while Clive had 'shown him some things' on banjo, he had never actually had lessons in the tent, though others he knew had. Rod told Clive that there was a weekly folk club round the corner and suggested that he go and play a few tunes there. When Tuesday came around they all went to The Crown Bar, where Archie Fisher ran a club. Clive introduced himself, played a few old banjo tunes and instantly made a lot of new friends, including 'a red-faced bloke in an Aran sweater.'

Robin Williamson, well known on the fringes of the Edinburgh folk scene, played guitar, fiddle and tin whistle. He had worked quite a bit with Archie, the two at one time sharing a flat and a residency at the Dunfermline folk club. Robin was also a ballad singer of considerable talent. Clive once compared him to Ewan MacColl in the way that he could deliver a traditional ballad so well that you could almost believe the events he was singing about had been his own experiences. Robin: 'My initial impression of Clive was that he was an interesting bohemian banjo player! What can you say?'

Hamish Imlach, a leading character in any story of the Scottish folk scene, remembers the 'evil-looking' monkey peeing in people's drinks in The Crown Bar. 'It belonged to an ex-miner from near Kilmarnock who had split up with his wife and become a very early freak, with the hair, the beard and the drug dealing.' Guitarist Bert Jansch was also very much a part of the scene at the time. Clive: 'The first time I met Bert was at a party. He was crawling over the floor in a state of considerable inebriation!'

In January 1963, Robin and Bert travelled down to London on the back of Robin's booking at the Troubadour club, with the specific intention of trying to gain a foothold in the London folk clubs, though Robin was actually more successful than Bert in his ambition at that stage. Robin returned in late March, Bert staying on a little longer. After a while Robin and Clive began to work as a duo, and began their own club night (later with Bert) at The Crown on a Thursday night. The Crown Bar was in Lothian Street, and was demolished in the early 1970s. It had a large back room, which could hold around one hundred people. Occasionally they hired guest performers, among whom was Davy Graham. Archie Fisher's Tuesday club still flourished, but a schism slowly appeared, Archie's club continuing to attract the more traditionally based singers, while the Thursday club began to appeal to those of more adventurous tastes. Before too long Bert returned to London to begin his climb to fame. Various regulars at The Crown Bar remember Clive singing music hall songs like After The Ball Is Over, The Spaniard Who Blighted My Life and The Girl (Boy) I Love Is Up In The Gallery, as well as American material such as The Lily Of The West (which Bert Jansch would later record, crediting Clive as its source) and British songwriter Cyril Tawney's Sally Free And Easy. Clive: 'When we first met, Robin was playing really simple Scottish songs, but beautifully sung with nice guitar backings. They made an enormous impression. And when we played together we started to experiment more, changing things around a bit, adding a bit of this and a bit of that. What we did was very varied.'

Society Buildings was quite a well-known stop on the beatnik circuit. Barry Miles, in his autobiography *In The Sixties*, writes about visiting it during his Easter break of 1963. He describes the inhabitants: 'Red, a huge man with flaming red hair and beard, chopping up tripe on the kitchen table with a claymore,' and his friend Robin The Poacher with whom he would head off to the Highlands in search of game, returning once with what they claimed was a wild boar, which they brought back to Edinburgh in Red's ancient Rolls Royce convertible and used every part of, even tanning the hide to make leather. You can work out their identities for yourself. Clive is referred to as Limpy, 'who, wearing a long black cape, had a gammy leg, which he dragged behind him like a character out of Dickens.' The book also describes the inhabitants' frequent trips to the Glasgow docks to meet freighters from exotic places with the intention of persuading sailors to sell them their dope at the lowest possible price. The strategy was to agree with all the other dealers not to buy anything until the very last minute before the ship had to sail again. They would keep the best for themselves and sell the rest on. Ian Ferguson remembers an exotic beatnik wedding taking place in Society Buildings around this time, an event which was fully reported in several local newspapers.

Ian admired Clive for his artistic talents as much as his musical ones, particularly remembering him spending a lot of time cutting strips of bamboo and weaving them into beautiful small boxes in the Japanese fashion. Miles mentions that the inhabitants of Society Buildings were so independent of the local economy that they even made their own ink, which sounds like a very Clive thing to do! Among the regular visitors were some schoolgirls, including a girl called Ash, and her friend Christina 'Licorice' McKechnie, who Clive recalls 'used to jump into bed with Robin Birch on her way home from school.' Licorice nearly became Mrs Bert Jansch in the summer of 1963, even getting to the point of having the banns published. However, Bert was dissuaded, rather too easily, from marrying Licorice during the course of a man-to-man chat with her father. Not long afterwards he went off to Morocco with a 16-year-old girl from Dundee called Lynda. As she was too young to get her own passport, Bert and Lynda got married (you can marry at 16 in Scotland without parental permission). After they returned they split up and never saw each other again. He doesn't even recall her surname. Licorice later took up with Robin Williamson and became a much-loved component of the Incredible String Band. When Miles came up to Edinburgh again in the summer break, for the purpose of marrying his girlfriend Sue, he found Society Buildings had been demolished.

At one point Clive, Robin and Bert shared (along with many other people), one of two flats opposite each other off a courtyard at West Nicholson Street. Bert Jansch would later write a song about these days entitled Three Dreamers (Robin, Clive and himself).

Clive, Robin and Bert in 1963.
Photo by Rod Harbinson

Bert has a great memory of Clive practising karate there: 'It was quite funny, really, he'd rigged up a wooden board with a bit of carpet over it and he was kicking it! Myself, Clive and Bruce somebody, he was an art student, we decided to go skiing up North. We had a little Morris Minor and we borrowed some sets of skis and put them on the back. Near Tomintoul, we got stuck, we were dressed for summer and we nearly froze to death. We never got to go skiing. That was the kind of thing we got up to.' Andy Scappaticcio, then part of the same Edinburgh sub-culture as Bert and Clive, had first met Clive when he lived in Society Buildings (oddly enough Andy had no problem with the monkey, describing it as perfectly amiable) and went on to share several addresses with him. He remembers the two flats as being constantly full of people, though he admits to being something of a weekend hippy, almost always having a job, which was something of a rarity amongst the West Nicholson Street crowd. 'Clive and I were simply good mates, with a shared interest in the consumption of marijuana and cheap accommodation.' Andy and Clive had several party pieces they would perform with Clive providing the music and Andy a recitation. Peter And The Wolf was one and Andy's take on the

Clive, 1963. Photo by Rod Harbinson

highlights from *Lawrence Of Arabia* another, though the latter usually collapsed into giggles before too long. Imagine Clive playing the theme music on banjo while Andy declaimed dialogue from the film: 'By the beard of the Prophet! To Aqaba!'

Later, Clive lived with his student girlfriend Mirren Scott in an attic flat in Nicholson Square. Rod Harbinson took a room in the same building, just down the corridor. In the autumn of 1963, during the Edinburgh Festival, Robin and Clive were among many artists recorded for a project which was released on the Decca label as *Edinburgh Folk Festival Vol.1*. The album featured an amazing variety of talent, almost all of whom would go on to greater things: Robin Williamson & Clive Palmer, The Ian

Campbell Folk Group (which at the time featured a fiery fiddler called Dave Swarbrick), Ray and Archie Fisher, Anne Briggs, Owen Hand, Lou Killen, Matt McGinn, Hamish Imlach, Nadia Cattouse and Dolina MacLennan. Other tracks were recorded, but not used, and there is a published photo of Bert Jansch taken at the sessions, showing him playing Robin's Levin guitar. Bert's own guitar had been stolen early in his career, and it would be some time before he owned another. When he was booked to play a club he would simply borrow an instrument from one of the other players present, who would doubtless boast ever after that Bert Jansch had once played their guitar. The following year, *Volume 2* was released, featuring more of the same from all the above artists except Robin and Clive, and adding one track by Jean Hart. All the tracks were recorded at Craighall Studios a few miles to the east of Edinburgh, an establishment owned by Waverley Records who had already issued some folk material, including EPs by The Corries, which explains their absence from the Decca albums. Robin and Clive performed Jazz Bo's Holiday, a short but sweet guitar/banjo duet on a tune written by Tarrant Bailey Jr. There is applause on many of the tracks to make them sound as if they were recorded in a pub or club. Photos of the sessions show that the studio had a stage area with tiers of seats opposite, which were occupied by friends and other musicians present. The sleeve notes say of the track: 'Jazz Bo's Holiday, a ragtime banjo piece is typical of the "curio music" that flourishes in odd pockets all over the folk scene. Robin and Clive... just blew into a club, played and sang, blew out again. Robin is quite well known locally as a singer. Clive – well nobody knows much about him except that he comes from around Nottingham, and plays, as you will hear, fabulous ragtime banjo.' No one knows quite where the idea of Clive coming from Nottingham came from, unless he was confused with Anne Briggs, who did come from that area. A mis-hearing of Edmonton, perhaps? All the participants were paid a one-off fee with no further royalties due. The fee was either £5 or £10, depending on who you ask, plus their taxi fare to the studio.

Nat Joseph, the project's producer, used the profits to build his own record company, Transatlantic, into one of Britain's premier folk labels. He had already issued several albums, the first of which were educational LPs offering advice on sexual matters (they became the subject of shock-horror stories in the Sunday tabloids, which of course only made them better sellers), as well as an EP telling you how to stop smoking. He eventually ended up signing many of the acts to his own label. The Ian Campbell Group, Archie Fisher, Owen Hand, Matt McGinn, Hamish Imlach, and Jean Hart all went on to record at least one album for Transatlantic.

Working as Robin & Clive, Williamson and Palmer began to get regular bookings all over the Scottish folk club circuit. 'There were a lot of clubs then, and it was quite well paid. We used to get £30, which was a lot of money. We were doing very well.' There were also frequent bookings in Sheffield, Rotherham and across the North of England.

Robin and Clive.
Photo by Ian Ferguson.

Musically the duo of Robin and Clive was great, and very satisfying for both participants, but on a social level this was certainly not always the case. 'Robin and I worked professionally together, but we never really got on that well, we didn't really have a lot in common. We didn't socialise, we wouldn't invite each other round for a drink, or anything like that. I had a lot of friends who were, how shall I put this, involved in the seamier side of things, like drugs. Not gangsters – they were all right, just a pretty rough crowd. They were nice to me; they were basically nice people. Robin didn't approve of this; he didn't even like long hair much. We had a lot of rows. We both had strong personalities. We'd even get to the stage of him saying let's go outside and have a fight!' Robin doesn't agree that things were quite as bad as that: 'We shared houses in Edinburgh and Glasgow for large periods of time. I did all the booking for Robin & Clive, and I'm not the world's greatest businessman... All that was done by me. One of the difficulties was in trying to get Clive to work.' Clive: 'The main difference between Robin and me was that I was a bit laid-back, whereas he was more serious. He was hard working. I was a bit lazy. He wanted to do something with his music. I just knuckled down when I felt like it.'

Billy Connolly first saw them perform at The Attic Folk Club, in Paisley. 'I couldn't believe how good they were. They were doing Uncle Dave Macon stuff like The Old Plank Road and stuff, but there was a kind of percussion involved in one of the songs and I always just presumed it was a drum. In the middle of the song Robin reached back and did the percussion with his hands on a guitar case. It sounded exactly like the record. They just blew me away. Some of these old players, like Clarence Ashley and Uncle Dave Macon, would sometimes make mistakes with the timing and do five bars instead of four, and then move along, they seemed to work on the system that if both of you do it it's OK, if you're playing with another guy. You can play a thirteen bar blues if you like, as long as both of you do it. I used to look on that as a mistake, on records, but Clive would play it exactly like them, the extra bar, there was something about the age of it seemed to attract him. It blew me sideways, because I had always looked on these extra glitches and notes as mistakes, but Clive did the completely authentic thing. And he always had rotten banjos! I always wondered why he played these terrible banjos. At one point he had a Clifford Essex drum, which was nice, but somebody made him a neck, a long neck, like Pete Seeger's with the extra three frets, and it was terrible, just a wiry smacking off the frets kind of noise. I always wondered why he didn't have a better one, but there you go. Robin and he used to do Scottish stuff as well, a myriad of songs from everywhere, English songs, coal miners' songs, American banjo-y stuff plus the Edwardian Joe Morley kind of playing. I remember them singing He Jumped Doon The Funnel Of The Clutha No. 20. It was about a guy called Rabbie Burns the diver. He used to jump off bridges into the Clyde. The Clutha is the old name for the Clyde; No.20 was like a dredger, one of those chug-a-lug boats that went up and down the Clyde. They used to sing stuff like that really well, and Robin seemed to have a bottomless pit of songs and interesting bits and Clive could play anything. It was brilliant, the folk scene was brilliant, because you had jazzers turning up, Diz Dizley doing Django Reinhardt, poems and all that.'

Robin: 'Billy is being a bit charitable. We used to do a mixture of Scottish, Irish, old-timey American songs and music hall songs. We were quite good, we were a bit better than a number of people. But what we were doing was very imitative. But it was imitative of a variety of styles.'

Clive and Mirren went to Paris together for a holiday in 1964. Clive: 'We were sitting drinking wine by the Seine when a black shadow fell on us. A man said, "Monsieur Pal-merr?" It was the same two guys who had arrested me last time. I've no idea how they knew I was in Paris, they must have had very efficient surveillance. This time they had handcuffs. As they were dragging me off I shouted to Mirren to take our papers and tickets and to go and stay with my father in London. I spent five days in a cell with about twenty illegal immigrants. It had no toilet, just a hole in the middle of the room. You had to sleep on the concrete floor and there was hardly any food. Then I was taken to the Tribunal and a man from the British Consulate came to represent me. The judge told me that "Your Embassy has taken an interest in your case." I faced a huge fine, maybe £5000, or a long prison sentence, and not being allowed back into France for ten years or so. The Consul told them that I was mad, and not responsible for my behaviour, and that I had been in prison several times in Britain, none of which was true of course. My case became something of a diplomatic incident. I was sent to Fresnes prison on the outskirts of Paris and released after six days. The cell was really nice, with French windows, its own toilet, and a wooden floor. I found some wax polish and polished the floor until you could see your face in it, just for something to do. The food was pretty good too, chicory salad and very nice soup. There was an Algerian there who had only one ear. He wanted me to teach him the lyrics to Lonnie Donegan songs so he could sing them to his friends, and he gave me cigarettes in return! I later found out that Fresnes had been used by the Gestapo when the Germans occupied France in the Second World War, and my cell had been used to hold and torture captured British agents. I swore to myself I would never go back to France again.'

Edinburgh is a small town socially, and Robin and Clive knew, and played with, all of their contemporaries on the scene, as well as an endless stream of visitors. During the 1964 Festival they put on mini-concerts in the afternoon at the Canongate Tolbooth featuring themselves and some of many traditional singers they knew, taking turns to hand out leaflets. The shows were always packed. Robin: 'We didn't charge admission, we just took a collection, and we got to play to loads of people that summer.' Clive in particular learned many things from jamming with visiting American musicians, and from records of acts such as Uncle Dave Macon, which were also beginning to be available at the time.

In November 1964 a student called Geoff Harden taped Robin and Clive's performance at the St Andrews University folk club. The first of the four songs on the surviving tape is the well-known standard Johnnie Cope, learned from the book *Hogg's Jacobite Relics*, a fine tale of Jacobite victory over the Government army though historically a little inaccurate, Cope being a considerably more competent general than the song suggests. Clive takes lead vocal and Robin plays basic strummed guitar, though his distinctive harmony vocals on the choruses are excellent. Robin takes over lead vocal for Johnny Lad, another song that the audience would have known well, though linked to a different tune from the usual one, Clive playing an extraordinarily intense banjo part behind it. The third track is easily the most interesting. Clive sings a bothy ballad called The Working Chap, adopting a slight Scots accent, but singing with complete conviction. Robin adds tin whistle and sings on the choruses.

But maybe, fren's, I've stayed ower lang
But I hope I hae said naething wrang
I only merely want to show
The way the puir folk hae to go.
Just look at a man wi' a housfu' o'bairns
To rear them up it tak's a' he earns
Wi' a willin' heart and a coat gey thin
He's workin' life oot to keep life in.

The fourth track is another crowd-pleaser, Hey Boys Do You Think I'm Fly? This is a Glasgow street song sung at high speed to the tune of Yankee Doodle with banjo and whistle accompaniment, and the song Billy remembers so well, with the lyric about the man who jumped off Jamaica Bridge down the funnel of the tugboat. The chorus is 'Hey boys, do you think I'm fly / It's only a wey ah've goat.' Fly means clever or cunning (not always used as a compliment) and Billy kindly translates the last line as 'It's just a habit I have.' The impression gained from the tape is of a very competent duo that always sought out slightly unusual material, or tried to do well-known material in an unusual way. Clive had picked up a few chords on guitar and would play it as well as banjo in the duo. 'Bert Jansch used to quite like some of the things I came up with on guitar,' he says.

Robin and Clive played a few times on Tyne-Tees Television on a show hosted by the well-known Edinburgh folk band The Corries, who at the time were a quartet known as The Corrie Folk Trio & Paddy Bell. They were the late Roy Williamson, who was often (incorrectly) thought to be Robin's older brother, Ronnie Browne, Bill Smith and Paddy Bell. Paddy left in 1965, Bill in 1966. As a duo of Roy and Ronnie, The Corries went on to become an institution in Scotland. Clive can remember having a row with Robin before one of these shows, with Robin telling him to get a haircut and stop hanging around with dope smokers. Billy Connolly, who saw them play together on many occasions, recalls that there were at least some concessions to show business. Robin and Clive would sometimes wear matching clothing: dark blue shirts with black polo necks underneath, grey slacks and black casual shoes.

Mirren's parents did not really approve of Clive, and tried to split them up. They insisted on her accompanying them on an extended trip to visit relatives in Canada. Clive was living in the top flat in Nicholson Square at the time. He would later recall how he felt the day she left, wondering how he would cope without her. He put on one of the few records they owned, an album of popular Italian music, and watched as the first snowflakes of the winter fell. He went downstairs to Alex in the grocer's shop at the foot of the tenement stair, who sold penny bags of coffee and individual cigarettes, and started to feel he might make it after all. He did, and they were reunited on her return.

Joe Boyd was an American blues and jazz enthusiast who had attended Harvard and become involved in the exciting folk scene that was blooming in early Sixties Boston, featuring characters such as Jim Kweskin, Eric Von Schmidt and Geoff Muldaur. After leaving university, Joe came to Britain several times as road manager and MC for package tours featuring legendary blues artists like Sonny Terry and Brownie McGee, Muddy Waters and the Reverend Gary Davis, all of whom were enormously influential on the British folk/blues scene at the time. Joe had briefly visited Edinburgh in the spring of 1965, hitching up from Newcastle where he had been helping Bill Leader do some recording. Bill had given Joe the address of Dolina MacLennan (who had sung on the *Edinburgh Folk Festival* album) and her husband George Brown. Joe was delighted with the hospitality he received, bemused by his host's attitudes to the peculiarities of the Scottish licensing laws, and shocked by Hamish Henderson's clumsy attempts to kiss him. After travelling around Scotland he hitched all round Britain meeting many of the greatest artists working on the folk scene at the time. He ended up in Padstow in time for the 'Obby 'Oss Celebrations in May before heading back to the US in June. He was booked to be stage manager for the Newport Folk Festival in the last weekend of July.

Joe returned to Edinburgh in October when he came to the UK to take charge of the Elektra Records office in London. He visited George and Dolina, who threw a party for him. The evening after the party George took Joe to a local pub to hear Robin and Clive play. They took their drinks into a dingy back room where a crowd of about thirty was waiting for the music to start. In his Sixties memoir, *White Bicycles*, Joe recalls the scene: 'Robin and Clive both had shaggy blond hair and were wearing heavy tweeds. Robin was graceful and relaxed while Clive seemed old beyond his years. To me, what they were doing was taking Scotch [*sic*] ballads that hadn't actually made the transatlantic journey to the Appalachians and making that journey for them with a few detours round the Balkans and North Africa. And I just thought it was fantastic; it was the most original thing I had heard in Britain really. They didn't take solos but complemented each other's playing with skill and wit. When George introduced us after the set, Robin conversed engagingly in a lilting, overly elocuted and thickly burred Scots accent. His manner was somewhere between a hippy and a 19th century parlour bard and he glowed with self-assurance. I was convinced I had found a star.'

One regular at The Crown sessions was Mike Heron, a trainee accountant from the Edinburgh seaside suburb of Portobello, who had been playing in rock bands around the town. He had gradually moved over to the folk scene after getting into the first Bob Dylan album, and realising that folk audiences actually listened to the performer whereas rock audiences 'either danced or they didn't.' Mike had started with piano lessons, eventually acquiring a ukulele after seeing someone play one at a Scout camp, and becoming envious of his ability to become the life and soul of the gathering. He recalls harmonising on Everly Brothers and Buddy Holly songs along with his friend Atty, both playing ukuleles. The ukes were eventually upgraded to guitars and Mike began playing in various Edinburgh rock groups. 'I was in one called the Saracens, which was a bit like The Hollies, a four-piece. Rock Bottom & the Deadbeats was an R&B band. It was little furry waistcoats and maracas, you know the kind of thing? We did lots of little gigs, dances. There weren't many gigs where you sat and listened to stuff but there were lots of social dances and engagement parties to do. There seemed to be a lot of work but it was all of that type. And then Dylan [arriving on the scene] coincided with the folk clubs becoming the gathering places of the time and all these people used to roll into folk clubs and they would actually listen to the artist and I was slightly brought over to that. That was initially what got me out of the rock bands because there was no chance anybody was going to listen to the songs, they were just either going to dance or not. I saw something else happening on the folk scene and saw that I could fit in on the edge of that.' As well as The Crown, Mike was already quite well known on the local folk scene, particularly for doing Dylan material. Andy Scappaticcio first met him singing in a bistro called The Stockpot in Hanover Street in mid 1965, 'murdering Mr Tambourine Man.' The Stockpot was run in the fashion of the basket houses in New York's Greenwich Village, where you played for tips from the diners. Mike also occasionally used to play in Henderson's vegetarian restaurant nearby.

The sleeve notes of the US edition of the first ISB album claim that Mike Heron joined Robin and Clive in 'late 1965'. They had put the word out that they were looking for a third member, a 'strummer' mainly, and Mike was one of two people they auditioned. 'I didn't get the job, I was the second choice. The first guy just thought they were too weird – "I don't fancy that, being on the road with these two, it's not for me!" – so I got it by default.' The could-have-been guitarist's surname is lost in history, though he was a regular performer at the club. His forename may have been Billy. Mike: 'So then the three of us got together and worked on a repertoire to keep what they had built up and to expand it in a direction that I could contribute to.' In later interviews Mike would often say (possibly with his tongue in his cheek) that Robin and Clive had decided to add another member after seeing how successful Peter, Paul and Mary were. Trios were obviously the way forward. Mike never worked out which one of them was supposed to be Mary.

Clive: 'I sort of didn't know Mike and then I did. I can't tell you the exact context of that; it's just too long ago to actually say. So basically I know Mike. As Joe Boyd says the String Band was the result of Mike being my friend and Robin being my friend. But not Mike and Robin being friends, it was an accident. So we've got Mike, Robin and Clive. We start doing gigs together, the audiences like it. We were trying to build it up, but there was only a limited amount of work. I think Robin & Clive had more initial success than the String Band did. We were doing odd gigs, but not getting long tours or anything.' The new trio were surprised to find that Mike's musical background caused some initial resistance in some quarters, with club organisers worrying that Robin & Clive were going to go all rock 'n' roll on them. 'When we first started playing as a trio, we couldn't get any work because they wouldn't book Mike Heron. The folk clubs would book Robin and Clive, but not Mike, they said he played rock 'n' roll! But that's what it needed, to make it more commercial.'

The reluctance was short-lived though, and Mike soon became an integral part of the group. He was confident in front of an audience, and brought his own exotic touches. He had a big solo number in the theme from *Zorba The Greek*, a 1964 film starring Anthony Quinn which featured a bouzouki tune that is inescapable in Greece to this day. Following a brainstorming session to find a new name they became the Incredible String Band, a name that would lose its real significance as the band evolved. The string band part came from the sort of music they played: American folk music played on stringed instruments. The expression 'string band' meant just that, in the way that brass band referred to music played on brass instruments. 'Incredible' was Clive's idea, it being a somewhat hip expression at the time, though they also considered 'Amazing' and 'Superior'.

CHAPTER 4

Balmore.
Bamiyan. Barlinnie.

4
Balmore. Bamiyan. Barlinnie.

'We felt that the boys had moved on now, it was a giant step. This was for the world, it wasn't just for us. This was big.' (Billy Connolly on the Incredible String Band album.)

C live: 'At some point I met Mary Stewart, I don't know how that happened but I met her. I ended up living at Mary's, at Balmore, just the two of us and her children. She was very into music and people used to visit her a lot.' Mary Stewart was a vet who lived at Temple Cottage, Balmore, a few miles north-east of Glasgow. She had split up from her husband and lived there with her five children and an ever-changing number of house guests, mainly drawn from her many friends in the climbing and folk music fraternities. Clive was very good with the children, keeping them enthralled for hours with his origami skills and helping them build models. He also learned to drive there, making good use of the long private roads. Mary would have liked to have been more than friends with Clive, but he was wary. 'She was quite a bit older than me. I take relationships very seriously, and I really just didn't fancy her.'

Ian Ferguson, who had first met Clive when he arrived at Society Buildings, ran a club in Glasgow with his brother in a basement flat below an Italian cafe in Renfrew Street. The owner used the flat only on Sunday nights to play cards with his friends, so the brothers persuaded him to let them run a soul music club there on Friday and Saturday nights. Once the band was set up there was hardly any room for the dancers, but the club was always packed, solely from word of mouth advertising. At that time there were few alternatives to the large dancehalls, and such clubs as there were had to apply for a licence, which was rarely granted, or be Members Only, with a 24-hour delay between joining and first admission. This was of little use to the average Glaswegian out for a good time on a Saturday night; he wanted to go to a club now, not Sunday! One way round that was to canvass likely-looking people on the street in mid-week, giving them free membership and telling them when the club was open. Basement clubs of this sort were considered much hipper than the big dance halls, and the cafe owner was delighted with how successful the venture was. The Ferguson brothers cast around for a new larger venue, and found it on the fourth floor of 134 Sauchiehall Street: two large rooms, plus several smaller side rooms, which had formerly been a Social Security office. The Italian cafe owner put up the financial backing and owned 80% of the business. You entered the club by means of a long corridor from the street leading to a tiny lift of almost unbelievably archaic design, a metal cage with a concertina-screen safety door. It was operated by a large brass lever in one of three positions: Up, Down and Stop. Forty years later, the lift is still the one thing everyone who ever went to the club remembers about it. Ian painted all the interior walls and windows black (even in the toilets) and installed a floating maple dance floor, a stage, a jukebox and a couple of one-armed bandits. One room was the dancehall, incorporating a raised seating area and an art-deco-style bar. The other room was filled with second-hand couches and armchairs and had a cafe. The lighting was low and the ambience just right.

Though several people who remember the club have implied that it had no fire escapes and was therefore illegal, this was not the case. Though there was no stairway by the lift as one might expect, there were two well-signed fire escape staircases, one at either end of the building. One led down past the Dance School on the floor below and came out on Sauchiehall Street itself; the other led down to an alley behind the street. In the fine Glasgow tradition of bestowing exotic names on the humblest cafe, cinema, club or dancehall, the cafe owner suggested calling it La Cucaracha. Just before the club was due to open, the cafe owner died. As his relatives untangled his many business dealings, they eventually discovered that he had owned an 80% share of what must have seemed to them like a potential goldmine, and started asking for some rapid return on his investment. Ian and his brother had to make money fast, and the only way to do that was to bend the rules on Members Only entry. The club was open from Monday to Saturday but could only afford to employ doormen on Saturdays. The gang culture was an almost inevitable part of working-class youth life in Glasgow at the time, and several times gang members would come back to the club mid-week after having been thrown out by the bouncers the previous weekend. On one occasion Ian was followed into the toilets by a youth with a knife, seeking revenge for some slight, and only managed to avoid being stabbed by keeping his head and talking his would-be assailant out of it. On another memorable occasion the staff on duty had to flee the club while it was wrecked by gang members. The lift was always the problem. It would sometimes burst open on the fourth floor and whatever had being going on in there would spill out into the club. It got very heavy sometimes. The police raided the club six times during its short life, and each time Ian was charged with running an unlicensed dancing club and allowing unlicensed gambling (the slot machines). On Ian's final court appearance, the Sheriff made it quite plain that another visit to the court would result in a custodial sentence. Ian's brother bailed out at this point, as he had a good job and any scandal would probably have led to his dismissal. So there were two choices: either close the club altogether or open it in a different form. At this point Clive was sometimes staying in the spare room of Ian's rented flat. Someone suggested opening an all-night folk club to run from 10pm Saturday to 6am Sunday. The dance hall area was filled with chairs so there could be no dancing (not that the folk crowd danced to their music anyway) and, as no alcohol would be sold, the club would conform to any legal requirements. The new venture was named Clive's Incredible Folk Club.

Courtesy of Ian Ferguson.

Clive took credit for the club's name: 'It was my name in the first place, and it didn't seem unusual that I should use it. Nobody was making a fuss about the Incredible String Band at that point. Not that I remember, though it was coming. When we started the club I thought – why not use that? I always thought it was a clever name.' It was decided to open the doors of the club at 10pm as (unbelievably by today's standards) the pubs stopped serving at 10.30pm, (and it was 10pm Monday to Thursday!) and as the folk fans tended to like a drink and the club could not sell alcohol, that gave them time to have a few drinks before the music started at 11pm. It also meant that guest acts could finish their other pub and club bookings before coming along. It was agreed that the Incredible String Band would be the residents and that they would organise support acts and guests each week. The club had a cafe selling coffee and Coke, sandwiches and egg rolls. Admission was five shillings. Clive: 'I said to the band that we could play there on a regular basis, but we even had rows over that. Robin said he wasn't getting paid enough. So I said "That's hard luck, that's all you're getting, that's the fee!"' According to Hamish Imlach, both he and Clive were being paid ten pounds each, with Robin and Mike getting five each.

Clive's Incredible Folk Club opened in late March, the membership cards stating that the club offered 'The best in Late Night Folk and Country Style Entertainment, Every Saturday from 11pm till Sunday at dawn.' An article in the *Daily Record* of 18/04/66 describing it as having been opened 'just a few weeks ago.' The *Record* sent along reporter Ellen Grehan to sample the delights on offer. 'On a Sunday morning between darkness and dawn, one hundred-and-odd young people whose ages ranged between 16 and 70, sat around in a room high above Glasgow, and sang folk songs. They sang of rebellions and young men killed for the cause. Protest songs against bombs and wars. Fishing songs, farming songs and songs of love. And there were a few who didn't sing at all, being too busy kissing in a corner.' Ellen's article does not specifically mention the ISB, though she admitted that she lacked the stamina to stay beyond 2am. She did mention that the audience could enjoy the music of Hamish Imlach, Matt McGinn, Alex Campbell and Bert Jansch. One of the guest bands on the night she attended was the Brian McCollum Folk Music Group from Newry in Northern Ireland. Ellen was pleasantly surprised by the fact that the band's pro-Republican material seemed to go down well with everyone. 'The kids, who very well might have got narked at hearing the same songs sung outside of the club, were joining in with a vigour that rattled the rafters.'

Hamish Imlach was the real stalwart of the club, acting as MC and plugging the club at his own gigs elsewhere. He would organise the singers, giving Billy Connolly the unofficial post of resident autoharp player whenever there were any Carter Family songs to be sung. He was also pretty good at calming down rowdier elements of the crowd: 'I would explain in a friendly way, "Look, the bouncers over there are bored, they haven't beaten anyone up all night. The only thing between them and you is me, would you like to take your money and leave now?"'

Clive became a good friend of Hamish's and would often accompany him to his other gigs to play short spots as well as occasionally providing an alibi for his romantic dalliances. A young guitar protégé of Hamish's called Ian McGeachy also used to come along and would shortly find fame himself under the name of John Martyn. John was seventeen at the time of the Incredible Folk Club, and has fond memories of the period. 'The Incredible String Band had very interesting ideas and were funky players in those days. Those were wild times and Clive was a remarkable man, a great musician and down to earth, absolutely no bullshit, he taught me lots of things to play. I used to follow people around. I didn't ask, I used to sit at the front and watch – it's the best way to learn. The best way to figure out how to do things is watch the fingers. I watched all kinds of people! Not rock 'n' roll, though, it was all folk for me. Davy Graham was my hero and still is. Hamish Imlach was a very underrated guitarist with a very strange style, a cross between flamenco and blues. His right hand was like a bee's wing. Very cool player.' The waistcoat John Martyn wore on his cover of his second album *The Tumbler* (and on several publicity photos taken at the time) was made by Clive.

Billy Connolly: 'You just arrived in this elevator into a room. I mean if there was a fire we would all have been barbecued. But that kind of added to the attraction. You would get all the hairy people and duffel-coat guys showing up, but also there would be drunk people showing up who'd go to anything that was late at night! It made for the most extraordinary atmosphere. It was a real sweatbox. I loved it.

Robin and Clive and Mike Heron were around all the time, in various bits and pieces, solos and duos and then the trio would show up sometimes. Mike would do blues I remember, he was a pretty damn good player on that funny wee Gibson he used to play, he would whack away on that, really well, playing old blues stuff. Plus his own stuff, which seemed very influenced by Robin, Sixties weird stuff. There was an amazing mixture of singers with old tinkers like Davie Stewart and his daughter Belle. They would show up and sing and I would play the Autoharp, that was my thing at the time. It was the most phenomenally jolly place! And it was a great place to get up and sing if you weren't getting gigs anywhere else, the way they used to do it on the folk scene, just give you the mike, you could go up and have a bash. I went about four weeks I'm sure, at least. I wasn't always available to go, because I was playing other gigs as well.'

*Mike, Clive and Robin
on stage at the club.
Photo by Ian Ferguson*

Ian Ferguson: 'The Incredible Folk Club regulars were an appreciative audience, sitting down listening, singing along, and no doubt having sly swigs from the half bottle. They really enjoyed the club, the novelty of being able to stay all night. The pubs closed at 10, the dancehalls at 11, after that there was nowhere to go but home, and who wanted to go home?' Though there was still the occasional bit of trouble, it was nothing like as bad as it had been when the club was La Cucaracha. Despite Ellen's estimate of a hundred-odd people in the audience, Ian recalls that the club could have held five hundred easily, though he cannot say for certain that it ever actually did.

The 'sly swigs' were in contravention of the club's rules, which stated forbiddingly: 'Consumption of alcoholic beverages in clubs is illegal therefore cannot be allowed on club premises. Any individual found in the possession of, or under the influence of alcohol will have his his/her membership confiscated, the management regret that under these circumstances membership fees cannot be refunded. The management reserve the right to refuse admission.' Presumably these were intended to impress the relevant authorities.

As an observer, Billy thought that Clive seemed uncomfortable with his role in the String Band at the time. 'I got the impression that the stuff that Mike and Robin were doing was more and more foreign to Clive, and not where he wanted to go. It seemed to me that Robin and Mike were developing along one direction and Clive didn't want to, his heart was elsewhere. The more esoteric and far out they got, the more uncomfortable he became. It ended up affecting how he stood on the stage; with them, but not of them.' Robin was unaware of this: 'It was certainly not conscious on my part. It wasn't deliberate in the slightest.'

After the club closed on Sunday mornings it became common for Ian, the ISB and other visiting acts to head out to Temple Cottage to catch up with their sleep before extending the weekend for a couple more days.

Wizz Jones, who had not heard from Clive for a while, was delighted to receive a letter inviting him and Pete Stanley, a bluegrass banjoist with whom he was working at the time, to play at the Incredible Folk Club. 'The club was amazing, featuring Davy Graham, Hamish Imlach, Archie Fisher and Owen Hand all on the same night – that was a gig to remember!' Afterwards Wizz drove back to Balmore, slept for a while, and was woken by the gentle tones of Archie Fisher playing a sitar outside his window.

Billy Connolly: 'Clive took me there one time after the club, and I slept the night, on the floor I might add! Alex Campbell was there as well, and Robin and Mike arrived later. I remember Mary saying "Who's that?", unhappy that this person she didn't know was in her house. But we became very friendly after that. I remember Clive did a wonderful talking blues about smoking which ended with the line: "Smoke marijuana – the thinking man's cigarette!" We sat and played for a wee while, I don't think he had met many people who frailed the banjo. I think he was the first frailer I had ever met, I thought I was alone on the planet.'

One of Joe Boyd's roles as London representative of Elektra was to act as a talent scout for the label. He came north in late March with the express intention of tracking Robin and Clive down and signing them up to record for Elektra. He had heard about the Incredible Folk Club and turned up at opening time one Saturday night to see the police arguing with people trying to get in. Unsure what to do he saw a guy with a guitar case approaching him, and correctly assumed he was on his way to the club. It was Hamish. Joe introduced himself and Hamish advised him to come to a cafe across the road from the club with him and wait there until the police had gone. He told Joe about Balmore, and Joe decided it would probably be a better idea to meet Clive and Robin there the following day. Clive: 'Joe Boyd knocked on

Mary's door when we were staying there. I didn't recall having met him before. He introduced himself, and says he's heard about us and asked if we want to make a record. I said yes, but there are now three of us.' Joe was introduced to Mike Heron and recalls that: 'He was short and solidly built with clumsy seeming but effective movements, a contrast to Robin's vague ethereal grace. He laughed at the slightest provocation, slapping his knee and teasing the other two constantly.' After tea and a few joints, Robin and Mike played Joe their latest songs. In *White Bicycles*, he writes: 'I was astounded; the songs were completely original, influenced by American folk and Scottish ballads, but full of flavours from the Balkans, ragtime, the Maghreb, music hall and William Blake. The combination of Mike's Dylan-tinged vocals with Robin's keening glissandos created harmonies both exotic and commercial. I had to have them.' Note that there is no mention of Clive...

Joe sent the band's demo tape to Jac Holzman, the boss of Elektra who, like Joe, was knocked out by Robin's October Song in particular. The demo tape had been recorded using equipment belonging to Alan Coventry, an old school mate of Mike's and formerly bass guitarist with the Boston Dexters. These were a raucous Edinburgh R'n'B quartet who dressed up in 1920s Chicago gangster outfits and fired starting pistols on stage. They were a great live act, and their lead singer, Tam White, is still regarded as one of the best blues singers ever to come out of Scotland. They were signed to Columbia and recorded several singles, including a highly rated cover of Ray Charles' I Believe To My Soul. The band had split by the end of 1965, Tam White taking guitarist Johnny Turnbull and adding a new rhythm section to form The Buzz.

One of many unsubstantiated rumours about the early days of the ISB is that they recorded an album for a small Glasgow label, to which Joe Boyd was forced to buy the rights to block its release. Mike has mentioned this in at least one interview. Clive later confirmed that he half-remembered something similar happening. Robin remembers that the label in question was Lismor, and thinks that there were certainly negotiations about them recording an album, though he cannot remember for certain if they actually got as far as going into a studio. Both Joe Boyd and Ronnie Simpson, who has run Lismor Records since 1980, know nothing about any album recordings. Ronnie: 'I'm sure there is/was only ever one Lismor. The first release was in 1973, so anything before that would have been with someone else. When we took over Lismor I recall that four record labels were going down and four more had just started. The ones going down were Scotia, Thistle,

Waverley and Scottish Records. Scotia operated out of a garage in Paisley, and had a very sparse release schedule, mostly of local talent. Thistle specialised in country dance, song and fiddle music. Waverley was based in Craighall studios in Edinburgh [where the Edinburgh Folk Festival albums were recorded] and went on to become a Scottish music production house for EMI. Scottish was run by a writer and broadcaster called Douglas Gray, who released everything from Early Music to Jean Redpath and Para Handy, folk song, fiddle music and spoken word. Knowing the make-up of all these people I cannot see them getting excited about the ISB. The hippy culture would have made all of them run a mile. I was heavily involved in the music scene then and can think of nowhere or no-one that would have done more than talk about an album. There were no real studios.'

Unless these tapes ever actually turn up, it is probably reasonably safe to assume that the recording session in question was the one with Alan Coventry. There seem to have been six songs on the tape, definitely including October Song and possibly Mike's Maybe Someday. Again memories are vague, but it is likely a copy was sent to Nat Joseph, as well as one to Joe Boyd. Robin had strengthened the connection with Transatlantic by backing Matt McGinn on his first album (released in 1966) as a member of The Balladeers, which featured Robin on mandolin and guitar, Hamish Imlach on guitar and Marianne Aarlberger on viola.

Elektra and Transatlantic both expressed interest in the ISB. Jac gave Joe the green light to make the record, albeit on a tiny budget, but Joe took it on himself to offer the band an extra £50 to swing them away from Transatlantic, who had also made an offer to match Elektra's. For an advance of £200, they agreed to sign with Elektra. Hamish Imlach: 'That was the luckiest break they ever had. Nearly everyone eventually had to leave Transatlantic in order to become famous, because Nat didn't push their records. He just recorded everyone, sat back and waited to see who would become well-known, then dusted off and re-issued his material. It was the Major Minor label, not Nat, that got the Dubliners into the hit parade with Seven Drunken Nights. Nat would rehash old tracks again to make compilation sampler albums. Through Nat's rehash technique I recorded eight solo albums for Transatlantic, plus a single and an EP but appeared on over thirty XTRA or Transatlantic albums.'

Clive, Mike and Robin came down to London to record their album in late May. They were booked to play at the famous Les Cousins club on Sunday 22nd while they were in London. The gig never actually happened, though Sandy Jones, for one, turned up to see them, remembering seeing them by the side of the stage looking none too pleased. Clive: 'The organiser had got the date wrong, but he admitted it was his fault and paid us anyway. We had been really looking forward to doing a gig in London. Mike and Robin played there later, but the original band never did.' The recording session was booked into Sound Techniques studio, in a side street off the Kings Road, near World's End in Chelsea. The engineer there was John Wood.

Joe Boyd: 'Mike, Robin and Clive came down and slept on the floor of my flat in West Hampstead. We piled in my car and drove to the studio on Saturday morning, and just started playing the songs, as you hear them on the record. John had lots of sessions Monday to Friday, but he gave us a cheap deal on the weekend.' Mike and Clive flew down to London by De Havilland Comet jet, having managed to get cheap stand-by tickets. Robin made his own way down (or may already have been in London). In an interview, Bert Jansch once mentioned a story which has since turned up a couple of times in print, about Clive and him getting very stoned one day in Edinburgh in late 1962 and deciding on a whim to take a plane down to London, neither having flown before. Clive doesn't remember it, but Bert still does, adding that they had to hitch back to Edinburgh afterwards!

The Incredible Folk Club opened for the last time in late May, possibly on the 28th. The only reason the club closed was money. Without financial backing, there was not enough coming in and the next rent payment was becoming due. Ian: 'We owed a lot of money, though fortunately no one tried to sue me. I honestly can't remember any details of the last night of the club. I presume I was there and I presume the Incredible String Band were there, I think I would remember if they were not. Maybe we just closed the doors at 6am and walked away?'

Hamish: 'We could have taken over the place for not much cash. Alex Campbell and others were keen that we run it as a co-operative, but I saw that I would have been doing all the work. I was already booking everybody, doing the paperwork, getting the money and paying it out, compering, trying to find who was on next – they'd probably be out on the fire escape having a joint or gone out to buy a fish supper. On the go the whole bloody night. I could see that I would end up moving the chairs, sweeping the floor and doing the bloody toilets as well. Then the other members of the co-operative would turn up for the share out of the cash. I wasn't interested.'

Ian promoted a Folk/Blues Concert in The MacLellan Galleries in Sauchiehall Street on 12th June, under the auspices of The Temple Cottage Folk Society. Featuring Hamish Imlach, the Incredible String Band and headlined by Bert Jansch, the concert was due to open at 7.00 and admission was 6/6. By 1966 Bert Jansch was one of the biggest stars on the folk scene and had long since based himself in London. At the time of the concert he had already released two influential albums, *Bert Jansch* and *It Don't Bother Me*, and had another two ready to be issued in August: *Jack Orion* and *Bert and John*, a duet album with John Renbourn. As the time for the concert drew nearer it became obvious he was not going to turn up. Ian had only a verbal agreement with him to do the gig. Clive was the brave fellow who took on the job of explaining to the audience that the headliner would not be appearing and offered a full refund to anyone who wanted it. No one did.

Temple Cottage Folk Society

Folk Blues Concert

at the McLellan Galleries
Sauchiehall Street, Glasgow

on Sunday 12th June 1966
at 7-30 p.m.

Ticket 6/6   Doors open 7 p.m.

Courtesy of Ian Ferguson

In the audience that night were Billy Connolly and his father, whom Billy had taken along to give him an idea of what he got up to on a Saturday night. Mr Connolly Senior was not impressed, turning to his son at one point and asking incredulously: 'You like this?' Billy remembers the evening well, recalling Alex Campbell doing a spot and also that the audience weren't too bothered about Bert not turning up. 'Bert was a sort of wispy fellow, there was a lot of word about him, but very few people had seen him. The scene was completely different then, there was a lovely bonhomie, people accepted a lot more. If you didn't turn up it actually made you more attractive. It made you kind of windswept and interesting, you know. It made you more unavailable, you weren't like Cliff Richard. You might not show up, you might show up in your pyjamas. There was a lovely acceptance of everything. The band seemed very jolly and happy on that night unlike the shifty uncomfortable stuff that had been. Clive played well, but it was a terrible banjo he was playing.' Following the concert, Ian and a few mates went to Iceland for a couple of months in search of work and adventure, though all the fish gutting jobs were taken and they ended up working as painters instead.

The MacLellan Galleries show was almost certainly the last time Robin performed with the first line-up of the ISB though he doesn't actually remember the gig. The trio had received an advance of £200 between them against future royalties on the album. 'I'd always wanted to go to Morocco, so we (Robin and Licorice) went. I got a variety of instruments there; I intended never to return to Britain really. I had an idea that I would stay there in some sort of garden, under a tree there, and study Arabic flute. That was as clear as I'd got my plan for life.' Robin had intended to live on the profit made from sub-letting his flat in Edinburgh, but currency restrictions meant that money could not be sent into Morocco and he was repatriated when his initial savings ran out. He was certainly back in Britain and staying at Temple Cottage by early October.

Clive and Mike both remember doing a few more gigs together in Glasgow, including The Glasgow Folk Centre, though neither can recall if they worked as a duo or separately. Clive: 'We did a show of some sort.' While Robin was away, Archie Fisher arranged a short solo tour of the Scottish folk club circuit for Mike Heron, who recollects doing a selection of his own and Bob Dylan songs 'with just guitar and a harmonica on a wee rack.'

The album *The Incredible String Band* (retailing at 35/6) is usually listed in discographies as having come out in June, though July may be more likely. The cover photograph had been taken by Joe in Moore's Classical & Early Music Record Store, on the corner of Poland Street and Great Marlborough Street, just up the road from the Elektra office. The trio is shown holding exotic instruments, none of which they actually played. Clive has an Asian folk fiddle, Robin what looks like a cello neck fitted to a crudely made triangular body while Mike holds some kind of unstrung harp/guitar hybrid. Allegedly they just walked in, asked if they could take a few photographs, picked the instruments off the wall and posed. Robin is wearing an exotic cheesecloth top ('his dress', according to Clive!) and Mike looks like he has just left his accountant's office, pausing only to remove his tie. Clive veers more towards the practical – a waterproof plastic coat which he had borrowed from Mary Stewart. 'It's a vet's coat, for doing the cows, and a shirt and a pair of trousers that were so enormous I had to pull them in with a belt. I didn't have anything to go down to London in.' He stands out as the only one with long hair. Under his lumberjack shirt is a very strange (LP-sized?) bulge. Clive, though admitting that the idea of him having nicked an LP or two is a good story, denies having anything concealed on his person, putting it down to the ill-fitting clothes.

The album featured some extremely strange sleeve notes about the members of the band having met a magic blackbird and spending every waking hour sitting astride logs which are floating down a river. The logs were a gift from a Golden Wonder potato, a friend of the magic blackbird. 'Everywhere they go they leave bits of themselves lying about all over the place, and if you didn't look at them very closely, you might easily think they were songs.' And that is probably the most sensible sentence in the whole piece... Almost everyone who has ever commented on the first ISB album has wondered why Clive seems to have contributed so little to it. Breaking it down, nine of the sixteen tracks are solo performances: five by Robin (including one instrumental), three by Mike, one by Clive. Three tracks feature just Robin and Mike, one features Robin and Clive. The remaining three tracks feature all three. The album is a melange of dozens of influences. The opening track Maybe Someday has a frantic fiddle part as well as the memorably odd line: 'I did not like the way her teeth grew.' Mike wrote short comments on each of the tracks and pointed out that this particular track displayed Bulgarian, Scottish and Indian musical touches.

Robin's October Song is undoubtedly one of the album's highlights. Robin claims it was the first song he wrote, in late 1965, inspired by a visit to Cramond Island, to the north-west of Edinburgh, (a place that would also inspire his later song The Iron Stone). In later years he would change the first line to: 'I never wrote a song before it' in live performance. If so, it is an amazingly mature piece of work. Certainly both Joe Boyd and Jac Holzman were mightily impressed, and Bob Dylan was even heard to praise it in one interview (saying it was 'quite good', a quote Robin has dined out on frequently since). It remains the Incredible String Band song that has attracted the most cover versions. For this track, Robin retuned his guitar to open D (DADF#AD), capoed at the fifth fret to play in G. Alternative tunings were nothing like as common on the British folk scene at that time as people now assume, and Robin was something of pioneer in using them. To this day he regrets that he has not received the credit he feels he is due for this. The lyrics of October Song are extremely fine, notably:

'I used to search for happiness, I used to follow pleasure
But I found a door behind my mind, and that's the greatest treasure.
For rulers like to lay down laws, and rebels like to break them,
And poor priests like to walk in chains, and God likes to forsake them.'

Clive thinks he was one of the first people ever to hear the song, remembering Robin coming round to see him, eager to play him his new composition. Mike's When The Music Starts To Play features fine interplay between his guitar and Robin's whistle. The opening line shows a nice sense of humour: 'All my life, and it's been a short one...' Clive only turns up once on the first side of the album, on the fiddle/banjo duet Schaeffer's Jig. At a mere 59 seconds, it is really just an interlude, though pretty typical of the old Robin and Clive sound. Though credited to 'Trad' it was actually written by Arling Schaeffer, an American mandolinist from the 1890s.

Mike's The Tree is a very interesting track, also in an open tuning, this time in open G (DGDGBD) capoed at the second fret. There are Indian influences in the sitar-like part, and Caribbean touches in the delivery, ('and de sun was shining brightly') which some attributed to Mike being influenced by Joseph Spence, the enigmatic Bahamian guitarist. The lyrics tell of how Mike had a tree he would visit 'in the dream hills where my childhood lay' and how the tree reached out to him when he was sad one day. The 'dream hills' was a term first coined by Robert Louis Stevenson to describe The Pentlands, to the south of Edinburgh; Stevenson had spent many happy days there as a sickly child in the village of Swanston. The first side ends in great style with Dandelion Blues, a string band-style number with both Robin and Mike on guitars. As Mike put it succinctly: 'Nothing to do with flowers and it isn't a blues.'

Side Two opens with How Happy I Am, a real example of the string band sound, with Clive and Mike on guitars and Robin on mandolin. The song owes a fair bit to the Reverend Gary Davis song of the same name, though the subject of the lyrics has changed a great deal. Mike had actually seen Gary Davies play live in Les Cousins while he and Owen Hand went down to London to take part in a CND protest march. Empty Pocket Blues is Clive's only original composition, but has become one of the album's best-loved tracks. It features two guitars and a lovely whistle part from Robin. The chord sequence is memorable too, with a very unusual change from D to Bb. Mike's sleeve notes mentioned that the title wasn't a joke, Clive having lived for two weeks on nothing but potatoes. 'He wrote this song and someone gave him a carrot.' There has always been a bit of friendly controversy between Clive and Wizz Jones as to the song's origins, Wizz having written a similar-sounding song called Teapot Blues. Clive: 'I know Wizz thinks I swiped it from him. We were both staying in Barnes and there was a guy there called Brian who used to play the piano, and was always playing bluesy stuff. I remember he got into playing this chord progression, and that stuck in my mind. Wizz went off and started to knock something together around that chord sequence and I was putting something together with it too. Brian was a pretty spaced-out guy and he came up with lots of funny chord sequences, and that's where Empty Pocket Blues came from.' Wizz: 'His name was Brian Kennedy, and he played that chord change, which comes from Beethoven or somebody, and he and I wrote some words to it. The following year Alan Tunbridge wrote some comical Cockney words to it and changed the feel of it. It was originally a slow blues, like Clive did it, and then we changed it into an up-tempo, jaunty, Cockney blues. When Joe Boyd wanted the Incredibles to do all their own material for the first album, Clive didn't have anything of his own so he quickly re-hashed that song and changed some of the chords. But it originally came from me and Brian Kennedy, then through Alan Tunbridge. So there were lots of people involved in writing it.' The song had something of a revival in 1970 when the Incredible String Band featured it, in a new arrangement, in their live repertoire for a while, and on a couple of radio broadcasts too. It also became a popular number in folk clubs.

Robin's Smoke Shovelling Song is another wonderful track, a blend of outrageous storytelling and the talking blues style. The end of the story, which has a frozen column of smoke melting to cover the town with the words of the song, is a touch of genius. His Good As Gone also struck a chord with many people, the realisation that the weather is gradually improving and that it will soon be time to set off on your travels again. 'My feet surely ache for the road.' Mike's sleeve notes, imagining that Robin was off being eaten by lions in Africa, obviously date from just after his departure in June.

Niggertown, again erroneously credited to 'Trad', is actually a composition by Joe Morley, composer of many other tunes that Clive would play live and record over the years. Mike's sleeve notes for this track suggested it was presented as something of a novelty item. 'All three of us include what are meant to be funny songs in our performances, but this piece of music from Clive always seems to bring the smiles running from miles around. No words, just notes dusted with laughter powder.' The title dates from times which seem unenlightened now, but black-face minstrel shows were a common branch of entertainment from Edwardian times onwards; the banjo was often seen as an inseparable part of that kind of music, with tunes written in London being given exotic titles like Downtown Dandies and Fun In The Cotton Fields. Everything's Fine Right Now is the perfect end to the album, and again soon became a folk club standard. It features the string band sound again, two guitars and mandolin with Clive on kazoo, and an irresistible chorus.

Billy Connolly loved the album: 'I was completely knocked out, both by Robin's stuff and by Clive's stuff. Everybody loved it; the whole scene was ablaze with the news of this extraordinary movement in music. Lyrics especially, the dream kind of lyric. I had heard them do some of the tracks, but I hadn't heard Empty Pocket Blues and Schaeffer's Jig before. The singing and the playing was lovely and everyone adored it. It had a very live feel to it, it wasn't manufactured super-produced pop music. We felt though that the boys had moved on now, it was a giant step. They wouldn't be around long; they wouldn't be fucking around in The Attic anymore. This was for the world, it wasn't just for us. This was big.'

Clive set off to travel to India with Ricky Boak in early July. 'I remember watching Wimbledon on the television about a week before we left', Ricky was (and still is) an incorrigible traveller and had already visited Asia the year before. Ian Ferguson still has a postcard he sent him from Kathmandu in August 1965. Clive: 'Ricky wanted to go to India and I was thinking about that, because the record hadn't made much impact. I was living at Mary Stewart's house when we were doing the planning. We thought about taking a van, but in the end we went on foot. It was all planned, and took a bit of organising.' He had saved about £140, mainly from busking, and he and Ricky set off, hitchhiking down to the ferry to the Hook of Holland, then through Belgium into Germany. As it was taking them too long to hitch through Germany, they took a train to Cologne and another to Belgrade. They hitched through Yugoslavia, Greece, then into Turkey. Clive did a bit of busking in Greece, which was both enjoyable and lucrative.

The standard route of the time was to head to Turkey, then into Afghanistan via Iran, travelling by train or bus. Visas were normally quite easily obtained at the border between each country. Unfortunately there were problems with getting a visa for Iran at the time, so they went south through Beirut, Damascus and Baghdad. At the time Beirut was still the Paris of the East and Clive busked there too, doing very well. They lived on the beach and dealt a little dope too. Language was never a problem: 'We just pointed at things! You'd go into a cafe and look at what other people were having and point at it and say you wanted one of those.' While in Beirut they applied for a visa to visit Jordan: 'They turned us down. I asked why, and they pointed at our hair and said, "We don't want Beatles in Jordan!"' Clive and Ricky headed east into Iraq instead, and then from Baghdad went to Kuwait, where they boarded an Arab sailing dhow for the two day trip to Abadan. 'They wouldn't give us a visa, they were terrified of spies at the time, but we got a transit visa which gave us just two weeks to get through Iran to Mashad. We went to Isfahan, one of the holiest cities in Iran, and couldn't find a hotel, so went to the police station and they sent us out with a lackey who found us a place. We had to sleep on beds on the roof, which was fine, but when people saw white faces on the roof they complained as they thought we were up there to try to look at their wives! So we had to move on. We tried to visit the main mosque and got through a couple of gates before these two crossed swords suddenly blocked our way, with two enormous blokes wielding them. We turned and left. Once when I used a water fountain in the main square, someone rushed out and cleaned it before anyone else would use it. In every village kids would throw stones at us. You'd just be walking and suddenly feel something hitting your back. They were little sods, but there was no point in chasing them, they'd just run off. Often we'd find ourselves sitting by the road, on a lovely warm night, smoking whatever dope we had, looking at the moon. It was very pleasant. You had to travel light, and most people would end up discarding most of the stuff they had brought.'

Entering Afghanistan, Clive was impressed by the stamp they put on his passport. 'They basically took half a potato and carved a design on it, inked it, and that was the stamp. Every day they made a new one.' The pair took a bus to Bamiyan in the Hindu Kush, a trip that took all day. 'The bus was full of sacks of spices and you had to sit on top of those. All the men on the bus had rifles, and they were constantly stopping to pick up some wildlife they had shot out of the windows.' Bamiyan was famous for two huge statues of Buddha, 53 and 38 metres tall respectively, carved into the sides of the mountain behind the town. Clive and Ricky climbed the larger Buddha and sat on the top of his head, a great feeling only marred by the nagging pain from a tooth Clive had had taken out in Kabul. 'We went to the tea-house and the people were very friendly. The local policeman was there, in his patched old uniform. They let us stay the night in a back room, for nothing.' The food was certainly nothing to write home about: 'Mainly powdered egg and slices of melon. Everyone in Afghanistan had dysentery. There were hamburger restaurants, but you'd see how they treated meat in the markets, just picking it up from the floor... The ice cream was disgusting too, it tasted like shaving foam. In every bar they had an old fashioned wind-up record player with a horn, and a boy working it, playing 78s, any sort of stuff, George Formby records even.' Travelling up to the mountains could be quite dangerous, but the mountain tribesmen accepted Clive and Ricky as they were, and treated them well.

The two then travelled through Pakistan to Kashmir, and down through India to Delhi. Ricky had worked out an elaborate swindle, which involved his having bought a substantial amount in traveller's cheques before they left. In Pakistan he reported them as lost. The company were sceptical but there were many street lawyers who were willing, for a fee, to issue a legal letter confirming the situation. Reluctantly the traveller's cheques were replaced. In the meantime Clive had obtained a student's ID card (again for a reasonable fee) with his photo on and Ricky's details. All he had to do was practise Ricky's signature. Though the lost cheques were cancelled, there was no real communication between the bureaux de change and it was easy for Clive to cash the original cheques while Ricky cashed the replacements. If it came to it, the man who cashed the originals could genuinely confirm that Ricky was not the person who had presented them.

'In the market in Delhi we met two high-caste girls who we got talking to, because they all speak English there. They showed us round the town. When they found out I played the banjo they said they had a little TV show, they sang together and they were looking for someone to play music behind them. They did traditional English songs and they asked me to back them. We met Aslam Ali, who was like an Indian Robin Day, spotty bow tie and all. It was very well paid. We also got to appear on their version of In Town Tonight; it was called something like On Town Tomorrow – they never get these things quite right! I met the musicians at the TV studio and they asked me to play for them. They didn't seem too interested until I played them some Uncle Dave Macon songs, and they really liked that – it was the rhythm they related to. The girls lived in a school, and I got a gig there as well. I was involved in a riot, with a couple of bricks narrowly missing me. The consulate rang me to warn me to stay indoors for a few days. I don't know what the riot was about. It's just something that happens at that time of year. It's the heat. We were moving around, a couple of weeks here, a couple there, just working our way round the country.'

Meanwhile, back in Britain, Robin and Mike were booked to be bottom of the bill support on a short tour by Elektra labelmates Tom Paxton and Judy Collins. The first date was on the 4th of November at the Albert Hall, followed by the Manchester Free Trade Hall the following night, the Ulster Hall, Belfast on the 8th and Birmingham Town Hall on the 12th. Lest Clive's absence be commented on by people familiar with the album, Joe Boyd explained in the programme notes: 'Most of the songs are written by Mike and Robin, the 2/3 [of the ISB] you will hear tonight. Clive is visiting a dream in Kashmir at press time.' While that may have implied that Clive would re-join the band later, Robin, interviewed in *Melody Maker* after the tour, made it clear Clive was not expected to rejoin. 'We may add a third member, but I don't think it will be Clive, even if he comes back from India. Our music is changing all the time, and I don't think his style would fit in with what we are doing now.'

Clive agrees: 'There was never any question of me being in the band, they didn't intend that and I didn't intend that. I wasn't interested in what they were doing at the time in the sense that I couldn't add anything to it at that particular point. Now I see it in a totally different context. We had basically agreed to dismantle the group, we hadn't had much work. We'd made a record, but we hadn't had any offers. We didn't see any improvement.' Clive now believes that he was possibly being sidelined even before the album had been recorded. 'At the same time, Robin and Mike were trying to do their own thing. I know now that they were actually rehearsing on their own, without me. They were into making money and being successful, and I was into that too, but I wanted to enjoy myself, and I wasn't willing not to see my friends just because they thought it was uncool. When I decided to leave, I think they were delighted. I was the catalyst for the String Band, and in many ways the catalyst for Robin, but a lot of what the ISB did I had very little to do with. What people know of as the String Band I contributed very little to, in terms of music. It was mostly their stuff, though there were a few little odds and ends that I put in. I wasn't even that enamoured with their [later] music, it wasn't my sort of thing. My function has always been very much as a catalyst for other people, I provide the initial push to get them going, then they go on and do their own thing. That's what happened with them.'

In the meantime the album had been getting excellent reviews, though the sales were still not that great. It would eventually reach the lower reaches of the album charts, but not until the Incredible String Band's popularity had grown considerably and they had recorded two more albums. Nonetheless the album was voted *Melody Maker* folk album of the year – 'a sound that will astonish and please thousands of people' – and earned a place in the top five folk albums of the year in both *The Guardian* and *The Observer*.

Clive's return from India was hastened when he ran out of money and caught a particularly bad dose of dysentery ('and how!'), losing two stone in weight – and he wasn't particularly portly in the first place. The British Embassy arranged for him to be flown back to the UK, leaving Ricky to find his own way back. Clive: 'I got back and went to London and stayed with my father.' Bill's second wife Hilda had died of cancer in the mid-Sixties, and her house had been willed to her children. Bill had moved to Enfield and had married for a third time, to Evelyn Dalby.

'Then I went up to Edinburgh, then Glasgow. Ricky had gone off in a different direction and come back a different way. Our original idea had been that we were going to meet up later on. I went to stay with Ian Ferguson in Glasgow.' Unknown to Clive, a substantial amount of money, set aside to buy a pony, had been taken from Mary Stewart's house at the time he left. When he returned he was horrified to find that he was being blamed for the theft, which he genuinely knew nothing about. Many years later Ricky confessed that he was the culprit, albeit for a bizarre reason. He explained to Clive that he had had doubts about his commitment to the India trip and took the money, knowing Clive would probably be blamed, to make sure he could not stay at Balmore any longer! Even though Robin Williamson later told Mary that Clive was innocent, she would never speak to him again.

Some of the houses in the street where Ian and Clive lived were frequently under police surveillance, due to the presence of a brothel or two and a lively trade in stolen goods. The police noticed a fair bit of coming and going from Clive's and Ian's flat and also recognised some of the faces. Ian thinks they may have stopped and searched one of them and found cannabis on him. The cannabis had been brought back from Afghanistan by Clive, strapped to his leg to get it through customs. According to Ian, it had turned out to be of pretty poor quality. On 16th December the flat was raided. As well as a quantity of cannabis, the police found five sugar cubes impregnated with more or less pure LSD. The LSD was not intended for sale, and Ian cannot remember who had given it to them. It had possibly been there for several months and they may even have acquired it when it was still legal. Ian tried it a few times, and Clive would later claim to have tried it only once. 'People used to tell me you could write fantastic music on LSD, but it didn't affect me at all. It was rubbish, I couldn't do anything. I just wanted to sit down.' Clive and Ian were remanded in Glasgow's notorious Barlinnie prison until they came up for trial at the Sheriff Court on the 30th of December. The prosecution went out of its way to paint the accused in the darkest colours as a serious threat to Scottish youth. LSD had only just been declared illegal in September (it had often been used in psychiatric medicine earlier in the decade) and the case was the first in Scotland to involve it. Clive and Ian pleaded guilty to charges of possession. In a case like this the usual penalty would have been a hefty fine, but the prosecution were so aggressive that the Sheriff felt out of his depth (Clive recalls he had no real idea what LSD actually was) and decided to recommend the case be referred to the High Court for sentencing. There are many subtle differences between the law in Scotland and England, a Sheriff being the equivalent of a County Court judge in

England. Barlinnie was a great shock, even though they were only on remand. They were split up and each had to share a cell with two other remand prisoners. While there Clive got talking to a 'public-school type' who was briefly in the prison. He had been a secret agent during the war, had been captured in France, and had spent some time in Fresnes prison, in considerably less comfortable circumstances than Clive had. The ever-creative Clive, unsure of how long they would be in Barlinnie, began to carve a chess set out of soap. He had only completed two pieces before they were set free. When the case was looked at more closely, it was realised that neither Ian nor Clive had any previous convictions, and so they were released on the 16th of January 1967, after being fined £100 each: 'Which took forever to pay off...'

Billy Connolly: 'It was a huge mystery for a long time; it was a bit like Chuck Berry going to prison. There were various people saying various things. I knew they'd gone to prison but I wasn't sure what for. The people who liked Clive didn't really care much, they were more hip. Hamish Imlach got busted at the same time; they found some hash in his car. It did your reputation no harm; people didn't judge you badly on it. If anything it made you even more attractive.'

Hamish was one of the few people who actually visited Clive and Ian in Barlinnie, a fact Clive was sure did not go unnoticed by the authorities. Hamish's bust did not actually take place until 1968, when he was careless enough to park his car in a space which blocked someone's access. His car was towed away and when the police searched it to try and find some clues to its owner, they found a substantial amount of hash in the glove compartment. Hamish had bought it in London as a favour for someone else, and was so eager to get his car back he had forgotten about it. He wondered why the police started rubbing their hands with glee when he turned up at the station to claim his vehicle...

CHAPTER 5

BACK AGAIN, *still* WAILING

5
Back again, still wailing

'Banjoland *was refused by every single company in* *London. That's probably a record!'*

*T*hinking it might be a good idea to get out of Glasgow for a while, Ian, Clive and Ian's girlfriend went down to London to stay with Clive's father. Ian and his girlfriend got their own flat in London shortly afterwards. Clive had been making him a grey frock coat, which he never collected. They would not meet again for over thirty years. Back in London Clive got a message to go to the offices of Elektra Records to pick up some royalties due to him and to arrange a photo shoot in the East End with Mike and Robin for a new picture to be used on the front cover of the American issue of their album, as the art director did not like the original cover photo.

'They paid my expenses for the day, my taxis etc. The suit I wore I had had made in India [by a tailor called Saville Roy!] – it was made in Kashmir out of cashmere wool.' Ian: 'It was a dreadful suit! I was always telling him not to wear it, but he really liked it.' The photo that was used was taken in a scrap yard in the East End, and shows the trio sitting in the body of a double-decker bus lying on its side. In contrast to the original cover, Clive now looks remarkably smart, wearing a shirt, tie and jumper under his suit, as well as a matching cap and polished brown boots. Mike and Robin are now studiedly scruffy. When the three met up again, Mike told Clive that he had known he was going to be busted, having noticed the police cars cruising about. Clive quite reasonably asked Mike why he hadn't warned him, and he replied that he didn't want to get involved! The album was released in America in the spring with new sleeve notes giving a history of the band. Mike's comments on the individual songs were retained.

From early 1967, Bert Jansch, John Renbourn, Jackie McShee, bassist Danny Thompson and drummer Terry Cox (who would shortly name themselves The Pentangle) began a regular Sunday nightclub at the Horseshoe Hotel, opposite Tottenham Court Road tube station. Seating 400, the club would become a base for the band for the next year. Their first gig as The Pentangle was in May 1967, and from June onwards the band would invite friends to do guest spots, Clive, Wizz Jones, Ralph McTell, Anne Briggs, Davy Graham, Les Bridger, Sandy Denny and Alexis Korner among them. During this time Clive was working as often as he could around the London folk clubs, one advertisement having him playing at the famous Les Cousins club at 49 Greek Street on Friday the 22nd of October. He was booked for the first slot from 7.30 – 11: 'Prompt start at 8. Clive Palmer. Very fine banjo player. Come early to obtain seats.' The practice was for the club to close and then re-open for the all night session from 11.30 to 6. On this occasion the evening guests were Ralph McTell and Bob Bunting, 'two new and interesting artists.' Folk fan Nick Burdett saw Clive a couple of times in this period doing floor spots at Les Cousins. A floor spot was an unpaid audition which hopefully would impress the club owners enough to lead to a paid booking. 'I'd just seen the ISB (Robin and Mike) at a folk club in Hampstead run by Leon Rosselson, just before or after *5,000 Spirits* came out. I expected Clive to have a broad Scottish accent but he sounded very London, to my amazement! He came across as a very unpretentious bloke who was going to play the music he wanted. We all loved it. He didn't mention the ISB, just got on with playing some American traditional songs on banjo and guitar. I think he also played a plucked string instrument he had made himself. I thought then that the musical path he was travelling was sticking to traditional music whilst Robin and Mike were more in line with the "expand your mind" music of the time.'

In the latter half of 1967, Clive teamed up with Wizz Jones, who had broken up his duo with Pete Stanley. Wizz recalls Clive playing several other instruments in their duo besides banjo: an Indian hand-blown organ, a Strohl violin (one of those without a normal body where the strings were amplified through a gramophone-style horn) and a balalaika. 'We used to do Those Were The Days but we used to sing it in semi-mad Russian, all these mad, stupid ideas. One thing I learned from Clive was the art of simplicity. It's so easy to over-adorn something and do too much. He had all the technique available, but it's having the technique, and not using it.' Clive and Wizz were booked to play on the BBC radio show Country Meets Folk, upsetting the producer by insisting on doing two duo items and one solo each when he was expecting four duo performances. The two songs they played as a duo were the well-known Come All You Fair And Tender Ladies and Swanoa Tunnel, the second of which was augmented by Brian Brocklehurst on double bass. What sounds like autoharp on Fair and Tender Ladies was just the overtones from Wizz's guitar. 'It had a lovely ring to it,' Clive recalls. Wizz: 'Working together was great, musically it was always good. It was nice to work with Clive for a little while, but it could be difficult. Once we were due to play at Sheffield University, and we arranged to meet up at my house in Balham and I was going to drive. He arrived late on his moped because he had broken down on the way over. He had got so annoyed that he threw a spanner at the bike and it went right through the vellum of his banjo. On another occasion the whole head had broken off his banjo and I remember him fixing it with Araldite [before Superglue, the strongest adhesive available], sitting with it in front of the gas fire trying to get it to cure faster before we could set off for the gig.'

Clive and Wizz did record together, but the result, an album called *Banjoland*, was to remain unreleased for nearly forty years. Peter Eden was probably best known on the folk scene for having discovered Donovan, managing him (in partnership with Geoff Stephens) and producing his first two albums for Pye during an extraordinary year ending in late 1965, when Donovan ended their contract. Eden mainly worked in the jazz field, though he also enjoyed folk and blues, going on to produce albums by Mike Cooper, Duffy Power and Heron, a Reading-based band who liked to record in a field near their rural cottage. He worked for labels such as Deram, Dawn, Island and his own Turtle label. Eden had heard of Clive and greatly admired what he had done on the first ISB album, so he got in touch and Clive was more than happy to accept his offer to make an LP. 'I was expecting new songs,' says Peter now, 'so it was a bit of a surprise when Clive came up with all these old numbers.' Seven of the thirteen tracks they recorded are Edwardian-style instrumentals, and the album ends with Coventry Carol, learned from a set of Christmas carols arranged for banjo, and printed in the journal of the Banjo Mandolin & Guitar Club. The title track is a lively Joe Morley composition which features Wizz on rhythm guitar, as does the next track, The Boy I Love Is Up In The Gallery, a music hall song made famous by Marie Lloyd which Mike Heron recalls Clive singing in Edinburgh folk clubs. There are three songs of the sentimental kind, whose influence clearly shows in some of Clive's own compositions. Two were learned from old 78s of the great Irish tenor Count John McCormack, and Smiling Through is a song one of Clive's brothers once sang in a competition. Tell Me The Stories Of Jesus is a song Clive and his classmates used to sing at assembly in primary school ('with an old lady playing the piano') which he had always liked. Here it is backed by Wizz's guitar, and Peter later had his friend, jazz arranger Michael Gibbs, write a string arrangement for it; until the album eventually surfaced many years later, it was rumoured that a Salvation Army band had been used, which would probably have worked very well. Peter paid for the extra musicians and for the sessions, which were held in Denmark Street's Central Sound Studios, and was very pleased with the results: 'I loved its roughness. It was an exact statement of how he was, and wonderfully at odds with what the rest of the world was preoccupied with at the time.' The album was a little short on playing time, but Clive had plenty of material and Peter could easily have recorded more tracks in the same vein. However, despite Peter's considerable efforts, there was not a record company in the UK that was interested in *Banjoland*. Clive: 'It was refused by every single company in London. That's probably a record!' Wizz: 'That was probably the last thing we did together, I think. I don't know why we stopped playing together; we just got fed up with each other I guess.' *Banjoland* was eventually released, with the addition of two of the Country Meets Folk radio tracks, in 2005.

The Pentangle's club at The Horseshoe was still going, and Clive was the advertised guest on the 11th of February 1968. Jo Lustig took over Pentangle's management the following month, and advised the band to withdraw from public performance for a period, after which he would re-launch them as a concert hall act – a favourite and proven business tactic of his. The last night at the Horseshoe was March 10th.

In 1968 Transatlantic released the album *Two Sides of Hamish Imlach*. Clive arranged some of the songs and plays banjo and kazoo on them. Archie Fisher plays concertina on various tracks and banjo on one track (I Got Fooled, on which Clive plays kazoo), along with Ray Warleigh on flute, John MacKinnon on fiddle and Martin Frey on tuba. There is also an uncredited blues piano player on a couple of tracks. Hamish's material is largely humorous, with a nod to the blues and a couple of Scottish folk songs including the sarcastic D-Day Dodgers. A later Hamish album *Old Rarity*, issued in 1971, opens with a track called Clive's Song, which Hamish credited to Clive. It's a minor key blues, opening with the lyrics: 'Been all around this great big world, just got home today,' which suggests that it may be a version of the traditional American song Don't Let Your Deal Go Down. Clive doesn't remember it at all.

CHAPTER 6

Fame, Stockrooms and Temples

6
Fame, Stockrooms & Temples

'Clive would sit, eyes closed, poetic features inscrutable as he played, enhancing his legendary status with every performance.'

 ate in 1968 Clive decided to move down to Cornwall, where he was eventually to team up with Henry Bartlett and Pete Berryman to form The Famous Jug Band.

Michael David ('Henry') Bartlett was born on the 3rd of May 1943, eleven days before Clive. Growing up in Mitcham in Surrey, about ten miles south of London, he became part of a crowd based around The Whitgift pub in Croydon, who shared his musical tastes for jug band, blues, jazz and folk music. Summer weekends were spent hitching down to Brighton, sleeping on the beach. Michael's physical stature, his beard and his attraction for the ladies led to him being nicknamed Henry VIII, augmented to 'King Henry' after winning a particularly hard-contested card game with the self-styled 'king of the beatniks' in Brighton one night. Among his compatriots on these trips were Ralph McTell and Rod (the Mod) Stewart. Henry used to say that Ralph McTell was the only person who still called him Mick. *Melody Maker* once called Henry 'one of the last surviving ravers of old. He has seen more dawns rise on Brighton beach than some of us have had hot dinners.' Henry first met up with Clive in the summer of 1960 around the time when Clive was doing his stint as a pavement artist outside the Tate Gallery. Clive's musical reputation had preceded him. Henry began running clubs to promote the kind of music he enjoyed, the first of which was in the basement of a coffee bar called The Olive Tree, on the Brighton Road in Croydon. Ralph and Wizz were both residents at various points, as was Jacqui McShee, who was accompanied by guitarist 'Little Chris' Ayliffe. Henry's club took place on Sunday afternoons, filling in those tedious hours between the pubs closing at two and everyone heading off to venues like Eel Pie Island in the evening. Later he ran a folk club at The Buck's Head, Mitcham, booking the likes of Malcolm Price, Pete Stanley, Wizz Jones, Bert Jansch, Alex Campbell, Davy Graham, John Renbourn and

The Dedicated Men. Later still he ran a club at the Red Lion in Sutton with Jacqui McShee, to whom he was actually engaged at one point. In early 1964 Cyril Davies died: he was of the founding fathers of blues music in Britain, and Henry was among those who organised a benefit concert at The Fairfield Halls, Croydon, to raise money for his widow.

In 1965 Henry met Johnny Joyce and Mac McGann at the Buck's Head. On a trip to Ken Collyer's Jazz Club, Johnny and Henry met up with Beverley Kutner, and Mac suggested they formed a group which became The Levee Breakers (after the Memphis Minnie song When The Levee Breaks, later given a sound thrashing by Led Zeppelin). The line-up was Mac on tiple (a Hawaiian instrument like a small guitar, with ten strings in four courses), harmonica, and rhythm board (an amplified board on which you stamped your foot in time), Johnny on 12-string guitar and Beverley on vocals. Beverley later married, and recorded two albums with, John Martyn. Band rehearsals were held at Henry's parents' house, and as they played blues and jug band music, they suggested that Henry should join in on jug. The jug used in jug band music was of the sort used for cider, usually made of stoneware. You played it by blowing across the open mouth like a flute and using your mouth to shape the notes. The sound produced was a satisfying low 'whump' and a good player could play bass lines using specific notes. As he was organising a club, Henry set about getting them bookings, and as he also possessed a reel-to-reel tape recorder the family bedroom became a recording studio, though unfortunately these tapes got destroyed. The band were spotted playing in a club in Tooting by Beatles associate Klaus Voorman (best known for designing the cover of their *Revolver* album and as a one-time member of Manfred Mann), and his interest led to their recording four tracks for Parlophone at Abbey Road Studios. The tracks were all jug band standards: Going To Germany, Stealin', Babe I'm Leaving You and Wild About My Loving, the last two being issued as a single. The band played all over the south of England, a definite career highlight being the night they shared a bill at Southsea Pier with Jesse Fuller, composer of San Francisco Bay Blues. Another fondly recalled gig was the opening night of the Orpington Folk Club at the Royal Oak in Green Street Green in Kent on the 17th of May 1965. Organiser Terry Sparks had wanted to book his own favourite singer, Paul Simon, but was outvoted as the others thought a 'name' act would be a less risky choice for the first night (not to mention the fact that Simon was asking a £12 fee). Terry remembers Beverley as a very sexy performer, as does singer/songwriter Ross Barlow, initiated into the world of folk music that very night: 'I'm sure she was the first girl I'd ever seen wearing a miniskirt!'

Henry later got Ralph McTell (though he was still Ralph May at that point) his first paid gig at the Orpington club. Later Henry and Ralph formed a band with Mick North from the Malcolm Price Trio on mandolin. The Strimmed Implements followed this, a band Henry put together with Ron Geesin (later to work with Pink Floyd on *Atom Heart Mother*) on banjo and piano, Brian Knight on guitar, Roger Churchyard on fiddle, Bill Shortt on washboard and Geoff Bradford on guitar. Brian and Geoff had both been involved with members of the Rolling Stones in the years before they became famous. Their strange name was down to a character in the Whitgift who was nicknamed 'Mr Winky-Wanky' and was an endless source of malapropisms. He'd meant stringed instruments. Several experimental line-ups followed featuring Bob Kerr and Jim Chambers of Bonzo Dog fame, and Mickey Sutton. They played several gigs around South London and had a residency at Osterley Jazz Club.

In the summer of 1967 Henry went down to Cornwall to stay with Ralph McTell for two weeks' summer holiday. Ralph had rented a caravan on a farm owned by a Mr Willoughby Gulachson, after whom he later named a guitar instrumental. Also on the spread, off the A30 near Mitchell, was The Folk Cottage, where Ralph was the resident singer. The Folk Cottage was an old granite farm worker's cottage, which had been gutted and turned into a club in the summer of 1965 with a snack bar downstairs and the concert room upstairs. It had a large crack in the back wall, supported by a baulk of timber, and the only toilet facilities were an Elsan chemical toilet in an outhouse at the side of the cottage, fondly known as Ye Olde Bog. On a busy night at the club it was often full to the brim. Fortunately there were plenty of other places nearby for those who preferred to pee al fresco. The Olde Bog had one very slight advantage, in that the container the chemicals came in served as a passable jug for Henry on at least one occasion. The Folk Cottage had been started by a local schoolteacher called John Sleep and a former oilrig worker called John Hayday.

Wizz Jones: 'We hit Cornwall, me and Pete Stanley, and we found out there was a folk club on a Friday night. Someone came to our gig and told us about it, and we went there. It was all very much, not traddy, but not much going on, it was mainly a load of teachers in Morris Minors... We kind of moved in on it, and said maybe we could run some other nights? So we ran Monday and Wednesday, and after the Friday night club we said we could run an all-nighter? They threw their hands up in horror! So we ran this all-night session, it just went boom, it was easy, in those days nothing was going on, it was underground, it was new and exciting, and it absolutely took off.' During the summer season the club was open Monday, Tuesday, Thursday and Friday. On Saturdays the legendary Cornish singer Brenda Wootton ran The Pipers Folk Club at St Buryans, near Penzance. During his holiday fortnight Henry played around the local clubs with Ralph, mandolinist Bob Strawbridge and 'Whispering' Mick Bennett (so named because of his very loud voice), who played the washboard. The combination worked well. 'We wowed them!' says Henry. At St Buryans Henry met Jenny, a young lady from Penzance whom he would later marry. He had no sooner arrived back in London when Ralph rang him to say that the two Johns wanted to give up running the Folk Cottage, and the opportunity was there for him to take it over if he wanted to. He wanted to. As soon as he was able, Henry returned to Cornwall and moved into a caravan in the field opposite The Folk Cottage with Mick Bennett. In October, Henry, Mick, Bob Strawbridge and Mac McGann (on double-neck guitar!) helped Ralph McTell out on the track Louise on his first album *Eight Frames A Second*, released in 1968.

At the end of the summer season, after the tourists had all gone home, The Folk Cottage opened only on Friday nights for the locals. Henry began a different booking policy, calling on many of the musicians he had booked and worked with in his London clubs. He could offer his guests a gig at the Folk Cottage on Friday night and one at St Buryans on the Saturday. When the 1968 summer season began again he would book guests for a week from Thursday to Tuesday, with a Saturday night gig at St Buryans thrown in. Whispering Mick ran the coffee bar, famous for its pasties, soup and curried shepherd's pie, courtesy of Jenny. Blues singer Gerry Lockran was one of the first artists to be booked regularly in Cornwall, followed by Michael Chapman, who came down as an itinerant singer when still an art teacher in Leeds. Up to this point, the Cornish folk clubs had relied on local guests and Come All Ye's which drew diverse audiences who joined in enthusiastically with the singing, perched on hard benches in outlandish venues such as the Count House, the predecessor of the St Buryans club, perched on the cliffs at Botallick. When non-local artists were booked on a weekly basis, the Folk Cottage may have lost something of its collective camaraderie, but it raised the musical expectations of the audience and there was no going back. There was no shortage of guests eager to visit Cornwall with their families; Derek Brimstone, Alex Atterson, and Wizz were all regulars.

Jenny Bartlett: 'They produced some amazing nights when the place was heaving and outside the yard was full of people sitting around chilling out to the music and anything else they could lay their hands on. Upstairs people sat on rows of uncomfortable benches facing the stage with its dark silhouette of a figure on the wall behind the performers. I remember The Climax Blues Band playing a Wednesday night for the take on the door, John Renbourn, Jacqui McShee, Tim Hart and Maddy Prior, Jo-Ann Kelly, Diz Disley, Bert Jansch, Noel Murphy and Shaggis all appearing there.' Shaggis, a.k.a. Davey Johnstone, was a young multi-instrumental wizard who later joined Elton John's band, where he remains to this day.

Mick Bennett is another Cornwall-based musician who plays a key role in Clive's story. He had arrived there in 1967, another Londoner who had one day just decided to jump on a train to Penzance, 'looking for adventure'. He came to Cornwall with no real preconception of what he would find, and ended up staying there. He had sung as a child, and his father enjoyed light opera and had a fine singing voice himself. Mick: 'I also had cousins of a musical bent and from an early age was encouraged to sing at parties etc. I loved this as I usually received money for my efforts. The literary side of things remains a mystery, as I'm totally untutored and self-taught. I'd started in showbiz as a Bluecoat in a holiday camp, the standard working class route in those days, but drifted into playing solo in London, mainly in Arts Labs. I'd sing a couple of songs unaccompanied, and then read some of my poetry. That went on for about eighteen months.' Mick enjoyed blues and rock and roll, but was more interested in poetry before he came to Cornwall. 'I went there to escape from my roots and the inevitability of factory work. I was lucky enough to meet Ralph McTell and Wizz Jones and others and the folk influence took over.' At the end of the season he spent some time in Morocco, a country he would regularly visit over the next ten years.

Another piece of the jigsaw had fallen into place when Henry was walking on one of the beaches at Newquay and was introduced by his friend Barney to Pete Berryman, who was busking. Henry: 'He was playing stuff like Hey Joe and he seemed quite good, so we invited him along to the club.' Pete was actually quite an experienced musician, having started out playing electric guitar in local Cornish rock bands in the early Sixties. In 1964 he was in a band called The Shondells (that was Shaun & The Shondells, not Tommy James & The Shondells of Mony Mony fame), who played on the London club scene and even had a single released on EMI. Inspired by Davy

Graham, he began to get more into playing acoustic folk/blues, and in 1966 he toured Britain with an Israeli folk group called The Haverim.

Pete, Henry and Mick had formed The Great Western Jug Band in 1967, along with John the Fish on guitar. John was originally from London and was almost regarded as an honorary Cornishman, well known for backing Brenda Wootton. He had started his career as a professional folk singer as a resident at The Count House. Bob Strawbridge was an occasional member of the band, too. The contacts Henry had made during the summer enabled them to do a tour of London clubs in the winter of 1967/68, playing venues like The Dungeon and the Bromley Folk Club at The Star & Garter. The summer of 1968 was another busy time for the Folk Cottage, with many students coming to visit and promising bookings for the end of the year at their colleges.

Clive had visited Cornwall often since his teens and finally made the decision to move down there permanently towards the end of 1968. Wizz Jones phoned Henry to make the arrangements, and Clive arrived around October. Jenny remembers him turning up at St Buryans one night wearing an overcoat he had made himself out of old army blankets. Henry and Jenny had married in September and moved to Penzance, so Clive moved into the caravan with Mick, who then left on one of his regular visits to Morocco.

Pete, Clive and Henry began rehearsing to form a new band. After some discussion, reminiscent of the brainstorming session which produced the Incredible String Band's name, they came up with The Famous Jug Band. It seemed like a good idea at the time. One night the trio decided to visit the Wadebridge Folk Club to do a floor spot and hopefully get a booking there. That evening the featured group were The Jayfolk, a female quartet from Truro. The group had been going for around four years, having been formed by Jill Johnson when she was fourteen, and, she says, 'all long hair and beads.' The band originally consisted of Jill, her two older twin sisters and her best friend, though the twins had moved to Canada in 1967 and had been replaced by two other girls. They had built up a good reputation and played at local festivals, clubs and hotels. At the time of the Wadebridge gig Jill was studying business at a local technical college. She was obviously the outstanding talent in the group. Henry: 'We were knocked out by her voice, and Pete was knocked out by the rest of her as well!' The FJB had a chat about it and decided to ask to Jill to join them on the forthcoming tour. She accepted immediately, but her parents weren't quite so keen on her giving up her college course. Henry: 'We actually had to go and meet her parents and have tea with them and get their approval – they weren't too sure about their eighteen-year-old daughter going off with all these long-haired scruffy gits!' The fact that Henry was married and seemed quite a responsible individual swung it, and Jenny thinks she may even have been expected to act as chaperone.

Famous Jug Band, winter 1968. Photo courtesy Market Square Records

On the 21st of November The Famous Jug Band supported Ralph McTell ('Transatlantic Recording Star. Guitarist /Songwriter and Britain's Representative in Austrian Song Festival') at the St. Johns Hall, Penzance. John the Fish was also on the bill, with both Clive and Pete receiving separate billing in addition. On New Year's Eve they played at The White Hart, Launceston.

Early in 1969 the four-piece FJB set off on tour. Jenny: 'They were a great mix. Henry was the front man with his laconic humour and always built up a good rapport with the audience. Though the other members of the band used to groan at some of the old jokes he regularly trotted out, people liked him and related to him. Clive would sit, eyes closed, poetic features inscrutable as he played, enhancing his legendary status with every performance. Pete's intricate guitar playing and songs gained him many admirers, while Jill, slim, small and shy with a dynamic voice, captivated everyone. The balance was good and the fact that they communicated well set them apart from many groups of the time who lacked this ability. Gigs were mainly in clubs and universities around Sheffield and the Home Counties. They appeared on the Radio One Club, and did several other radio shows. They gained a following amongst the people who would see them on the university and folk club circuits, many of whom would visit the Cornish clubs in the summer.' While they were in London Wizz Jones phoned them up and suggested that they contact Pierre Tubbs. Pierre was Head of Creative Services for United Artists/Liberty Records, and had recorded Roy Harper's *Folkjokeopus*. He felt sure that the way ahead was to record people with original material, so Roy suggested that he record some original people, specifically naming Wizz Jones and Clive Palmer. Pierre recorded the Wizz Jones album for UA, and, when he heard from the FJB, invited them to come and see him with their instruments for an impromptu audition. Henry: 'We played there and then in his office, just ran through some numbers, and I think he was quite taken with Jill's voice. He said "Let's do something".' Pierre: 'I loved Jill's voice. That's why I signed the buggers!'

According to the sleeve notes for the album, the meeting took place in February, and the album was recorded soon afterwards. The sessions took place over a couple of days in a small basement studio in Putney. Wizz Jones recalls Clive telling him that he had made a rule that if there was a woman in the band there were to be no

Famous Jug Band February 1969.
Photo courtesy of Pete Berryman

81

relationships, but nature took its course and Jill and Pete became a couple after she has split up with her previous boyfriend, a nice young chap from Truro who was studying dentistry in London. His name was Roger Meddows-Taylor and he was also a musician, eventually doing rather well for himself as the drummer in a band called Queen. The FJB embarked on a tour taking in London, Cambridge and Sheffield. The Sheffield gig was a memorable one. Pete: 'We had played the Highcliffe Hotel, a great folk club run by Win White and compered by the outrageous Tony Capstick. After the gig we found it was snowing and very cold, and the four of us were travelling with our instruments in a little ex-Post Office Morris Minor van. The hill down to the town was steep and slippery, but no need to worry – Clive went into his expert persona and decided he would drive – down the pavement.' The next morning Jill received something of a culture shock when the band were driving around looking for somewhere to get a hot meal. Jill: 'It was cold and snowing and Clive said he knew a place we could go for dinner. He took us to a Salvation Army shelter!'

Even before the album was released, Clive was starting to become frustrated by his role in the Jug Band. 'Henry was booking us gigs and making a mess of it, so there was some friction there. He would exaggerate the fee to get us to do the gig. Pete and Jill were making decisions together instead of individually. I'd more or less exhausted the artistic possibilities of what I wanted to do.' Liberty released a Famous Jug Band single, The Only Friend I Own/A Leaf Must Fall in May. It gathered some airplay and did the band's reputation no harm at all. It was reviewed on Radio One's Round Table show, where new releases were listened to and commented upon by guest celebrities, in this instance Eric Clapton. Eric was guardedly non-committal, saying that 'anyone who can strum a guitar is a friend of mine.' A later gig at Sheffield University in the same month was also memorable. Clive was travelling in a minivan with Henry and Jenny, who was six months pregnant at the time, (Pete and Jill travelled separately) and Clive announced he would do all the announcements on stage that night, something Henry usually did. The stage was made up of blocks pushed together to make a larger area – but not pushed together quite closely enough. They opened with Saro Jane and Clive got as far as the first line before suddenly disappearing. His chair leg had fallen down the crack between two parts of the stage and he was catapulted backwards. Pete: 'I remember the incident being a source of great comic relief for us as the tour was becoming a misery because of the tensions between us and Clive. He re-emerged smiling.' The end came shortly afterwards. Clive had a row with Henry when he found out from a promoter how much less the agreed fee for a gig was than what Henry had told him it would be. The next morning Henry, Jill and Pete arrived at Clive's caravan and told him they had decided to try it on their own and wanted him to leave the band. 'I said that was fine. It wasn't acrimonious, I wasn't bothered.'

Clive's departure left a gap though, and Pete and Jill approached Wizz Jones about joining the band in Clive's place. He remembers them coming round to his home in Balham to rehearse, and the new version of the FJB did a recording session for the BBC at The Paris Cinema, in Lower Regent Street, London, on the 29th of May. Four songs were played on the John Peel show on the 11th of June, including the old jug band standard Going to Germany, Black Is the Colour, Pete's I Don't Need No Orchestra and Common Or Garden Mystery, an Alan Tunbridge song from Wizz's repertoire. Tony Wilson interviewed the band for an article to promote the new album published in *Melody Maker* on the 21st of June entitled 'What! A Jug Band from Cornwall?' The article mentioned their Peel session, an appearance on TV in East Anglia and noted: 'Clive Palmer, banjo player and international traveller extraordinary was with the group [and was shown in the photo accompanying the article] but has since hit the road again and so Whizz [*sic*] Jones has stepped in to take his place on gigs.' Wizz sounded cautious: 'I want to stay in London, I just can't move down to Cornwall, though the lure is strong. I'm definitely working with the group professionally, but I shall still be working in folk clubs solo.' He said he saw things as still being in the experimental stage until they had worked together a bit more. 'And we're going to have to use amplification in some places. We feel we could perhaps use more instruments. If we get the opportunity we could work with another guitarist.' Pete added: 'But we are mainly an acoustic group, which is our appeal.' Henry: 'We haven't really got the usual jug band sound. We do some of the old stuff just to show we can do it.' The article went on to say the band were hoping the album would help them move into bigger gigs, especially on the university circuit. There was no shortage of new material, Alan Tunbridge was going to be writing some songs for the band, and Pete and Alan were planning to start writing together. 'So the group will be featuring lots of original things – a welcome change from the jug bands who try to sound like a scratched 78 recorded in 1927. The Famous Jug Band have no great expectations except to play their music as often as they please, as well as they can. And if fame and fortune isn't forthcoming – well there's the peace and quiet of

Cornwall to relish and the Atlantic to paddle in. Some people have all the luck.'

No one is too sure if any gigs were done with Wizz in the line-up, though he soon chose not to throw in his lot with the Jug Band. At the time he did not feel comfortable in a group context, having had a bad experience when he had been asked to replace Gordon Giltrap in Don Partridge's band. He could also make more money as a solo performer, which, having a family to support, always had to be the major consideration.

Meanwhile Clive had wasted no time in recruiting Folk Cottage regulars John Bidwell and Tim Wellard, as well as Mick Bennett, to form the Stockroom Five. Tim recalls Clive turning up unexpectedly at the Folk Cottage and saying to him and John Bidwell: 'I've left the Jug Band, let's do something!' They were surprised, but pleased to accept.

John Bidwell was from Rejerrah, a village near Newquay, and had played in a schoolboy rock band called The Monarchs while at Newquay Grammar School, ('we never really got out of the rehearsal space') though he wasn't particularly into electric guitar, choosing to borrow one when he needed to. The repertoire of the band was typical of pre-Beatles pop, mainly Buddy Holly, Eddie Cochrane and Shadows material. Tim Wellard, a year younger, also played in the Monarchs. He was born in Malta, his father working for GCHQ, and the family moved around every three years as part of his job; he had arrived in Cornwall in his teens. John and Tim were both caught up in the folk boom of the time, initially from records. Their first live folk experience was seeing Nadia Cattouse, at a nearby club called The Smugglers' Den in Treballan, near Cubert. Nadia was a singer from Belize who was very popular on the British folk scene at the time with her Caribbean-flavoured songs and calypsos. She had also appeared on the same Edinburgh Folk Festival album on which Robin and Clive made their recording debut. As well as guitar, John had played banjo from about the age of 16. In 1964 he went to Bradford University to study chemistry, but dropped out after a year. However, there was a thriving folk club in Bradford called The Topic, and it was there that he started to hear more English folk material from the likes of Martin Carthy & Dave Swarbrick, and also attended bigger concerts to see Alex Campbell and the McPeake Family. John returned home, getting a job with English China Clay, a major employer in Cornwall. In 1965, Tim went up to London to study Law but, like John, only completed a year of the course. He decided he just wanted to play folk music: 'The cause of my downfall!'

The Stockroom Five's name has often been a source of confusion, especially as they were always a quartet. Their name has also appeared in print as The Barrelhouse Five, an error possibly caused by it being translated into German and back again at a later date. The origin of the name lay in John's attempts to start a folk club in the unused storeroom of a hotel in Truro. The scheme fell through, but what was printed on the door of the room they had hoped to use sounded like a good name for a band: Stockroom Five. Clive was later to describe the band's music as 'being much more to my taste' than that of the FJB, and they played American old-time music, especially songs by Clive's old favourite Uncle Dave Macon. Clive played banjo and occasional fiddle, Tim guitar, Mick percussion and John played both five and six-string banjos, plus guitar. All four of them sang. John had bought a six-string banjo in order to lend authenticity to the Uncle Dave numbers; Macon's guitarist Sam Magee had played six-string banjo on some recordings, having bought a brace of matching six and five-string Gibson Mastertone banjos in 1928 in a music store in Baltimore.

The Famous Jug Band's first album, *Sunshine Possibilities*, came out in July on Liberty. The opening track is Can't Stop Thinking About It, a song by Alan Tunbridge which had been part of Clive's and Wizz's repertoire. Clive starts the song with a staccato two-chord pattern on banjo, with Henry's jug sliding in below, while Pete shows off a few flashy guitar licks in the intro. The lyrics are blackly humorous:

He was missing when I found him.
He was dead as the car around him.
In the rain the siren was sounding.
Now he's lost his no-claims bonus.

Clive takes a confident lead vocal, with Pete and Jill in support.

Nickolson Sq. features Jill on lead vocal, backed by just Pete's guitar and the others on vocals. Clive insists that the song is not autobiographical, even though he did at one point occupy 'a little room tucked away in the rooftops' in Nicholson Square when he lived in Edinburgh. He Never Came Back is a novelty number, originating in the turn-of-the-century American Vaudeville scene, performed unaccompanied, almost in barbershop style. A Leaf Must Fall follows, usually considered to be Clive's finest hour as a songwriter. It tips a hat to Jacques Brel's song Ne Me Quitte Pas (a.k.a. If You Go Away) and makes sense of Pierre Tubbs' comments in the sleeve notes about Clive looking 'like a poet should look'.

And if they ask where you are, I'll say that you have flown.
Before you died of cold. And while your wings were strong.
And that I love you still. And that all will fade.

Pete follows with an instrumental Shakey Train Blues, and side one ends with the single track The Only Friend I Own, also written by Pete. It's a good fun song, with Clive on banjo and lead vocal, and on this they sound like a bona fide jug band. Side 2 opens with a gorgeous version of the traditional Scottish song Black Is the Colour, with both Clive and Pete on guitars, and Jill singing her heart out. She had sung this song in the Jayfolk, but Clive changed the arrangement, basing it strongly on Hamish Imlach's version. Saro Jane follows, a lively jug band standard with a brilliant jug solo from Henry. Train On The Island is another US import, group harmony over Pete's 'train guitar' with a flurry of bluegrass banjo to end. The last three tracks are Berryman compositions and all feature Clive on fiddle, with a coarse style which owes a lot to old jug band records. He had only started playing fiddle since he arrived in Cornwall. The Main Thing is a tirade against false gurus, and Breakfast Blues is a light number with a good tune and lyrics about the sheer hell of having to get up in the morning to go to work. The album's title track is a fine ending to the album:

There's a million of us together, just soaking up the weather
Beneath the orange trees
So we'll leave our cares behind us, if you're lucky you may find us
Way beyond the seas...

Reviews were all good, mostly praising the variety of styles and musicianship. *Melody Maker* called A Leaf Must Fall 'haunting – one of the best tracks on the album' and thought Nickolson Sq. 'Beatlish'. Pete's 'good modern material' was also praised, and the whole was 'highly entertaining. The Famous Jug Band lifted this particular type of music from out of 1929 and planted it very firmly in 1969.' In *The*

Guardian of 31/12/69, Robin Denselow compared the FJB album with other recent releases in the same field by the American Jim Kweskin Jug Band and the Panama Jug Band from Britain. 'Best of all, on Liberty, there's the Famous Jug Band, which includes founder member of the Incredibles, Clive Palmer, and the expansive jug blower who backed McTell, "Henry VIII". Their new album contains almost all new material, from whimsy to chanson, and is curiously reminiscent of the first Incredibles album. It certainly shows that jug bands need have nothing to do with musical crudity and clichés: the banjo and guitar playing is excellent, Henry's jug miraculously follows a difficult bass line, and against this they build delicate songs of wistful good humour. The influence may be Memphis, but the mood is London bedsitter.' Even *Titbits*, a popular weekly not normally known for its musical insight, liked the album: 'Tracks are a mixture of pop and folk and it is very distinctively played – adding up to 35 minutes of sheer listening enjoyment.'

Sunshine Possibilities was undoubtedly an artistic success, even though sales were not that great. It was influential, several of the songs becoming folk scene standards. Jenny Beeching and John the Fish both recorded versions of A Leaf Must Fall, while Tony Capstick recorded The Only Friend I Own. Scotland's JSD band did their own version of Sara Jane, recording it on both their first and third albums and releasing the second version as a single. The title track of the album also appeared on a Liberty Records sampler *Son of Gutbucket* in the same year.

Christine Quayle was another member of the Cornish folk scene whose path would later cross with Clive's. She had come down from the West Midlands at the age of 15 with her parents. Her father, Eric Quayle, had left business life to try his hand as a writer, buying a house out on the cliffs near Zennor, a quarter of a mile from the next nearest property. He eventually had 13 books published and was also known for his collection of 10,000 antiquarian books, specialising in early children's fiction. Chrissy was enormously inspired by the wildness of her new surroundings and would stand on the headland to sing and play her guitar. The locals started calling her 'The Mermaid of Zennor' after a well-known local legend:

A young fisherman called Matthew Trewella had a beautiful singing voice, and when he sang in church his voice carried out to sea, where it was heard by a mermaid. Some versions of the story give her the name of Morveren, though others say that was simply the old Cornish word for a mermaid. Anyway, the mermaid was unable to resist trying to get a look at the singer, so put on human clothing and attended church, always sitting at the back and causing everyone to wonder who she was. After her clothes fell open one night and her true identity was revealed, she fled back to the sea, but Matthew followed her; when she declared her love for him he agreed to join her under the sea. They were never seen again, and a carving, thought to be at least 500 years old, of a mermaid complete with comb and looking glass can still be seen on the end of a pew in St. Senera's church in Zennor. It is said that Matthew's singing can still sometimes be heard coming from below the waves.

In 1969 Chrissy started the Mermaid Folk Club, which she ran for three years, in a barn adjoining the Gurnard's Head Hotel. The club was open three nights a week, two of which were compered by local singer/songwriter Mike Silver, and the other by Bob Devereux.

Bob, another future Clive Palmer collaborator, had been born in Dorking in 1940 and had studied art at Kingston Art School (a year ahead of Eric Clapton and two years ahead of John Renbourn). Though he later started his own advertising agency, he never liked it and eventually, fearing he was turning into a collar-and-tie man, his wife suggested they move down to Cornwall. They bought a cottage in St Erth and Bob has lived there ever since, making a living as best he can from painting, writing, and printing. In 1969 he started a weekly folk club in St Ives called Mask, in Porthmeor Road, where (as 'Mask') he performed his poetry with guitarist Jim Hughes. He also compered one night a week at the Railway Hotel in Penzance. Mask performed a mixture of songs and spoken word pieces, the best known of which was the 25-minute Arnold, set in a street market with Bob playing all the various voices between songs. They also developed a piece called Yellow Dwarf which was constantly evolving, almost like a soap opera. Bob: 'We'd always leave the audience on a cliff-hanger, which we'd resolve next time we played that venue. It was a good way of getting return bookings!'

The Stockroom Five lasted from about May to September of 1969, and were very popular with the public, though there was still a certain amount of fallout from Clive's having left the FJB. For example,

Henry would never give them a booking at any of the clubs he had a hand in, including the Folk Cottage. The Folk Cottage was not normally open on Saturdays, as that was the night of Brenda Wooton's club at St Buryans, so the band approached the farmer who owned the Folk Cottage and arranged to run their own session. They also had a residency at Wadebridge Folk Club, and John recalls a gig at an event called The Cornish Wrestling Championships, which didn't go down quite so well! 'When we started to run the Folk Cottage ourselves we used to plaster Clive's old Ford 100E van with posters and drive around with Mick calling out the details of that night's gig through a megaphone. I also used to go up and down the beaches at Newquay with sandwich boards advertising that night's gig – they were always full and it's a shame there aren't any live tapes as, to coin a phrase, the joint was jumping.' Another regular gig for the band was in a church hall at Newquay each Sunday evening, run by a singer who put the Stockroom Five on after he had sung his own material. Unfortunately he soon found that the Stockroom Five had become the main draw. Jealous of this, he ensured his sets got longer until one night he announced they could only do two songs instead of the half-hour they had planned. This of course did not go down well with the band, and they said so. The next week he did the whole night himself and left them no time to play at all. The audience started slow-handclapping until the Stockroom Five came on stage and got ready to play. The singer walked over to Clive and put his hand on his strings to stop him playing, before walking away. Clive was furious, jumped to his feet and grabbed his banjo by the head and swung it at him. John: 'It missed him by a fraction of an inch, fortunately. If he had hit him it might have been murder, you know how heavy a banjo is!' Clive went after the singer, the two having to be held apart by their friends as the argument continued outside. The vicar diplomatically solved the problem by giving the Stockroom Five their own night in the hall, which went on to prove popular in its own right. Tim proudly recalls the Stockroom Five being 'an outlaw band' and says that they were more than once refused service in pubs because they were so scruffy, a story confirmed by Pete Berryman. The FJB and the Stockroom Five developed a certain friendly rivalry, playing much the same circuit of gigs. Though The Famous Jug Band were not exactly classy dressers themselves, Pete says the Stockroom Five were 'real freaks'. The band never recorded officially, but several tapes exist showing just how enjoyable the Stockroom Five's music was. A tape of Clive's unrecorded material in circulation among fans starts off with two of their performances, both excellent. Rise When the Rooster Crows has often turned up in Clive's repertoire over the years, and is an Uncle Dave Macon song, as is Been a Waggoner, which has the great line:

I'd rather ride a wagon and go to hell, than go to heaven in an automobile!

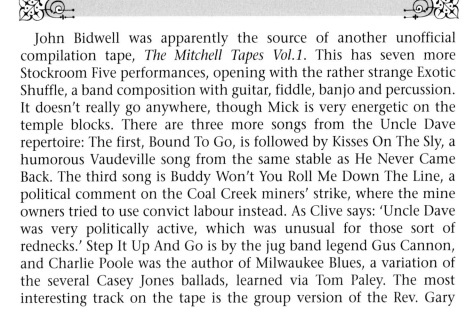

Uncle Dave Macon

Uncle Dave Macon did indeed run a haulage business at the turn of the century, in Kittrell, Tennessee. His company rejoiced in the title of The Macon Midway Mule & Wagon Transportation Company. David Harrison Macon had been born in 1870, his father being a farmer and a former captain in the Confederate Army. In his early teens, the family moved to Nashville, where they opened a hotel for 'theatricals' passing through the town and playing at the Vaudeville theatres; Dave learned many songs and stories from the guests. Much later he played the banjo and performed comic routines for the amusement of his neighbours in Tennessee, until he was discovered by a talent scout in 1918, and his musical career began. He first recorded in 1924 and went on to spend 15 years as one of the most popular turns on WSM's Barn Dance radio show, the predecessor of The Grand Ole Opry.

John Bidwell was apparently the source of another unofficial compilation tape, *The Mitchell Tapes Vol.1*. This has seven more Stockroom Five performances, opening with the rather strange Exotic Shuffle, a band composition with guitar, fiddle, banjo and percussion. It doesn't really go anywhere, though Mick is very energetic on the temple blocks. There are three more songs from the Uncle Dave repertoire: The first, Bound To Go, is followed by Kisses On The Sly, a humorous Vaudeville song from the same stable as He Never Came Back. The third song is Buddy Won't You Roll Me Down The Line, a political comment on the Coal Creek miners' strike, where the mine owners tried to use convict labour instead. As Clive says: 'Uncle Dave was very politically active, which was unusual for those sort of rednecks.' Step It Up And Go is by the jug band legend Gus Cannon, and Charlie Poole was the author of Milwaukee Blues, a variation of the several Casey Jones ballads, learned via Tom Paley. The most interesting track on the tape is the group version of the Rev. Gary

Davis song Twelve Gates To The City, which Clive sings over the others chanting in a similar manner to that later used on Scranky Black Farmer on COB's *Spirit Of Love* album. It was presumably taped at a rehearsal as someone can clearly be heard saying: 'I'm really lost here!'

Tim married his girlfriend Liz when he was twenty-one and they rented a semi-detached cottage from a farmer for £1 a week at Zelah. The one next door was later rented by Mick Bennett. Though 'we didn't want to be bread-heads,' Tim occasionally took work as a labourer on building sites and for a while worked as a milkman. John stayed with Clive in the Folk Cottage caravan for most of this period. The career of the Stockroom Five was set to end at the conclusion of the tourist season in September. Their last gig was at the Folk Cottage, after which the club would only open once a week, on Fridays, to cater for the local trade. At the end of the night, Stephen Val Baker and his sister Demelza, thoroughly impressed, introduced themselves. Their father was the renowned Cornish author Denys Val Baker, and the family lived in an old sawmill near the River Fowey, about a mile north of Fowey town itself. They were an interesting family to say the least, who would play a large part in Clive's life for various reasons for years to come.

Denys Val Baker had one son, Martin, from a previous marriage. His second wife, Jess, a potter, had two children of her own from separate previous relationships, Gill and Jane. After Denys and Jess married they went on to have three more children: Stephen, Demelza and Genevieve. Stephen played piano and guitar, and Demelza had picked up a pair of clay bongos on a trip to North Africa and was just getting into playing them, though she had yet to perform in public. Stephen and Demelza invited the band back to their house.

Martin had attended Falmouth Art School, then gone up to London in his late teens to study at Hornsey, returning to Cornwall in 1965 to work as a litho printer. Strangely enough he had met Clive before. In 1963, he had driven up to the Edinburgh Festival with three friends, among whom was Jonathan Baker. They arrived in Edinburgh with hardly any money: 'I had ten shillings, someone else had a pound and the other two had nothing.' Jonathan, a talented classical guitarist, somehow knew Clive, and they all ended up staying with him, Bert and Robin at West Nicholson Street. Another person he met in that summer was Donovan Leitch, who spent a while in St Ives. Donovan knew Jane Val Baker, and at one point Martin loaned him a tent to live in. Two years later Donovan was a huge star, and came down to St Ives with a film crew to make a documentary about his life, *A Boy Called*

Donovan. He roped in some of his old friends, Martin included, as extras, to recreate the summer of 1963 for the princely sum of £3 a day each. One scene called for them to be filmed cooking mackerel and potatoes round a camp fire on the beach, but no mackerel were to be had in St Ives that day, so the film company sent six over from Newlyn, by taxi! Some of the party scenes were a little too authentic, and when the film was shown on TV in January 1966, the sight of beatniks openly smoking dope directly led to Donovan being busted later that year. In 1966 Martin had organised a fund-raising folk concert for CND, and caught the gig-promoting bug. Later that year he ran a series of folk concerts at The Winter Gardens, Penzance. Among others now forgotten, he booked Shirley Collins for £10 – from which she had to pay her train fare from London. She was supported that night by Jonathan Coudrille, who mightily impressed her by picking her up at the station in his Rolls Royce! Martin also booked local talent including Cyril Tawney and John Sleep and the banjo player Hedy West 'who, being American, wanted £25, half up front.' These gigs began his career in music promotion, which continues to this day. Martin didn't stay long at the Sawmills, later getting a place of his own in St. Ives. The Sawmills was situated on a tidal creek draining into the western side of the River Fowey, and when the Val Bakers bought the property it came complete with three chalets and a houseboat, which unfortunately later sank. The creek entered the main river by passing under a railway bridge, which carried the single-track branch line from Lostwithiel to Fowey. No longer used by passenger trains, it still carried several goods trains a day, taking china clay down to Fowey docks for export. At that time the easiest way to get to the house was by boat or by parking in Golant, a village a little further to the north, and taking a fifteen to twenty minute walk along the railway line and then by the creek. The only other way was to take a circuitous footpath through the woods. Denys Val Baker always believed that part of *The Wind In The Willows* had been inspired by the creek. Kenneth Grahame used to visit Fowey and stay with his friend Sir Arthur Quiller Crouch, who used the thinly disguised setting of Fowey in his novels as Troy Town. *The Wind In The Willows* reference is in the first chapter, in which Mole has met Ratty and been taken on a trip down the river in his boat. They turn into a backwater, where they intend to picnic, and Grahame describes them passing into what seems like a little landlocked lake, with a mill house and a water wheel. In his book *Life Up The Creek*, Denys described the frequent visitors who would turn up at The Sawmills, usually in response to an invitation from Demelza:

'What the staid and conservative people of Golant, or even the jolly train drivers, made of the visitations I often wondered. More than once I would look out of our kitchen window just in time to catch a glimpse of an extraordinary procession of colourful individuals – men with hair down to their shoulders, girls in sombrero hats, some individuals whose sex was impossible to tell – no matter; they all wended their purposeful way towards our quiet little haven. Once it was literally a pop group, the Stockton Five [sic], who played at the Mitchell Folk Club; five of them in a line bearing guitars and other instruments. Mysteriously, it always seemed to me, these huge hordes were usually swallowed up into the tiny confines of either Stephen's chalet or the one Demelza now used down on the quay, and all we ever heard – and it was to be fair, pretty melodious – was the playing of guitars and zithers, and maybe the latest Beatles or Rolling Stones record on the hi-fi.'

Clive and Mick went back to London for the winter. Around this time they recorded a track at Regent Sound, Blues In More Than 12 Bars, for Ralph McTell's third album, *My Side of Your Window*, which was released in time to be voted Folk Album of the Month for January 1970 in *Melody Maker*. They had been doing a spot of domestic carpentry work for Ralph, and he rehearsed them in the morning, then took them into the studio. Done in just two takes, Clive played fiddle and banjo, Mick percussion. Described in the sleeve notes as 'a double-edged ragtime tale on how to succeed' it was certainly not one of Ralph's more memorable songs.

When the farmer refused to renew Tim's and Liz's lease at Zelah due to the hippy carryings-on of the summer, Denys offered to rent them the largest chalet at the Sawmills, a substantial building with a kitchen, living room and two bedrooms, which they were pleased to take up. John went back to his parents in Newquay for a while. Having made the connection with Demelza, John and Tim joined her in The Novelty Band, who basically played English traditional music. The only tape of them I have heard is their version of Wild Mountain Thyme, with Demelza on tabla, Tim on guitar, and John on recorder; the band also featured autoharp and dulcimer. The Novelty Band played all over the Cornish folk club circuit of the time, including the Rose Folk Club near Perranporth, which was the new venue for the Folk Cottage; the Mitchell venue had closed as the farmer had sold the land. They also played the Tankards Club in Falmouth, and other venues in Liskeard, Truro, St Just and Penzance. Some of these clubs were a fair distance away and they rarely earned much more than their travelling expenses. The obvious move was to open their own club, and they had the ideal venue on the top floor of the Wheelcat Pottery in 19 North Street, Fowey, a shop which the Val Bakers owned and used as an outlet for their pottery. Demelza and John applied for a music licence but reckoned without the good folk of the town. A local shopkeeper started a petition against the club, although they only wanted to open it once a week, and on the day of the hearing at Lostwithiel, no fewer than twenty-one citizens of Fowey turned up to make sure that their application was turned down.

In the early spring of 1970 both Clive and Mick came back down to Cornwall and took a cheap winter let on a caravan at Brighton Cross, near Fowey. Eventually, they also moved to The Sawmills, and joined with Tim, John and Demelza, the new combination being named The Temple Creatures.

Their name was, according to Clive, 'based on the stone guardians one sees outside temples in Siam and Indonesia.' The Temple Creatures were a very different kettle of fish from the Stockroom Five, playing Indian influenced music and original songs by Clive and John. With Demelza on percussion, Clive played balalaika, guitar, banjo and fiddle. John's main instruments were an Indian hand organ and dulcimer. Tim played guitar. Mick was the main vocalist and played tambourine. John added that the band had lots of other less obvious influences besides Indian, including Scottish, Irish and Arabic music. 'We didn't bother much with influences from individual sources.' They band seems to have been up and running by the spring, securing a regular gig at the Railway Hotel, Penzance, every Thursday. John had borrowed the Appalachian dulcimer he used in the band from a friend and altered the bridge to make it buzz like a sitar, which had become an important part of the group's sound. One night, while they were loading the van to set off to a gig, it met a curious end. It was not in a case, and was simply forgotten and left on the roof of the van as they drove off. After balancing for a while, it inevitably fell on the road and was smashed to pieces. They didn't realise what had happened until they reached the gig and put two and two together. With a pretty good idea of where it might have fallen, they went out in search of it the next day, but no trace was ever found. The dulcimer had been a very good one, built by the American maker Homer Ledford, and John of course had to tell the guy he had borrowed it from. John offered to pay for the damage, but the owner, about to head off to India, was unfazed. With another gig a few days away, they needed a replacement fast, and, finding some good quality pine sheet in the old sawmill, Clive and John made a new one. It was built quickly and cheaply, using large staples for frets. They installed a sitar-style bridge from the start, with the strings passing over a flat piece of hard bone in front of the bridge. Gradually deepening the slots in the bridge until the strings started to buzz lightly on the bone, they got the sitar sound they were after. They called it a dulcitar, later fitting it with a contact mike pickup so it could be amplified. They were delighted with their new instrument.

The Indian hand organ John played was the same instrument Clive had used with Wizz Jones, which Ricky Boak had brought back from India. It was played with the right hand while the left worked the bellows. One advantage of the instrument was that individual notes could be kept open by unhooking the springs that kept the keys shut, which produced a particularly effective drone. Clive described it in an interview: 'It's almost unique over here. The reeds are very good and it's got a lot of volume.' It was even more unusual, as at one point Clive's father had painted it green with designs all over it.

In April, Colin Hill, the social secretary at Launceston College, organised an event at the Youth Centre as part of the Launceston Music Festival. A friend who was a local journalist suggested he book Chrissy Quayle and The Temple Creatures if he wanted some good contemporary folk music. The stage was decorated with branches and logs from a nearby wood to give it a more rustic appearance. Colin read some of his psychedelic poetry and a few friends were added to the bill, including a flamenco guitarist and a folk/blues trio. The event was a great success. Colin's main memory of the event is of the band arriving in a Volkswagen van. 'I shall never forget the way they tumbled out the side door into a very stoned heap. They were utterly amazing; the sound was kind of East-European gypsy with Indian raga overtones and a little traditional folk. Little John's Indian hand organ was the keystone to the sound.'

At this time Denys Val Baker and his wife Jess had gone to Bermuda for around six months as she had been offered a temporary job to teach hand-throwing techniques to the workers in a new pottery factory there. They left the house in the hands of Stephen, Demelza and Genevieve. Clive and John shared a chalet on the creek below the house, and Mick was at one point living in a lean-to tent nailed to a tree in the surrounding woods, something Clive also tried for a while. As well as The Temple Creatures' residency at the Railway Hotel, the small Town Hall at Fowey became a regular gig that summer, even though it cost all of £3 a time to hire. Tim: 'Eventually they wouldn't let us use the hall any more. They said it was too dangerous as we used to have candles everywhere. We were just a bit too hippy for them.' After a while Tim and Liz left the Sawmills and the band, citing bad vibes caused by a fall-out with Demelza. They moved to Redruth and Tim took a labouring job. Mick left at the same time.

The band continued as a trio of Clive, John and Demelza; Chrissy Quayle occasionally appeared with them, playing a bit of flute and adding backing vocals, though she had a showcase number of her own in She Moves Through The Fair. Chrissy: 'That summer the place became a kind of commune with lots of windswept and interesting characters coming and going. People taking acid. It was an eye-opener for a middle-class girl like me. It changed my life really! No one had any money and everyone ate very little food, mostly dry bread and wasp honey, and a few spuds. I remember Clive being furious when he found that some hitchhiker who had turned up had taken one of his teabags! He'd only had about seven to last the week. I would come and go depending on when we were rehearsing or doing gigs.' Unsurprisingly, the locals began referring to the place as Cannabis Creek.

Meanwhile Clive's old band, The Famous Jug Band, released their second album, *Chameleon*, in June 1970. They had continued to work as a trio, and were starting to do pretty well. Liberty Records had advanced them the money to buy a Transit van and a Simms-Watt PA system, though they had to carry a publicity board for Liberty to every gig they did. They also had a sponsorship deal with the Cornish Mead Company and gave out free samples in miniature jugs emblazoned with the FJB logo! In the last weekend in June they were booked for the National Jazz, Blues and Rock Festival at Reading and during the summer of 1970 had three regular gigs per week in Cornwall alone: The Folk Cottage, The Railway Hotel in Penzance every Wednesday, and a club in Redruth. *Chameleon* was a fine album, though very different from their first. The majority of the songs were by Pete, whose songwriting had improved considerably in the interim.

The Temple Creatures were booked to play in the gym at Launceston College on the18th of July, a benefit of sorts for Colin Hill, who, through a series of unfortunate circumstances, had lost a bit of money promoting Pete Brown and Piblokto! two weeks earlier. The band turned up in a battered Hillman Husky, and were somewhat embarrassed to find they had forgotten to pack the hand-organ. They didn't feel they could play without it and cancelled the gig. Colin and his friends went to see Fairport Convention playing at the Van Dyke club in Plymouth instead. Clive doesn't remember the gig and thinks it unlikely they forgot to pack the organ. 'It was as big as an oven! Even we couldn't forget to pack that.' He does think that the problem may have been that the organ would not work properly for some reason. Another memorable booking for the Temple Creatures was at Perran Round, an old heritage site (a sort of amphitheatre) at Rose, near Perranporth, where they supported several other well-known folk bands and acts.

Martin Val Baker also promoted two gigs featuring the best of the local talent, headlined by the Temple Creatures, at The Guildhall in St Ives. They drew crowds of around 400 and even made money. 'We thought about a hundred people would turn up, we couldn't believe it when we opened the doors.' The gig on the 21st of August featured The Temple Creatures, Kris Gayle & The Jazz Roots, Mike Silver, Chrissy Quayle, Bob Devereux and High Speed Gas. A poster for the second event, just under three weeks later on the 10th of September, called the headliners Clive Palmer's Temple Creatures, giving the line-up as: 'Clive Palmer. Ex-Incredible String Band. Violin, Balalaika, Guitar, Banjo, Harmonium. John Bidwell. Dulcitar, Hand Organ. Demelza Val Baker. Bongo, Tabla, Congo [*sic*] Drum.' Admission was seven shillings, with a reduction of one shilling for Mask club members. The local paper reviewed the Temple Creatures' performance favourably: 'Led by Clive Palmer, an original member of the Incredible String Band, the group is completed by John Bidwell of Newquay, and Damelza [*sic*] Val Baker, daughter of writer Denys Val Baker, formerly of St Ives, now living at Fowey. The group owes its distinctive sound to its use of a variety of instruments, including an Indian hand-organ, brought from India by Clive Palmer and believed to be the only one in the country; a Russian balalaika, and a dulcitar, which is a cross between the American dulcimer and the Indian sitar and was hand-made by the group.' The article specifically praised a song based on the Gentle Jane legend. John: 'I wrote that song. The story goes that she went mad (gentle in Cornish parlance) when her husband failed to return from a fishing trip. She reputedly haunts the bay near Wadebridge which is named after her, waiting for her love who will never return.'

She is wrapped in a coat, much thinner than skin.
And she waits for the boats that will never come in.

Poster for Temple Creatures St Ives gig.
Richard Morton Jack collection

Vernon Joynson's book *The Tapestry of Delights*, which covers the music and recordings of many obscure British bands, has a brief section by Jon Newey on The Temple Creatures, which mentions a demo tape featuring Raga Danjit, Till Death Comes Away, and She Moved Through The Fair. The band were very pleased with the demo, giving it to Julia Creasey to pass to Roy Guest, a well-known promoter in the folk field. Clive: 'It got lost. She might have put it in the bin for all I know, we didn't make any copies, unfortunately.' There are a few tapes of The Temple Creatures around, largely featuring instrumentals, notable for Demelza's powerful percussion, including Raghupati which was also, in a considerably more dynamic version, part of the Incredible String Band's repertoire at the time, though they punningly retitled it Raga Puti. John: 'It came from an album by Ananda Shankar, loads of people were doing it.' The album in question was the self-titled 1970 LP by Ananda Shankar, Ravi's nephew. One of the songs that has survived on tape is Child Of The Season, a John Bidwell song which is very much in the style of his later Eleven Willows. Another song from this period that would later turn up again was Mick's Music Of The Ages. Around the end of September, Clive left the band. The rumour was that he was going to India with a bag of apples, intending to meet up with a friend under a specific arch in Delhi! He actually went to Scotland.

After Clive's departure, a Welsh friend of Demelza's called Gwilliam joined the band. John remembers him doing 'a little bit with the hand-harmonium.' Around October, John, Gwilliam and Demelza went to London as The Temple Creatures, intending to pick up other musicians there. Gwilliam didn't stay long. Demelza remembers a guitarist from Belfast called Sparky playing with them briefly, but John doesn't. The duo of John and Demelza met up with Judith Piepe, a London social worker and folk club organiser who had been well known for offering help and accommodation to up-and-coming folkies in the mid-Sixties, including Paul Simon and Al Stewart. Her boyfriend was Stephen Delft, who would go on to become Britain's best known guitar technician in the Seventies, counting The Incredible String Band among his many clients, as well as being a fine guitarist in his own right. Stephen briefly joined The Temple Creatures after meeting them when they played The Marquee in Wardour Street, and helped to tune Demelza's tabla drum which was 'damp, slack and being difficult.' Judith had actually known Demelza's father before he had moved to Cornwall, through a shared interest in writing poetry and short stories. She got behind the band and managed to get them mentioned in the *New Musical Express* of 14/11/70. The accompanying photo showed John playing the dulcitar, Stephen playing a lute, and Demelza on her Moroccan clay bongos.

Judith was reported as feeling 'they will gain fame just as Simon and Garfunkel did.' The music had changed, becoming a lot softer, especially after Stephen joined. He rehearsed with John and Demelza at Judith's flat and recalls they played at least one December gig at the Marquee, where Judith was running folk nights some Wednesdays, and

JUDITH PIEPE (centre) with her cat and three folk artists whom she feels will gain fame just as Simon and Garfunkel did. They are the TEMPLE CREATURES, with STEPHEN DELFT (blond). They appear at the Marqu on December 2.

The Temple Creatures.
Richard Morton Jack Collection

a few other gigs, including one in the club in the crypt of St. Martins-

In-The-Fields, just by Trafalgar Square. Stephen had some doubts about the band's name: 'I am sure they knew the historical significance of "Temple Creatures" – religious cult prostitutes – but this didn't seem to worry Demelza or John, and I doubt whether one in a hundred of the audience would even have thought about it. It was a time of fanciful and eccentric names for bands. Demelza had a pair of tablas, which she played well, and with passion, but she wouldn't accompany some kinds of music: "Because the tablas wouldn't like it." She would also sometimes make complex malapropisms; the one I remember clearly occurred when I was describing a treadle lathe, which was a foot-powered woodturning lathe. She said, "Oh yes, a treble lathe, I saw a Hampstead do it once." She had mixed up treadle and treble and treadmill and hamster and Hampstead. She was actually referring to a hamster running round in a cage wheel! At the time I was being a musician and running a musical instrument business, and needed to schedule times for rehearsals in between repair work for customers. I think Demelza and John were living to a more casual timetable, and inevitably we had different views about arriving on time for rehearsals. We finally split when they contacted me more than a day late for a missed rehearsal, and didn't seem particularly bothered about it.' Despite all the good publicity they had received, the Temple Creatures failed to break through, and Demelza later admitted that they should have just stayed on in Cornwall. They split up, Demelza going on to get involved in session work.

The Famous Jug Band had contemplated splitting up at the end of the summer season, taking a month off to think about it, but had decided to add another member instead. They were now being managed by Ralph McTell's younger brother Bruce May (Ralph's real surname is May), who had suggested they move up to London and base themselves there. Pete had met Welsh guitarist John James in April and greatly enjoyed jamming with him as they had similar styles. He had considered forming a band with John before thinking that it would be better to carry on as The Famous Jug Band, 'playing the old songs with a different approach.' John joined in September and they set out on tour, but it became obvious by the second gig, at The Theatre Royal in York, that it was not going to work: 'All the weaknesses came out.' John left. Henry, Jill and Pete played some memorable gigs on the University circuit, sharing stages with acts as diverse as Fairport Convention, Roy Harper, Family, The Who and Ralph McTell. At the 1970 Sheffield University Rag Ball they were on the same bill as Georgie Fame, The Kinks, Ike & Tina Turner, The Strawbs and Steeleye Span. The FJB were on in the refectory when the Kinks were on the main stage. Henry: 'Everyone left to come and see us! The Kinks complained because they were left playing in front of a handful of people, which was quite good!' As well as his jug, he had acquired a double bass by the name of Bessie, which he originally used mainly as a prop. He gradually became a perfectly competent bassist. In an interview in *Sounds*, Pete told Jerry Gilbert that he was considering doing electric material in the band and even adding drums and a horn section. Nothing came of these plans, but an advert in *Melody Maker* produced keyboard player Tim Rice (not the well-known lyricist), who was playing in a South London rock band called Skunk. They rehearsed and recorded some demos for a projected third album with the four piece line-up, but the tapes are now lost. The FJB lasted until April 1971, *Melody Maker* announcing that 'The Famous Jug Band are to break up following singer Jill Johnson's decision to leave and return to her home in Cornwall.' Jill elaborates: 'When Clive left I had become the lead singer and straight man to Henry's shtick. I preferred the music we did latterly, which was mostly written by Pete, but it was far more exacting, and demanded much more in the way of performance than some of the old fun-loving Jug Band stuff we used to do. By the time we were recording the third album, I was really sick from stress. I knew that I had to leave because I was too sick to continue, but I was devastated because it was the only thing I had ever wanted to do. I believe Pete drove me back to Cornwall, dropped me off at my parent's house – and then left! I didn't hear from anyone for another twenty-five years!'

After Clive's sojourn in Scotland he returned to Cornwall and moved into a caravan near Mylor, owned by the Russian emigre father of a friend of Robin Birch. Mick joined Clive in the caravan and they briefly formed a band with Tim Wellard called Burning Bush. The trio only ever played one gig, at the new Folk Cottage club in the church hall at Rose. Several of the songs that later appeared on COB albums (albeit in sometimes considerably altered arrangements) dated from this time, including Spirit Of Love, Wade In The Water,

When He Came Home and Solomon's Song. Clive originally played Spirit Of Love on concertina, an instrument he was toying with at the time. 'It was an Anglo-concertina (one where you get a different note on the pull and the push), and I bought it new from a music shop. I don't think I had a banjo at the time, and I used it for composing.'

CHAPTER 7

The group...
are going to be a huge success

7
"The group... are going to be a huge success."

'I did the whole COB record, listened to it again, and thought "Oh my God..." and then people started saying, "No, it's really good."'

n early 1971, Jo Lustig was approached by CBS Records to provide them with some acts in the progressive folk genre, CBS believing that this had a good chance of being the Next Big Thing. Jo was more than happy to offer some of his clients the chance to produce a pet project each, as this could only serve to increase their industry profile. The project gave the producers the chance to acknowledge their influences and settle a few artistic debts. John Renbourn produced Wizz Jones' *Right Now*. Wizz: 'John always championed me; he followed me around right from the beginning when he was just a kid. He probably felt he owed me.' Bert Jansch produced Anne Briggs' *The Time Has Come*. Ralph McTell had long admired Clive's work, and was pleased to be able to do his old friend Mick Bennett a favour too. He offered to produce the album which became *Spirit Of Love*. The fourth album in the series was *Almanac*, a concept album with twelve songs related to the signs of the zodiac by a trio called Therapy. Later reduced to a duo of Dave Shannon and Fiona Simpson, they went on to be one of the most popular folk club acts in the Seventies. The third original member was Sam Bracken, who later replaced Dick Gaughan in Five Hand Reel.

None of the CBS albums would go on to sell particularly well. Ralph: 'Jo was a high-powered, old-style New Yorker – pushy, strong and committed. He'd had success with Julie Felix and the Pentangle, amongst others, and practically everyone else on the folk scene had passed through his hands at one time or another. He deserves more credit for that than I think he gets. Yes, he was a businessman – but what's wrong with that? He was devoted to his artists and did a lot of good for them. Anyway, his reputation allowed him to get a deal from CBS, and he asked me if I knew of any good acts. I mentioned Clive and Mick Bennett and he asked me to produce them myself.' Clive: 'There were a number of labels that wanted to sign folk bands at the time. Sales didn't really matter to Jo; he just got a flat payment from the record company. The main reason he set up the deal was to give Ralph some production experience, I think. Ralph was his main interest, really.' Clive called up John Bidwell, who was still in London. Clive and Mick jumped into a car and came up to London to sort out the details, staying with Robin Birch in Notting Hill. They then returned to Cornwall to rehearse for a short while. Mick remembers this period slightly more romantically than Clive does.

'The three of us found an abandoned caravan in the woods in Mylor, near Falmouth, and decided it'd be a great place to get our heads together and make some new music, so we squatted there. We were always incredibly broke, though – everything Ralph says on the back of the first record about living off digestive biscuits is true. John was the only Cornishman among us, so he had his parents nearby and perhaps didn't stay in the caravan so much, I can't remember exactly. Anyway, we'd sing and play all day long, then play live in the evenings. As for the songs, I used to go for long walks – it was easier then, there were fewer fences up – and dream them up as I went.' The poverty and hunger were real enough. If all else failed they could drive over to John's house where his mum was always willing to cook them egg and chips. They returned to London, Clive and John moving in with Clive's father in Enfield while Mick stayed with his parents in Islington, and arranged for Jo Lustig to come to Enfield to hear them play. They practised all day, and when Jo turned up asked if he'd like to hear what they sounded like. They played him one number, he said: 'Fine, lovely, that'll do...,' and left! The new group's name was Jo's responsibility, as no-one in the band had any ideas that made sense. Seeing Clive's past with the ISB as a good selling point, he came up with Clive's Original Band. Clive wasn't initially keen. 'It suggested that this was the band I had before the one I was in before the one I was in... It sounded a bit stupid to me, but I sort of went along with it because it was nice to make a record.' Despite frequent claims to the contrary COB never stood for Clive's Own Band (or Clive's Other Band). All participants also always referred to it as 'cob' rather than 'c.o.b.'

John: 'I remember us all trying to think of what to call ourselves and coming up with ideas that were just embarrassing. I think it was a bit of a relief when Jo came up with COB, to be honest. The fact that we were theoretically going out under Clive's name didn't bother us at all. If anything we probably thought it was best to take advantage of his name. Jo was quite funny, but essentially in it for the money and empire. We went round to his place for band meetings every now and then, but he wasn't involved on a day-to-day basis.' Clive later told an interviewer that the album had taken six weeks of preparation, but was recorded in just four days. He gave most of the credit for getting things together to Jo Lustig: 'Jo told us to take our time; there was no rush. He gave us time to develop our ideas and gave us a free hand with them. He helped us a lot in telling us how to handle what we did. If we'd been left to ourselves, we would have made a lot of mistakes.'

Ralph had just moved from his council flat in Croydon to his own house in Putney, a stone's throw from his favourite pub, The Half Moon. From mid May COB rehearsed there most days, Ralph inviting his new accompanist, Steve Bonnett, to contribute to the sessions. Jo Lustig's current master plan for Ralph's career was to move him out of the folk club scene into the concert hall circuit, and market him as a singer/songwriter, with Elton John providing the role model. With this in mind Ralph had been casting around for sympathetic musicians to form a band. Steve had been recommended by both Tim Rice (who had recently joined The Famous Jug Band, managed by Ralph's brother Bruce) and the owner of the local music shop, Bob Kerr. He had played bass and flute in Tim's band, Skunk. After a jam with Steve, Ralph told Jo to offer him the gig and he did: £15 a week retainer plus standard Musician Union rates for gigs and recording sessions. This was a pleasing upturn in Steve's fortunes, both musically and financially. He had just got married, just failed to get the job of replacing Greg Lake in King Crimson (Gordon Haskell being the lucky man who did) and was in fear of eviction from his flat. Still only 20, Steve was a multi-instrumentalist with a great deal of experience playing in a wide range of styles and venues. He had played Yank Rachell-style blues mandolin with Jo-Ann Kelly in folk and blues clubs, soul in Mod bands and tenor banjo and bass in several eccentric outfits led by Bob Kerr, who had regular gigs playing 1930s jazz to gangsters in illegal gambling joints.

Steve: 'I tended to talk to John about my parts, as he was the one most likely to know the chords. Clive often retuned and improvised and so wasn't always sure what the chords he was using were. I guess with John playing harmonium he had to work out the chords in a more conventional way.' The harmonium was Ralph's; during the recording sessions, John used the studio's electric organ. Clive also made himself useful by building a new staircase for Ralph's house, which is still in use to this day, despite his insistence to Ralph that a good carpenter should do everything by eye and did not need to measure anything. His woodworking skills were put to good use by Jo Lustig too, when Clive laid the rosewood floorboards Jo had imported at considerable expense for his own flat. Jo had considerable style in the way he managed his artists. Steve got an insight into Jo's management style at the 1970 Isle Of Wight Festival, when Ralph McTell had come offstage following a particularly fine performance and Jo was trying to persuade him to return for an encore. Unaware of this, the DJ started playing a record and was physically attacked by Lustig for ruining the moment. Steve also recalls driving to a festival gig with Jo in a Mini along a temporary road laid over the mud of the site. The Mini came off the track and several fans came over to help get it back on the road. Steve naturally got out to assist and was told off by Jo: 'You're the star; they've paid to see you, let them do it!'

On Monday the 24th of May COB entered Marquee Studios to record their first album. Ralph: 'I can safely say they were the most difficult sessions I have ever been involved with. COB were loose and undisciplined, totally unaware of recording techniques. They never counted bars or anything like that, and didn't seem to understand the need to keep outside noise to a minimum. I remember having to ask Clive not to sniff when he played the violin because the mike was right by his nose and he'd say, "It doesn't matter, who cares?" to which I'd reply, "It does and I do!" At one point he fell asleep in a vocal booth and I faded up his snoring. That's not to imply for a minute that he was casual, simply that his attitude to recording was laissez-faire, he was Mr. One-Take. John was relaxed in the studio but Mick was nervous. The harmonies were very complicated and took forever to get right. Clive loved hypnotic, repetitive choruses, but on record I felt too much of that chanting style would get boring, so I tried to get them more focused than they had to be on stage.' Steve expands on this: 'Not being the person whose neck was on the line, I was able to shrug it off as charming eccentricity, but I do remember doing loads of retakes because of people forgetting that you have to face the microphone for it to work! They would also jam along and chat in the corner of the studio when overdubs were being done. I had to do some of the bass parts as overdubs, because the song structures were different every take, but some of the tracks were performed more or less live. We had rehearsed the songs at Ralph's house, but they were still subject to change, random bars added or subtracted, even in one case a new section appearing on the day. Some of the instruments were not at concert pitch, or in tune with each other. They had a very ethnic approach to tuning anyway, which led to the nightmare of having musicians who were ill at ease in a studio having to do overdubs on tracks that were of varying structure. Despite all this I enjoyed the sessions and thought they were very creative. Remember we were still mentally in the Sixties, when being organised and professional was still frowned upon as a sign of a closed mind. I remember when I turned up to do a show with Ralph in a suit and having a French journalist berate me for selling out! We had fun making the album, it felt low key, just like a bunch of friends making music just how they wanted. I was barely aware of being in a studio; there was none of the angst I normally associated with recording. The Marquee studio was a modern but small place, not state of the art but comfortable. It was just a bunch of blokes sitting around playing. Clive and Mick seemed impossibly old, not just in years, they felt like they were from some distant rustic past, operating to rules older than time. They both had a haunting frailty about their voices even when they spoke, which was wonderful. Despite that, Mick always seemed to be laughing. John, who I always picture wearing lots of bright coloured wool, was more like me, a hippy with some kind of pop music sensibility lurking under the surface.'

The album's title track, Spirit Of Love, was seriously considered to have potential as a single, and was recorded in a special session on Wednesday the 26th. Four female voices were brought in to add to the chorus, belonging to Christina Bonnett, Gillian McPherson, Chrissy Quayle and Reina Sutcliffe. Christina was married to Steve, who was also responsible for inviting Reina to the session. Reina and her husband Mike worked in a record shop in Putney High Street and also ran a band called Down In The Flood, who introduced many local musicians to the joys of country music. They lived in what Steve describes as 'a classic hippy pad on the edge of Wandsworth' and often hosted jamming sessions. Reina had several other claims to fame. She was one of the Electric Ladies on the cover of a certain Jimi Hendrix album, complaining many years later to Q magazine that the photo 'made us look like a load of old prostitutes.' The ladies were paid £5 each if they went topless, £10 if they were nude. John Peel claimed to have been her boyfriend at one time, and had fond memories of driving her from Edinburgh back to London and singing her the entire Lonnie Donegan songbook on the way. Her father was the well-known comedian Sid James, and she was actually named after Sid's mother. Chrissy Quayle's musical career was also in the ascendant at the time. By the end of the year she had recorded a self-titled album for RCA with a band called Daylight, featuring herself, songwriter and guitarist Mike Silver and guitarist Steve Hayton, who had been a member of the American band Daddy Longlegs. Daddy Longlegs had been touring England and Chrissy had met Steve Hayton in Penzance. Getting together to jam with Mike Silver, they were so pleased with the result that they recorded a demo and sent it to RCA, who signed them straight off on the strength of it. Though basically a trio, they were augmented on record and on some gigs by the rhythm section of Spike Heatley on double bass and Tony Carr on drums, who had played with Donovan among many others. The fourth female vocalist, Gillian McPherson, was another one of Jo Lustig's ever-growing stable of folk artists, having signed with him in May. Originally from Belfast, Gillian would shortly record her own album for RCA (produced by Danny Thompson), entitled *Poets Painters And Performers Of Blues* and released that September.

After the recording was finished the band had another demonstration of Jo's style. Clive: 'We were invited round to hear the master-tape of the COB record, but the studio hadn't actually got the tape to him, and he rang them up to ask where the tape was, and really, the air was turning blue... all this old American heavy manager stuff – if you don't get this tape down here, you'll never work again! Really heavy. I didn't feel I really wanted to be part of that. But he got us lots of work.' The trio then went back to Cornwall and possibly played some gigs locally as COB, opening the evening for some of Martin Val Baker's promotions. Martin certainly promoted an early COB gig as headliners, at The Guildhall in St Ives, on 4th June. They were supported by the Ron Smith Quartet, Bocvum and Iris Gitten. Martin distinctly remembers COB, complete with all their instruments, arriving at the gig on two mopeds, Clive's BSA Bantam and John's Lambretta! This was quite possibly COB's first ever gig, though Martin doesn't think so: 'We would have made more of it.' Tickets for the event read: 'Introducing from London, next booking Royal Festival Hall, Clive's Original Band. Clive Palmer, Little John & Whispering Mick.'

At the end of May Bert Jansch had released *Rosemary Lane* to great critical approval, his first solo album for a while since he had joined

Pentangle. On the sleeve he says that the traditional title track 'has been a hot favourite with me since hearing Clive Palmer sing it about five years ago.' Clive thinks that Bert had actually learned it from Robin Williamson rather than him, though now Bert considers it may actually have been from Anne Briggs; both Anne and Clive used to sing it. In a later interview Bert talked about what he had learned from Clive. 'If you heard him on his own you'd either love him or hate him – Clive is likely to sing a 30-verse ballad, whether you like it or not. But the man has influenced me more than anyone else, in every way really. He had a quality of singing in his voice; if you hear him on his own it really comes through. It's as though he's a hundred years older than he actually is. His knowledge of music is immense.'

Jo Lustig had taken a lease on the Festival Hall for the 30th of June to showcase Van Morrison. When Van's manager withdrew his artist (which did not please Mr. Lustig, a man never afraid of litigation) Jo managed to persuade Bert to play his first solo concert since Jo had taken over the management of The Pentangle back in 1968. He also decided to add Anne Briggs to the bill and to use the event to showcase COB. It was originally intended that Steve Bonnett play with the band, but Ralph was offered a BBC2 In Concert TV show on the same night, which naturally took precedence. The concert was a great success, critics particularly praising the fact that the three acts complemented each other so well.

Telegram to COB
Courtesy Shirley
Palmer

COB opened with an unaccompanied Wade In The Water. Among the other numbers they played were Music Of The Ages and When He Came Home, ending with Spirit Of Love for which they were joined by the choir from the record: Christina, Gillian and Chrissy, along with Mike Silver. No-one can recall if Reina was there or not and Chrissy herself can't remember performing that night. To COB's surprise, an encore was demanded. Thinking on their feet, they did Spirit Of Love again, in the best 'plug the single' tradition. Andrew Means, reviewing the event for *Melody Maker*, was disappointed with the choice of encore, feeling it had ended the band's set on an anti-climax. That apart, he was impressed: 'Their set contained a highly original approach to music. Clive Palmer's songs explore obscure yet highly productive angles of approach, building on a wealth of international folk and pop styles, nevertheless expressing definite characteristics of their own.' In *Sounds*, Jerry Gilbert called them 'Clive Palmer's latest brilliant creation.' But, he went on to say: 'I only hope that this time he will persist and allow the group to develop logically. If this happens, the group... are going to be a huge success.' Jerry interviewed the band at length at 'their Enfield home' a week after the concert. Clive talked at length about the band's instrumentation and mentioned that 'what we want is a reed sound – perhaps a crumhorn because the recorder is too flimsy.' He mentioned that he had given up playing the banjo with the exception of one track. He also commented on the evolution of the group. 'We've been working together for about three and a half years off and on, but now we've reached something really worthwhile, and after travelling through all these stages we've come to some kind of a settling point. With Temple Creatures we went through the heavy Indian thing, but we found that you run out of ideas when going through a phase. Now all the kind of work we've done in the past is beginning to bear fruit because we've never been at the stage where we've had that kind of flow before.' Clive was bold enough to suggest that COB was the logical conclusion of his musical wanderings. 'If people are insensitive they will see me leaving groups merely as a pattern, but it's a natural artistic thing to change, and the thing we are doing now isn't changing at all basically. For instance, Robin [Williamson] and I worked together for a long time but we weren't very close, so what we produced was a reaction to each other rather than an inter-action. But this band has always been very close on a personal level, and because there's only three of us we can control it so much easier. We can make much more of a finished job of it, but we still use rough edges because they are effective. One of the things that's gone wrong with traditional music is that it's got smooth, but our image tends to be very primitive in a way because we don't go in for fine detail.'

Photo of COB from
Sounds 24/07/71

● *COB: have been allowed to mature*

Jo Lustig had tried to get COB on the bill of the 1971 Cambridge Folk Festival, but had left it a little too late. They attended the festival anyway (as they always did), and arranged to play in the club tent, where acts not on the main bill have a chance to perform. COB managed to cause a minor controversy when they walked off stage on being told they could only perform two songs. The band felt they would not have had enough time to get into a worthwhile set. Clive was unrepentant. 'At Cambridge we didn't play because ethically we disagreed with that sort of regimentation. If I was in the Albert Hall and in the same position I would do the same.' *Melody Maker* of 2/8/71 printed an interview with COB which had taken place in the beer garden of an Enfield pub. Wittily headed 'Clive on the COB', the article noted, amongst other things, that they already had enough material for another album. Clive brushed aside comparisons with the ISB, and was keen to explain the 'Original' in COB: 'I can't think of anything we do that has been influenced closely by anything outside. We are trying to get as close to an original thing as we can. When we started off with the String Band we were much more connected from my point of view. With the later developments they didn't have the weight to hold them down. Their later stuff I don't think has the power to hold them down. My original reason for getting in trouble with the Incredibles was laughable really. I was heavily into smoking.' Mick added: 'It's a question of lifestyle really.' Clive also said the band intended to expand their instrumentation, adding harmonium and twelve-string guitar to the instruments they had used on *Spirit Of Love*. But, he hastened to add: 'Not electric. Electric for me is nowhere. I can't use it.'

In an article in *Disc* ('Cob try not to be corny...' – the second of these puns in two weeks), Clive told the interviewer: 'For a while I was playing music which was based on influences I picked up when I was

CLIVE PALMER (right) with JOHN BIDWELL AND MICK BENNETT

Clive on the C.O.B.

in India, but I've passed through that stage. We've also passed through the stage of being self-indulgent as many artists are. Our songs are not purely personal. Anything you produce is not complete until someone enjoys it. Nothing happens until it's reflected by someone else. There is a tremendous psychological build-up before we do a concert. We couldn't do one every night because we don't think it's honest to turn it on just like that. We work up to it and give a better performance because it's more of an occasion. It's like a ceremony.' *Disc* expected COB to play some concerts to coincide with the album release, but warned: 'They don't expect to tour because it would be too exhausting. Having taken three years to work together as writers, and a year to work at being a group, they don't want to rush things now.' COB signed with the Chrysalis Agency, who got them gigs supporting bands like Fairport Convention and filling in for cancellations.

Spirit Of Love finally came out in December. The artwork was very pleasing: a painting of Clive, John and Mick. Clive is smiling on John who is playing the dulcitar, while Mick has his eyes closed and his arms full of books, doubtless full of the mysterious subject matter that led German author Horst Pohl to aptly describe COB's music as 'mystik folk.' The sleeve was a semi-gatefold with a single layer of card for

the front of the sleeve. This, one felt, was

somehow inferior to a proper gatefold sleeve, which no self-respecting album could come without in those days. The opened sleeve featured a photo of all the lyrics written out (rather too neatly) on various pieces of paper, insides of cigarette packets etc pinned to a cork tile notice board. Ralph wrote the sleeve notes for the album, which threw light on the inspiration and internal workings of the band: 'With the talents of Mick and John it seems that Clive has found a solution to the question of challenge. Whereas in the past it was largely left to Clive to decide direction, in this band each member sets the others off and provides new stimulus. In John, Clive has found a musician of similar tastes and great ability and in Mick a lyricist, poet and vocalist and together they keep enthusiasm bubbling all the time.' The notes also say that Clive, 'though best known as a banjo player, now plays everything but banjo and had to borrow one for one number on this album.' This isn't quite the whole story. Clive had actually sold his Clifford Essex Concert Grand banjo to Ralph. 'I was skint!' He wasn't too sorry to sell it as it had originally been made to take gut strings and never sounded quite right with steel strings. Clive mainly used John's guitar with COB, though he had a nylon-string guitar of his own. John's was a Levin Goliath steel-string jumbo, which he still has today and he says plays better than ever. Clive used several open tunings, often based on banjo tunings, with EGCGCE being one of the commonest. He soon acquired another banjo, a cheap East German one with a distinctively shaped head, which he bought in a second-hand shop and played for another twenty years. COB's devotion to the cause of music was also mentioned: 'All the guys have known hard times, two winters spent living on potatoes, flour and water in an old caravan miles from the nearest road, but all the time making music.'

In the end the title track was never released as a single, which was a pity. The song is a simple two-chord (G/G7 to C) strumalong, but catchy nonetheless. Clive plays guitar and takes the lead vocal, with Ralph adding a simple but effective guitar solo. John is credited with playing organ but it is barely audible. Steve plays bass and adds an uncredited piano overdub – the only one to survive of several overdubs he did at the sessions. Some percussion can also just be heard, courtesy of Mick. The line 'Seven times down and eight times high' is from a Chinese proverb about life. Mick: 'I usually took songs to the band fully formed, with words and melody, but John came to me with the tune to Music Of The Ages written on dulcitar. I had access to Denys Val Baker's library, and I suspect the lyrics came about after reading Buddhist literature, in particular *The Secret Of The Golden*

Flower – A Chinese Book Of Life. The instrumental track Banjoland would bring a smile to the grumpiest face. Clive and John play it straight from the sheet music in the old style with John playing the second part and Mick on washboard. Mixed in the background are the sounds of children playing on a beach. Wade In The Water, the number they used to open their Festival Hall show, ends the first side, sung unaccompanied with Ralph banging a drum in time.

Scranky Black Farmer, a traditional Scottish bothy ballad, opens the second side. It originally came from the agricultural area of Buchan, in the North East of Scotland, one of the richest sources for traditional song in Britain. The hired unmarried farm workers lived in communal cottages called bothies that were legendary for their lack of comfort and poor quality of food. The men sang songs reflecting their daily work, and of their romantic aspirations. Clive had often played in the clubs around this area and had a great love and knowledge of the bothy ballads. The songs also frequently mocked the meanness of their employers and Scranky Black Farmer is definitely in that category. Scranky is a fairly uncommon Scottish term meaning thin, mean or lean. Despite the air of mystery the band give the song, it is simply about a sailor who decides to try work as a seasonal agricultural labourer, and gets taken on at a hiring fair. He very soon realises that he was better off at sea. You can just imagine his misery when Clive sings:

The wind it doth beat and the rain it doth pour
And aye yon black farmer he on us does glower.

The song had been collected by Gavin Greig and James Duncan in the early years of the twentieth century and Grieg was of the opinion that the farmer in question was one Daniel Skinner, who leased Earlsfield farm from 1863 to 1882. Clive plays guitar and John plays dulcitar, with Mick unusually playing the organ (he could play a bit of guitar and keyboards but usually preferred to be seen as a front man). A strange but effective 'Aum-ba Oo-da' chant runs all through the song, giving it a slight atmosphere of menace which is somewhat at odds with its actual lyrical content.

Evening Air follows, and calms things down nicely, a beautiful, gentle song in waltz time with Clive on guitar and John on dulcitar and recorder, with Ralph's production getting a fine warm sound from the instruments.

Sitting here on a summer's evening
Star-drawn patterns across the sky
And all the dreams that I had forgotten
They come again to fade as soon

The band had asked for a cello player on some of the tracks, and Ralph arranged for Ursula Smith, then with The Third Ear Band, to overdub some parts. Her cello on the last three tracks adds greatly to the depth of the group sound. Serpent's Kiss is a very intense song lyrically and musically. Mick: 'It was a poem which I feel became an unsuccessful song – and, on rereading it, I'm not sure how successful it was as a poem. Sweet Slavery was a love song with an underlying theme I used a lot in those days – the spirituality of love and / or physical love transcended.' When asked at the time what he thought Serpent's Kiss was about, Clive shrugged it off as 'inscrutable Mick.' Mick didn't really know either: 'As I left the studio, Ralph asked me what it meant. I told him, "Don't ask me, I only wrote it!"' When He Came Home is a perfect ending to the album. The cello part almost physically echoes the pain the subject feels on returning to his hometown after a period of exile.

When he came home all the troubles
Of the world were at his feet
And his poor heart was aching
As he gazed along the street
And nothing was quite the same
As he dreamt that it would be.

The song is the only one on the album to feature John playing the Indian hand-organ. Towards the end of the song, he starts up a riff, which is picked up on cello by Ursula, who starts to improvise on it and then is joined by Mick on percussion as the song speeds off into the distance.

Making *Spirit Of Love* the *Melody Maker* Folk Album of the Month, Andrew Means wrote: 'It is astounding how unique Clive Palmer's brainchilds [*sic*] are. This album completely justifies his reputation as an innovator. COB is unlike anything on the folk scene... The tunes are often unpredictable on first hearing, the melody lines taking courses which no one else would dream of... A number of songs, notably Spirit Of Love and When He Came Home, contain a repetitive pattern, a single mantra phrase that builds up its own impetus. The lyrics and instrumentation contain a similar individuality. Mick Bennett appears to be responsible for the lyrics. If it is him, he has written some stimulating verses. Clive Palmer only touches the banjo, for which he was once renowned for one track, Banjo Land. Mainly he plays guitar and sings.' In *Disc*, the reviewer gave it three stars: 'Whatever Clive Palmer takes in hand, he makes a success then promptly leaves it. However he looks as if he might settle awhile with COB (Clive's Original Band) and their first album *Spirit Of*

Love (£2.30) shows great promise. As the instigator of the Incredible String Band, it's easily heard just how much his influence contributed to the Incredible's initial success. As they seem to have forsaken what seemed to be a winning formula, Clive has picked it up again, with a few more embellishments, and has presented it with his two able musicians Mick Bennett and John Bidwell. A little of the Indian atmosphere remains with the hand organ and the singing style, but much is original Clive, John and Mick. They tried out some of the numbers at a Festival Hall concert in the summer and they went down extremely well. This album should, too.'

In *Folk & Country* magazine, Eric Winter compared the album to the early Incredible String Band: 'Much of the music on *Spirit Of Love* should be allowed simply to flow over you. That way you'll soak it up and feel pleasantly drunk on it – the combination of the record and a bottle of wine is too much to contemplate. There's a certain classicism about most of the tracks, which I believe guarantees survival. In a world where folk outpourings come by the million, survival is at best a chancy business, moreover.' However, Eric did not get Scranky Black Farmer at all, surprisingly failing to appreciate that it really was a genuine traditional song. 'It has me a bit worried. The tune is clearly akin to All Things Are Quite Silent and the song is credited 'Traditional arranged Palmer' but COB have added a chorus – Aum-ba aum-ba aum-ba aum-ba etc – and I don't know whether or not Clive is pulling our collective legs.' That track aside, Eric was very impressed: 'The record is refreshingly real, as opposed to the mass of plastic "fake-music" uttered month by month. I wish I could convey in mere words the pure delight the LP gave me in the listening.'

Norman Davison in the Newcastle-based *Journal* thought Scranky Black Farmer 'ingeniously arranged' and considered both the title track and Wade In The Water ('not the spiritual of the same name, but a gayer piece') 'good examples of the fertile application of vocal arrangements that have gone into this absorbing piece of musical interest.' Maurice Rosenbaum in the *Daily Telegraph* considered both Scranky Black Farmer and When He Came Home 'outstanding.'

Clive initially had his doubts: 'I did the whole COB record, listened to it again, and thought Oh my God... and then people started saying, "Oh no; it's really good". Like you were going to throw something out, but people say "Keep it, it's really good".'

To promote their series of folk albums, CBS issued a six-track maxi single, designed to be played at 33⅓ rpm. Entitled *A Folk Sampler*, it featured one each track from Therapy, Anne Briggs and COB on each side. The two COB tracks featured were Sweet Slavery and Music Of The Ages. It came in a picture sleeve with drawings and short bios of each artist on the back, based on the album's sleeve notes, adding: 'With such talents as these it's hardly surprising that their first album *Spirit Of Love*, produced by Ralph McTell, displays what fine music is all about!'

On the 21st of January COB supported Ralph McTell at Royal Holloway College, Egham, and again the following night at The London School of Economics. On January 25 they played The Medway Folk Centre at the Old Ash Tree pub in Chatham. The Tuesday club night was run by Geoff Harden, who had recorded Clive and Robin at the St. Andrews Folk Club back in 1964. Despite its grand title, the Folk Centre was basically a folk club, albeit in a very large room with a P.A. Geoff booked most of the acts on the scene at the time, Richard Thompson, Hunter Muskett, Al Stewart, The Boys Of The Lough, John Martyn and The Woods Band (featuring Gary Moore on that occasion!) among them. COB played for an agreed fee of £30. Geoff always regretted turning down the chance to book Planxty. Why? They wanted £40! COB drew a respectable audience of 120. Despite takings of £32.25 on the door and a profit of £1.90 on the raffle, the band's fee and an advert in the local paper left the club with a loss of 95p. As was his habit, Geoff recorded COB's performance, and the resulting tape remains an intriguing record of the band in the period immediately after the release of *Spirit Of Love*. By now John had acquired a harmonium, bought for £20 in a London junk shop, and was concentrating on that and the dulcitar. Clive moved between guitar and his recently acquired clarinet (another junk shop find, at £7). What is most interesting about the tape is the band's introductions to the songs, giving the inspiration and in some cases the name of the member who wrote it. On record all COB songs were co-credited Palmer/Bidwell/Bennett. John Bidwell has explained that was actually quite fair, as, for example, while When He Came Home was basically his song, the riff at the end and the arrangement would not have happened without the input of both Clive and Mick. They open with I Told Her, featuring a strong vocal and tambourine from Mick, Clive on guitar and John on harmonium. Music Of The Ages is almost identical to the recorded version, and introduces the dulcitar, which they had obvious problems getting into tune with Clive's guitar, so much so that Geoff stops the tape for a short while. Mick then announces that, as it is all going wrong, they will do something silly, and introduces Bones, which certainly cheers things up, with Mick adding some remarkable/extremely annoying (depending on your taste) scat singing over the top. Sweet Slavery follows with the vocal and organ parts being the same as the recorded version, but with Clive now playing clarinet instead of guitar. The first half ends with Wade In The Water, in a new arrangement featuring guitar and harmonium. Mick tells the audience: 'Originally it was intended to be a protest against all the things that's happening to the Earth, but it didn't turn out that way. It's more like a gospel song now.'

The second half is slightly more dynamic, opening with Oh Bright Eyed One. For Scranky Black Farmer Mick moves over to the harmonium. The chanted backing vocals have been dropped from the new arrangement, but they produce a powerful extended version, with John really getting into it on dulcitar. Blue Morning: 'A new song, one of those happy/sad songs' is in a primitive state at this time, though the music and chorus are fully formed. Mick bravely gets the audience to clap along before the song has even started, giving Clive and John time to get in tune. The verse lyrics almost sound as if Mick is making them up as he goes along, including a piece about 'leaving on that midnight train' which would be absent from the later recorded version. On When He Came Home the opening harmonies are (deliberately?) dreadful, as is Mick's scat singing. Fortunately they recover their composure by the end. Clive plugs the interview they had done that afternoon for local radio, and Mick says that *Spirit Of Love* 'keeps changing all the time, and this is the of-the-moment version.' It seems slightly slower than the album version, with John's harmonium prominent, as are the individual vocal harmonies. The last song of the evening is announced as the pub's last orders bell can be heard. Mick tells the audience: 'We've been out of folk clubs for the last six months or so, and it's nice to be back. This is called The Lion Of Judah, which is written for, and dedicated to, The Emperor Of Ethiopia, Haille Sellassie. The Lion of Judah is one of his titles.' COB do a powerful version, with Mick on his best vocal form of the night. The inevitable cries for an encore lead Clive to announce an 'old Hebrew song', an instrumental which Mick (accurately!) says 'sounds like a lazy camel trying to get across the Sahara.' Mick plays finger cymbals here, with Clive on clarinet. The tune would turn up again in Clive's repertoire many years later under what was presumably its proper title: Erev Shel Shasha Nim.

On Friday, the 26th of May, COB were booked to play at the Great Western Express Festival at Bardney, near Lincoln. The event ran over the Bank Holiday weekend and billed itself as 'The Festival They Couldn't Stop' as the organisers (the actor Stanley Baker and Lord Harlech) had undergone enormous legal hassles to put the festival on. They took out adverts in the rock press begging the fans to behave themselves, warning that if things went badly it could lead to a total ban on future large scale festivals in Britain. The bill was an incredibly strong one. For £4.50 you could see The Faces, Joe Cocker, The Beach Boys, Rory Gallagher, Humble Pie, The Groundhogs, The Incredible String Band, Wishbone Ash, Stone The Crows, Lindisfarne, Slade, The Strawbs and dozens of others including up-and-coming outfits such as Genesis and Roxy Music. *Melody Maker* quaintly announced that 'in the mornings between 10am and 1pm there will be outdoor folk singing, in a tent if wet.' The tent was then to be used for a series of Giants Of Tomorrow showcases, featuring bands like Skin Alley, Capability Brown, Magic Carpet, Patto and Gnidrolog, none of whom lived up to their billing. Flyers were issued for the 'Great Western Folk Express – The Festival Within A Festival.' The bill on Friday was Al Matthews, COB, Derek Brimstone and Johnny Silvo & Dave Moses. On Saturday the folk tent was to feature Hamish Imlach, Harvey Andrews, Bridget St John, Colin Scott, and the JSD Band, who undoubtedly would have livened things up a bit. On Sunday the tent featured Mick Softley, Anne Briggs, Jonathan Kelly and The Boys of the Lough. The compere for all three days was the Edinburgh-based singer-comedian Bill Barclay. Clive: 'The place was decimated by a hurricane the night before; it smashed up all the caravans so there was no accommodation. It was all muddy. Typical disaster festival.' Or, as the *Lincolnshire Echo* so eloquently put it on the 27th of May:

'Festival fans fight wind, rain in pop swamp.'

Hamish Imlach had been playing in Droitwich on the Friday night and arrived at the site at 4am: 'I was supposed to have a caravan to sleep in and had the paperwork to get me through the gates. Thousands of people were still arriving. I got through but couldn't find anyone to direct me to the caravan, and ended up sleeping in the car with cement sacks over me until seven am. It was freezing and pissing with rain. I squelched through the mud to learn that the marquees had blown down, so we wouldn't be performing but we would still probably get our money.' However, the folk singers, the only ones with acoustic instruments, had a great session in the artists' bar, Mick Softley going round all the big stars with a cleaned-out ashtray to collect money for their drinks. At nine am on Sunday word came round that the acoustic artists would be put on the main stage. Hamish wasn't keen. 'I was talking to Clive Palmer and he said his group were going to go on the main stage. I said, "Ach, if you go on I'll go on. We only had to do three numbers each anyway. I can do that even though I'm wrecked." We went up, eleven o'clock on a Sunday morning, the start of the official programme, and there was a fair crowd sitting there. They were all pissed off; soggy, harassed by the police, ripped off by everybody. I chose the right songs, in the right place at the right time. I got three encores, everybody going daft, Stanley Baker shaking me by the hand and offering me a ride in his helicopter!' Clive adds: 'We went down alright, everybody did. The organisers accepted defeat and just put everyone on for half an hour in succession. You couldn't see the audience, they were sheltering under plastic sheets.'

In June COB were reviewed supporting the rock band Argent at The Gliderdrome, a huge venue also known as The Starlight Rooms, in Boston, Lincs. It was well known for its revolving stage, which often broke down. This was an unlikely pairing of bands, but COB acquitted themselves well: 'They played an excellent and varied set of folk based numbers, featuring the strong vocals of Mick Bennett and the multi-instrumental ability of John Bidwell on dulcimer, balalaika, and specially organ, which produced a very full sound.' COB supported Argent again at The Roundhouse in London around the same time. Clive also remembers COB supporting Eclection in Boston.

John: 'Nice gigs floated our way through Jo, and from them we earned enough to live off. We'd get together a couple of times a week to rehearse at Clive's dad's place. At gigs we weren't always miked up by the same people, which was occasionally a problem, though a friend of Mick's called "Mad" Roger Blackmore regularly helped us out.' Clive: 'He was a great roadie and driver but you couldn't stop him drinking. He'd sleep it off in the van, and then he could drive forever.' The band often had to sleep in the van after gigs.

On the 14th of July COB released a single on Polydor with Blue Morning on the A-side backed with Bones. Again, Ralph McTell was the producer and it was specifically recorded as a single, Jo insisting it should be commercial and radio-friendly. Blue Morning is basically the same song that the band had played at Chatham but the lyrics had clearly been refined. Steve Bonnett adds crisp electric guitar and reggae-style bass, and the result is quite pleasing, though hardly what COB sounded like live. Bones might actually have had more chance as the A-side. Again Steve adds bass and piano to the basic track; he had actually stopped working live with Ralph nearly a year previously, when Ralph decided not to pursue his idea of forming a band, but they still remained friends and saw each other socially. Steve had since worked with several other Lustig signings, including Gillian McPherson and Julie Felix. Julie had formed a backing band with Steve and 'a couple of guys from Daddy Longlegs' (presumably including Steve Haydon, who had played in Chrissy Quayle's Daylight). Julie had been delighted to find they were all born under the same star sign, feeling sure this was a great portent of success; she was to be sadly disappointed. Bones is based on a Matt McGinn song called The Dundee Ghost about a poltergeist disrupting a house, the first two lines of the first two verses of both songs being more or less identical. Clive adds the 'bones, bones ba-ba-ba-bones' part. Live, Bones often became Balls! Ralph: 'I remember Jo sending copies around with miniature bottles of whisky, the idea being that it would help the DJ through a 'blue morning' at work, but it did no good and I don't believe either tune ever got as much as a single spin.' Both Mick and John would later admit that they regretted issuing the single. Mick: 'It wasn't true to us and I didn't like it, but we were desperate for money. They were both Clive's songs, but we each wrote a verse of Blue Morning.' John: 'I liked the counter-melody of Blue Morning and thought it was a good number overall, but I'm not sure if it was a good idea to release it as a single.'

Rosalind Russell interviewed the band for *Disc* just before the Cambridge Festival in July. She didn't quite know what to make of Blue Morning either. 'A somewhat surprising single starts off like a reggae number, then slips into (an) old 78rpm cum 1930-ish type of jig-along romance. After a few listens, it becomes quite compulsive. The addition of percussion has done good things for the band. They are hoping it

COB (LEFT TO RIGHT): CLIVE PALMER, GENEVIVE VAL BAKER, MICK BENNETT AND JOHN BIDWELL

COB are trying again . . .

AFTER their dazzling debut as warm up band at the solo Bert Jansch concert in London last year, COB have lain quiet. They were signed to CBS on the strength of the show and brought out an album last summer with that label. Now, this time round with Polydor, COB are trying added

record the album. I don't like hanging about in the studios. We put down the straightforward ones first and get them out of the way. That way we have something behind us, then we do the tricky ones. The last album was made in about a week.

"There are going to be a few changes this time. For a start it's going to be a 'live' album, with

will get some airplay. It's not exactly what you'd expect from COB. It was done without any premeditated idea of what it was to turn out like, a kind of experiment. When I first heard it, I thought it was reggae, but on closer listening, it reminds me of an old 78 – that's not the quality, but the kind of mood it's sung in.' It was certainly true that Mick sung Blue Morning in a manner more suited to a 1930s dance band crooner. The *Disc* article also announced that COB had added 'a lady drummer, Genevieve Val Baker.' Clive: 'Genevieve is a very good drummer. She is an old friend from Cornwall. We spend a lot of time there. Genevieve's sister is a drummer too, but she doesn't play professionally. We didn't have any percussion on our first album, and now we have a lot more rhythm and can experiment a bit more.' It was generally agreed that Genevieve was not as technically competent as her sister Demelza was, but her personality fitted in better with the band. At one rehearsal she remembers being asked to play a very simple percussion part. She really couldn't see how it fitted in. Clive restarted the song and suddenly told her to stop. The song just fell apart, her small part having been the key to the whole structure of the piece.

Russell reported that the band intended to record their new album shortly, then take a holiday. The songs had all been worked out over the last two months, and they did not anticipate spending much more than a week in the studio. The new album was to be more than just a collection of songs. There was to be a 'kind of theme running through it, enough to connect all the songs with each other.' Clive: 'I'm sure the LP will be very good this time. The last time we hadn't been together for very long. I think it'll take about a week to record the album. I don't like hanging about in the studios. We put down the straightforward ones first and get them out of the way. That way we have something behind us, then we do the tricky ones. The last album was made in about a week. There are going to be a few changes this time. For a start it's going to be a 'live' album, with practically no double-tracking or effects. The only session man we'll have will be Danny Thompson on bass if it's convenient for him at the time. The rest we'll be doing ourselves. And of course having the drums makes a big difference in itself.' Russell, in common with almost every interviewer he had at this time, could not resist asking Clive why he had left the ISB.

'If I hadn't left [when I did] I would have left soon after. I wouldn't still be in the Incredibles. I never saw eye to eye with Robin, it seemed important to him that he should succeed, that he should be noticed. When you worked with Robin you worked for him and not with him. Now someone like me, I wouldn't work for anyone, I work with people. In our band all the members have to be on an equal footing. Otherwise there's not enough interaction. COB wouldn't be successful if I was influencing them strongly. I've never been sure about what I want, but I don't think it's to be noticed. I knew this band was going to work out.'

COB in Ralph McTell's back garden. Courtesy Shirley Palmer

COB played the Cambridge Folk Festival in the last weekend of July in common with a great number of Mr Lustig's clients including Ralph, Barry Dransfield, Gillian McPherson and Wizz Jones. The poster for the event featured a large number of cartoon people spelling out the name of the festival. In the letter M is a figure seated at a drum saying: 'It's not as

The Dubliners
Artie and Happy Traum
Derrol Adams
Alex Campbell
The Boys of the Lough
Steve Tiltson
John James
Mike Coopers Machine Gun Co
Alex Atterson
C.O.B.
Alan Taylor
Barry Dransfield
Wizz Jones
George Deacon & Marion Ross

Ralph McTell
Gillian McPherson
Oak
Totem
De Cameron
Jasper Carrot
Peter Bellamy
Pete Sayers
The Radio Cowboys
The Southern Ramblers
Brian Golbey
Pete Stanley & Roger Knowles
The Down County Boys
Brian Challen's New Frontier

Weekend of July 28 29 30
Cherryhinton hall grounds
All day buffet and bars
Camping sites available
Car parks and full facilities
Grand Ole Opry Tent
and Club Tents
One day ticket £1.00
Weekend £1.70
Tickets: Guildhall Box Office
Phone Cambridge 57851
and 77 St. Phillips Road
Phone Cambridge 48025
also main agents

windy as Lincoln!'

Andrew Means, reporting for *Melody Maker*, certainly enjoyed himself. 'The standard throughout the weekend was ridiculously high. Not only were the famous playing and talking and drinking in all parts, but the usual anonymous groups were swinging away in every corner. Oak, though hardly unknown, led many a shadowy session, trailed by an impressed Clive Palmer. Clive's Own Band [*sic*] played with refreshing tightness, as did Decameron and Hunter Muskett.' The following week COB went into the studio to record their second album, again with Ralph as producer. He had learned his lesson from recording *Spirit Of Love*. The new album was recorded using vari-speed. This meant that they had so-called 'tuning tracks', so if things went out of key you could speed them up and slow them down until they sounded right with each other. Unfortunately the engineer recorded the whole LP at too fast a setting, so when it came to be pressed it had to be slowed down. Ralph: 'If anyone ever finds the master tapes they'll have a surprise!' Danny Thompson came in for one day only. He brought his small son with him, who had wanted to see what a recording studio looked like. Danny played double bass on three tracks: Sheba's Return, on which he used his bow to powerful effect, Lion Of Judah and Chain Of Love. Demelza Val Baker also joined her sister in some of the sessions, the two being thanked as 'the amazing Val Baker girls' on the sleeve. Demelza played drums and percussion on Sheba's Return/Lion Of Judah, tabla on Eleven Willow and congas, the instrument for which she had become best known, on Heart Dancer. Genny played bongos on four tracks, and added vocals to three. According to the box containing the master tape, *Moyshe McStiff And The Tartan Lancers Of The Sacred Heart* was recorded and mixed by the 8th of August. At the end of the session the master tapes went to Polydor, though Ralph claims that neither he nor any of the band ever received any payment for them. Danny Thompson was apparently the only one who did get any sort of payment – a box of 25 copies of the finished album, which he immediately sold! Clive: 'We never saw any statements or received any PRS royalties.'

When the album sessions were over, Clive and Mick were interviewed in *Melody Maker* for an article entitled 'The compelling mystique of COB.' 'Most groups concern themselves with smooth sound reproduction, stage presentation and hard-hitting songs. COB remain virtually oblivious to those standards. As they recognise, their indifference to presentation and the visual aspect of a gig is a shortcoming, and one that they expect to eliminate in time. But freedom in approach also brings its advantages. It is precisely this that distinguishes them, for more resourceful degrees of imagination are sadly lacking in acoustic music today. COB's songs are surreal, their instrumentation and arrangements are unlikely. Their music is disturbingly abnormal, so the group has never found itself in a cosy category, with its own recognised type of venue and brand of followers.' The interviewer then commented on Clive's reputation for leaving bands: 'The fact that they avoid personality clashes and all have musical ideas to contribute to the group has ensured that it has lasted.' The *MM* bravely had a go at explaining the new album's title, or perhaps it was simply the band's then-current version of what it meant: 'The title points to the group's influences – Mick's interest in Jewish history, the effect of Scotland upon Clive and Catholicism on John. Nevertheless the tracks demand concentration; Sheba's Return/Lion Of Judah and Solomon's Song are particularly rich in imagery and owe their content to Mick's Jewish history and Clive's absorption in the Kabbalah and occult books in general.' Clive explained his fascination with Eastern music: 'I think it's the freedom, especially the musical freedom. It has tremendous vitality. They live life to the full, it's so positive and when it's feminine it's so feminine. Everything's so clear cut. The trouble with so many Western traditions is that they are so mixed up.' Clive also mentioned his ambitions for the band, talking of adding a bass guitarist (Steve Bonnett once said he might have joined COB had it not been for his contractual obligations elsewhere), and even of COB working with an orchestra or a theatrical group, though he doubted that money would be available to do this. They were unconcerned that COB was out of touch with the music scene, Mick mentioning that he had only bought one album that year – Dick Gaughan's *No More Forever*. Mick explained that he was just about to go on a trip to the Shetlands, partly to explore the music there, and intended to investigate Balkan music after that. 'They claim they are not concerned with the fashion of the day, and not prepared to make compromises in exchange for popularity.' On the 5th of August COB (though the poster called them COBB) supported Sandy Denny in an open-air concert at the Well Hall Open Theatre in Eltham, South London.

In the September issue of *Folk Review* (previously *Folk & Country*) , it was announced that Pentangle would be starting a mammoth British tour on the 8th of October lasting two months, with Wizz Jones and COB in support. Before that they would be touring Australia, New Zealand and Scandinavia. Editor Fred Woods quipped: 'With all this rushing around it won't be long before Pentangle has the corners rubbed off it! Geddit?' What few people realised was that by now the members of Pentangle were thoroughly sick of the whole thing, and each other. A recently released DVD of Pentangle performing on a French TV show around this time shows them as a pretty miserable bunch, only Danny and Terry looking as if they were even vaguely getting any pleasure out of the proceedings.

On the 20th of September COB appeared in concert at The Basildon Arts Centre, sandwiched between Gillian McPherson and Bridget St. John. The programme claimed that 'the group demonstrate the vitality and spontaneity of the early ISB, but with their own special flavour.' An advert appeared in the folk press in October introducing a new label from Polydor called Folk Mill. Three albums were announced: The Peelers – *Banished Misfortune*, COB – *Moyshe McStiff And The Tartan Lancers Of The Sacred Heart* and Barry Dransfield – *The Barry Dransfield Album*.

The Peelers were a trio of Tom Madden (guitar/5-string banjo/vocals), Joe Palmer (guitar/dulcimer/vocals) and Jim Younger (concertina/whistle/mandolin), who played traditional folk material from Irish, English, Scottish and Australian sources. Barry Dransfield usually performed with his brother Robin as the Dransfields (managed by Jo Lustig) but his Folk Mill album was completely solo. Lustig had worked the brothers hard, as was his way, and was far from pleased when they turned down a lucrative recording deal with Warner Brothers which he had brokered. After seeing Barry support The Johnstons (an Irish folk group featuring star-to-be Paul Brady) at a gig at the Queen Elizabeth Hall Jo began to re-appreciate his potential and offered him a solo deal.

The COB album was the only one of the three to receive a full gatefold package, the inner sleeve carrying the lyrics to the songs and a small photo of the new four-piece line-up (the same photo that had accompanied the *Disc* article in July), all smiling and looking slightly windswept. The painting on the outside of the sleeve appeared to be laden with symbolism. It featured a stark desert plain with mountains in the distance. Three knights are rescuing a naked girl from the clutches of a dragon. Two are dressed in Middle Eastern/Crusader style (one wearing what may be intended to be a tartan sash) and are plunging lances into the dragon's body. The beast's tail is wrapped around the girl, and a vision of a bleeding heart wrapped in thorns and crowned with flames shines light on to the shield of the third knight who is about to decapitate the dragon. He is dressed in full

medieval armour. His shield features the grail motif and his face, visible beneath the open visor of his helmet, is black and stony. The Polydor Folk Mill logo appeared in the bottom right hand corner. It has to be said that it is not a particularly attractive cover (though some think otherwise), but it was certainly an intriguing one. The cover was the work of artist Paul Whitehead, who simply painted the image suggested by the album's title.

Ralph: 'It was a light-hearted, throwaway title, really, and we were all pretty astonished when the art department came up with that amazing cover. In fact, we had high hopes of the album selling, but it turned out to be a little too out there even for those enlightened times. Still, we felt vindicated just to have got the songs right.' The title has caused a fair bit of interest over the years. There is little doubt that 'Moyshe McStiff' was one of several joke names for Mick Bennett, based on his mixed Jewish/Scottish ancestry. Clive and John were The Tartan Lancers, and 'The Sacred Heart was just for fun, a throwaway addition really. There's nothing deep for people to read into it. It doesn't mean anything apart from the wordplay on Mick's name, which also describes the music quite well, I suppose.' Ralph McTell added that The Tartan Lancer was the name of the nearest off-licence to his house in Putney. Steve Bonnett recalls it was on the Lower Richmond Road, near the corner of the road where Ralph lived. John, however, claims never to have heard of the establishment.

The album opens with Sheba's Return, an instrumental featuring harmonium and Clive's multi-tracked clarinet; he had written the melody around a phrase on clarinet. Danny Thompson came up with an extraordinary bowed double bass part. 'Danny lives in a world of his own. He just knows exactly what to play,' says Clive. Lion Of Judah started out as a poem after Mick became fascinated by the life and times of Haile Selassie (or Highly Unlikely, as Mr Thompson used to call him). Growing up in Finsbury Park, Mick had become exposed to Caribbean music quite early on through record shops catering to the Windrush generation. Solomon's Song is closely based on the first and second chapter of The Song Of Solomon in the Old Testament, but slightly re-arranged, and arguably, improved. For example the St James version of the first verse is:

I am black, but comely, O ye daughters of Jerusalem,
as the tents of Kedar, as the curtains of Solomon.
Mick sings:
I am comely because I am black
As the tents of Kedar, as Solomon's veil
John's song Eleven Willows, (incorrectly titled Eleven Willow on

the sleeve) on which he sings lead, harks straight back to the Indian influences of the Temple Creatures. Genny sings a beautiful harmony part, based on the Indian principle of 'tala'. This is used by teachers of the tabla drums to get their pupils used to singing the rhythm patterns used in playing. The deceptively simple pattern here is actually a complex 11 beats per bar, made up of a 4-3-2-2 pattern. The lyrics are very strong, too:

> *This valley is a cradle for the sun and for the silent one*
> *Who wears the coat of many colours.*

The first side ends with I Told Her, a song which predated the band's formation and had gained a great deal of confidence since its Chatham airing. Clive now plays guitar and John strums balalaika, giving the song quite a Russian feel, with Mick on lead vocals and tambourine and Genny on bongos. Mick boasts that he has no conscience about breaking a girl's heart; after all he had told her in advance that he could not love her. He has another love in his sights. It's obvious how much Mick enjoys performing this song, ending it with a laugh and a joyous 'yippee'.

Bright Eyed One is a charming track, with a simple lyric, finger-picked guitar and harmonium, and Clive and Mick harmonising beautifully. Chain Of Love was largely written by John, and features the lovely line 'To travel in your warm and wooded country', which describes parts of Cornwall beautifully. John admits he was thinking specifically of the valley of the River Fowey when he lived at Golant. Pretty Kerry is a particularly subtle song, both in its lyrics and in its backing, with Clive's seemingly simple but ever-changing banjo pattern and the understated whistles, played by both John and Mick. Mick deliberately wrote the song in traditional style, basing the lyrics on a conversation he had overheard in a Camden pub. They concern a young man walking home from work one evening and meeting Kerry, who has been forced into prostitution to support her child when her lover has been arrested. The young man agrees to sleep with her, but is haunted by what he has done; ultimately it seems that Kerry knew from the beginning that this would happen, and enjoys the power she has gained over him.

> *And the cry of her small child, seemed so cold and hungry*
> *As I left in the morning quietly*
> *Be it seed time, be it moonshine, be it sunrise, be it harvest*
> *Would that I could forget this travesty*
> *But from somewhere inside me, a voice seemed to say*
> *Peace of mind you shall not find, you shall not see.*

Mick: 'Martha And Mary started life as a poem called Hands Of

Mary and developed into a song with the same intention as Sweet Slavery. I took the words and melody to Clive, who worked out the chords. He was extremely good at finding that special chord, and even to this day I don't know which ones fit that tune.' The Martha and Mary in question were the ones from the Bible, the sisters of Lazarus, whom Jesus raised from the dead. 'I still read the Bible; it sprang from that, and probably taking LSD!' The song is probably the finest on the album, with Clive's delicate balalaika interweaving with John's finger-picked guitar.

Jerry Gilbert gave *Moyshe* a surprisingly lukewarm review in *Sounds* on October the 14th. 'It's an album that won't appeal far beyond COB's loyal band of followers, but as far as criticism goes one can only fault the vocals, which should have been stronger. The texture of the sound is brilliant throughout although the quality of the compositions is perhaps not as high as on their first album.'

Andrew Means in *Melody Maker* was a little more impressed, though he thought that Mick's lyrics sometimes seemed 'curiously aimless.' He made the point that COB were one of the very few bands about who actually challenged the listener's imagination. 'They launch into sound with an apparent fearlessness for the consequences. In accordance with the laws of chance some wild elements spring from this attitude, but excess is a small price to pay for worthwhile originality. They move from the magnificent, threatening theme of Lion Of Judah to the Irish traditional flavour of Pretty Kerry. It's not apt to term *Moyshe McStiff* development. It's a continuation along similar absorbing paths of exploration.'

Bearing in mind Clive's comments in the *Disc* interview, was *Moyshe* a concept album? Probably not, or, as John said, 'only in the most abstract way.' Nonetheless, one American author, calling himself The Lama, had a pretty good try at explaining it as a concept. In a long essay on the album published on the Internet, he writes: 'The closest I've come is the image of a late-medieval crusader-knight, who at the end of his career has returned to England, where he contemplates upon the many years of travel, his Christian faith and the Church, as well as family life at his rural homestead, with faint echoes of a long-gone childhood. His mind moves freely along these axes of space and time. Layers of time atop each other, like cultural sediment, England in 1972 and the 14th Century, Jerusalem in the 14th Century but also in the days of the first Christians.' The Lama ends by saying that *Moyshe* is 'as far as I am concerned, the greatest LP ever recorded in England.'

Thinking about it now, Clive feels that the songs are linked by period and feel, in the same way that a painter has, say, 'a blue period.' He doesn't think that the songs were linked by a narrative thread, though 'perhaps they were, and we just weren't aware of it!'

The Pentangle/COB tour kicked off in the Davenport Theatre, Stockport, on the 8th of October, before heading north to Scotland with dates in Edinburgh, Aberdeen and Glasgow. On the way to Edinburgh Clive took a slight detour and went to visit the Incredible String Band, who by then were living in a row of estate workers' cottages on land owned by the Tennant family, about 6 miles down the Tweed valley from Peebles. After the Scottish dates the tour headed south again and played all over England, travelling up and down the country, with gigs most nights. On the 28th the tour played the Royal Festival Hall in London. At Clive's suggestion, there was a surprise addition to the bill, the 75 year old traditional singer Willie Scott, a retired shepherd from the Scottish borders. He stood alone on the huge stage, leaning on his crook, and went down extremely well.

Wizz: 'I don't know whether it was meant to be [Pentangle's] farewell tour, but it certainly turned out that way. It had kind of gone sour, they'd been going for so long that I think it had got a bit automatic for them, but the amazing thing was that the management chose to put Clive's Original Band and myself on the same bill, which made the whole thing a bit impractical. I think the idea was to give Clive's band and myself a bit of a leg up, but really the bill was top heavy, I thought. Either Clive's band shouldn't have been on or I shouldn't. But we were all glad of the tour. Economically it was ridiculous [Clive recalls COB being paid £500 a night on the Pentangle tour]. Bert and John weren't speaking at all, Danny was drinking a lot, in fact everyone was drinking a lot! I did OK because I was solo, and you can always win in those circumstances. COB were doing some good stuff, but it was a real shambles of a tour. Pentangle were at the end of the line, they weren't together, they didn't care any more.' In the November issue of *Folk Review*, Karl Dallas wrote that Pentangle had 'represented a bedrock of stability for five years so far. Another four of the same or similar, will not be too much to settle for.' Indeed.

The tour was generally well received but in Croydon the *Croydon Advertiser* reviewer obviously caught Pentangle on a bad night: 'The small and disappointed Fairfield Hall audience drew one consolation from Sunday's folk concert – that of hearing Wizz Jones... [who was of course a local boy]. Wizz Jones's act had one ingredient missing from the other two on the bill – direction. Clive Palmer's COB [that's how they were billed] sang some pleasant songs, making little impression. One felt that Palmer himself had something to say, but his associates were playing in a world of their own. Mary and Martha [*sic*] a song about happiness, featured good vocals by Mick Bennett, but soon the act went off into strange instrumentals, such as Boom-Boom [presumably Bones] and eastern songs like The Lion Of Judah. Clive's Incredible String Band origins came out in one glorious song Let It Be You. Why didn't they pursue that angle and find some direction?' Pentangle were dismissed as 'a major disappointment – they sounded dated, and played overworked songs with overworked rhythms.' Clive would later describe the tour as 'hard work. We just got polite applause – we were either ahead of our time or behind it. Still, the tour enabled me to have some very nice holidays in Cornwall on my motorbike. £500 a gig at that time wasn't bad between three people. That tour did us a lot of good; we started to make some money.' Clive was forgetting that there were four people in the band at the time – though Genny was actually paid a smaller share of the gig money than the other three. This took a while to come to light as Clive would hand the band their wages in brown envelopes. Genny didn't mind at all as she was only eighteen, getting to play in some of the biggest venues in the UK at the time, and just glad to be a part of it all, but both Mick and John thought it was unfair when they found out. All the hard post-gig partying took its toll (Genny recalls seeing Bert finish off a whole 24-bottle crate of beer by himself one night), as, three gigs from the end of the tour, Danny was taken to hospital with a heart complaint, and the last dates were cancelled. The first issue of the *Melody Maker* in 1973 had 'Pentangle Split' as its main front page story.

In early 1973 COB, now a trio again, began a weekly residency at Bill Knox's pub at Putney, The Half Moon. Clive: 'We built that up from nothing to nearly full up, about 300 people. It was amazing, I was the most surprised person, we found that the group could build an audience and they really liked us. At that point we were playing the same things that were on the albums plus we were doing Flowers of the Forest and various other things. We were doing The Road To

Dundee, which is still Bert Jansch's favourite song. It's one he always asks me to do.' Sean O'Rourke of the JSD Band, who were based in London at the time, saw them at the Half Moon a few times, recalling that they played sitting down, with Clive mainly on banjo and clarinet and John on guitar. 'They played very gentle, flowing, melodic and lyrical stuff then.'

Around this time Clive met Shirley Ward at a party and invited her along to see COB play one night at the Half Moon. She reciprocated by inviting him to accompany her to a performance of *Parsifal* in Covent Garden. Clive fell asleep. Shirley: 'Well, Wagner does have its boring bits!' Shirley Halpin (her original surname) had grown up in Hampstead with her divorced mother. She had been interested in folk music from an early age, remembering hearing Sonny Terry and Brownie McGee on the radio and feeling that this sort of music was different and exciting. She was also drawn to left-wing politics, joining Young CND at the age of 13. When she was 15 her first boyfriend was a folksinger and she was also a member of the Anti-Apartheid League and the Young Communists. At sixteen she ran a folk club in Watford booking an eclectic range of guests including Lou Killen, Derroll Adams and the Young Tradition. She married a drama student called David Ward when she was 19 and sang with him in an un-named trio, also helping to stage plays. The marriage was not a great success, her husband moving too far away from his original political principles: 'I left him on my 21st birthday!' Shirley had first met Clive as long ago as the winter of 1968, when she was down in Cornwall with a friend and was introduced to him at The Folk Cottage. 'He was sitting downstairs in a rocking chair by the fire. He didn't say much, was a bit inscrutable, but he had a very warm smile, a cool guy.' In 1972 Shirley began working as a PA to Ken Woollard, the greatly respected organiser of the Cambridge Folk Festival, and for many years worked as the stage manager for Main Stage 1, a post she occupied until 1997, several years after Ken's death. She remembers speaking briefly to Clive at the 1972 festival, though she knew Mick Bennett very well socially from the London folk club scene. Shirley's day job was as a secretary, and she also contributed the occasional article to *Folk Review* magazine. After a while she and Clive moved in together.

COB came to a sudden halt one Friday night in March 1973. Clive: 'Mick and I were always arguing. Mick's one of those needly characters, you know. I'm very patient, but I do have a limit. We were doing a residency in Putney, and we were packing the place out, doing very well. But I was in the throes of getting married at that time, I was pretty busy, preoccupied. John and I had a... dispute on stage. Basically, John was drunk. I'm not forgiving about that sort of thing. When I'm on stage I expect people to be professional. I was very disappointed. He was basically too drunk to play, and that's not really good enough. So all I did was pour a pint of beer over his head. He was upset... but I'd made my point.' John: 'I can't speak for Clive or Mick, but I didn't feel bad about the break-up at the time. My personal view is that we split up because we weren't really changing direction. We always played acoustic, and perhaps should have done more in the electric sphere. For one reason or another the broadcast media never picked up on our records, so our music was always more evident live, that's when people would show us their appreciation. We never chased success though; our personalities precluded it, really.' Mick: 'It was a serious struggle keeping it all together. The residency at the Half Moon was great, but because we never had any money we started squabbling about petty things and it all became a bit much. It's a shame, because if we'd been able to afford it I'm sure we'd have developed further musically.' The band had already accepted several bookings for gigs and festivals up to the summer, so Clive decided to recruit two new musicians to cover the dates COB were committed to doing, including the Norwich Folk Festival in the second week in June. He also decided that the new band would play old-time and jug-band standards, rather than the old COB repertoire. Clive had recently met up with Henry Bartlett again, and he was invited on board, as was guitarist Chris Newman, who was backing Fiona Stuart, a singer who shared Shirley's flat. Shirley had met Fiona on the folk scene and had written about her for *Folk Review*. Clive and Henry would occasionally join Chris to back Fiona on some of her gigs.

Henry and Clive at the Norwich Folk Festival. Photo by Shirley Palmer

Since the FJB split Henry had formed another band which gigged around South London; the membership included Chris Ayliffe on acoustic guitar, plus electric guitar, drums and Henry on double bass or electric bass guitar. Henry had moved into courier work, mainly antiques, and eventually he and his friend Mike Allenby formed a partnership to go into the antiques trade themselves. A trip down to Dorset with £150 capital and a Transit van proved the beginning of a long and satisfying career for Henry, who enjoyed the trade immensely. He developed a great feel for furniture, and loved the wheeling and dealing and the characters he met working in the field. Henry and Mike opened a shop in Kew, and later in Wandsworth Road. Chris Newman helped Henry out with his business on the odd occasion.

Chris Newman had received a great deal of encouragement from Diz Disley, a popular guitarist on the folk club circuit. Chris regards himself as having 'served his apprenticeship' with Diz. He was initially unsure about joining COB: 'I was a bit sceptical about being part of what was effectively COB Mk II, but was delighted when I realised that the entire repertoire was going to be old-time material – something I've always had an interest in. Among the songs I remember we did were The Darktown Strutter's Ball, and Uncle Dave Macon songs like The Wreck Of The Tennessee Gravy Train.'

Clive, Henry and Chris at the Hull Folk Festival, Saturday, 9th June 1973. Courtesy Jenny Bartlett

After honouring its remaining commitments, COB called it a day. Clive had by now decided that he wanted to do something else: 'It was the end of a good few years of mucking about. It seemed like a good time to give it a rest.' In September he started a year-long full-time course at Merton College in Musical Instrument Technology, where he learnt how to make and repair musical instruments such as guitars, woodwind instruments and pianos. The man running the course was John Bailey. John had made a guitar for

Mike Heron, as well as being featured in the 1969 Incredible String Band film documentary *Be Glad For The Song Has No Ending* in a scene where Robin, Licorice and Leaf the dog visited his house. Robin was thinking of buying a hurdy-gurdy and was filmed trying various instruments John had built. John also wrote a couple of books for the English Folk Dance & Song Society (EFDSS) on how to build guitars and dulcimers. Around this time John Renbourn played Clive an album by the Northumbrian smallpipes player Billy Pigg, which impressed him enormously. He found a book on how to make and play the pipes at Cecil Sharp House (headquarters of the EFDSS) and, working from photocopies of the pages, started making his first set of smallpipes. The Northumbrian smallpipes have a quiet, sweet tone, and the bag is filled by air from a set of bellows under the player's arm. Clive learned a lot of new skills in making them, including how to use a lathe and the long drills needed to hollow out the pipes. Learning how to play them took some time too.

Clive regarded himself as having ceased to be a professional musician when COB's commitments ended, though of course he never stopped playing. He undertook a series of day jobs, but his and Shirley's ultimate intention was always to live in Cornwall. After Shirley's divorce came through, they were married on the 26th of January 1974, with Henry Bartlett as Best Man and Jenny as Matron-of-Honour. Clive's jobs during this time included working in a picture framing shop in Soho, and, perhaps more satisfyingly, a few months making clarinets for the well-known musical instrument company Boosey & Hawkes. He was offered a job working for a French company making woodwind instruments but turned it down as it would have meant spending three months training in France. He then spent a year working for a company that made dental and medical appliances and instruments. A photo in a trade magazine shows the staff, including details of how long they had worked for the company – thirty years in one case. Standing at the back in a brown coat is 'Mr C. Palmer (one year).' Clive walked out of the job not long afterwards, following a disagreement over a Health & Safety issue.

In the meantime John Bidwell had been working very hard at learning to play the metal Boehm-system flute. John was sharing a flat with another Cornish musician called Jake Walton, who played guitar and dulcimer and was something of a Donovan fan. He had been part of the Cornish folk scene too, being a one time resident at The Folk Cottage, and had supported the Stockroom Five and Temple Creatures on numerous occasions. Jake had recently graduated from Reading University (where he ran the folk club) with a degree in psychology and had got involved in a programme to teach guitar to children in secondary schools. Knowing a good thing when he found it, he had also got some of his friends from the folk scene jobs in the programme, including John Bidwell and Jenny Beeching (who would later record a version of A Leaf Must Fall). Jake had also formed a duo with Roger Nicholson, almost certainly the best dulcimer player in Britain; he went on to play on most of Roger's albums. John's and Jake's flat was in Bedford Hill, only a few streets away from where Wizz and Sandy Jones lived, and John and Jake often dropped round to visit. Sandy was getting back into playing the banjo after a lapse of a few years and was working her way through the material in John Burke's *Book Of Old Time Fiddle Tunes For Banjo*. Wizz: 'I came back from Germany and Sandy had been sitting around playing music from the John Burke book with Jake and John.' Wizz already knew versions of most of the material in the book from old Folkways albums and of course he was very familiar with bluegrass from the years he had spent with Pete Stanley. The new combination became Lazy Farmer, with Wizz on guitar, John on flute and guitar, Jake on dulcimer and guitar and Sandy on banjo. Jake: 'It was very much a social thing – meet round at Wizz's house and bring a few cans.' At the time they saw it mainly as a fun band with no real intention of gigging. The Jones family usually headed down to Cornwall for the summer season, and Lazy Farmer did a few formal gigs then, headlining at the St Ives Guildhall on the 10th of August, supported by Mask, Mike Silver and Chrissy Quayle. Shortly afterwards Sandy decided to take a few lessons from the American banjo player Tom Paley, who held classes at Cecil Sharp House. Following one lesson they headed for a music session in a nearby pub and met up with a young banjo player from Nottingham called Don Coging, who was also well versed in the John Burke repertoire. In October Wizz recorded a solo album for the Bristol-based Village Thing label. Entitled *When I Leave Berlin*, it was issued in the following spring and included four tracks featuring Lazy Farmer, two of which also featured Don, who was credited separately from the band, though he soon joined them officially. The album also featured Bert Jansch, and a cover version of Robin Williamson's First Girl I Loved.

Mick Bennett also wasted little time in putting a new band together following the demise of COB. Named Scarlet Runner, it featured Mick, with Tim Wellard and Thom Podgoretsky on guitars and Sandy Spencer on cello. They played songs by Sandy, Mick and Tim. Mick: 'Thom Podgoretsky, or Podo as we called him, was an interesting fella, an American, although he and I didn't get on too well and I eventually sacked him. Scarlet Runner didn't really end, it mutated through the Wheal Barrow Band to Crooks And Nannies.' Martin Val Baker put Scarlet Runner on at the St. Ives Guildhall on the 25th of May 1973, and again on the 18th of July. They also played the Medway Folk Centre in Chatham on Tuesday the 17th of December, following an impressive floor spot earlier in the year. Pete Berryman came with them and was separately billed. They drew a crowd of 70, and were paid £30, with an extra £5 for Pete. Two days later they were back in Cornwall, playing the Penwith Gallery in St Ives. Mick also made an appearance on Ralph McTell's 1974 album *Easy*, adding his powerful vocals to the title track, which was even released as a single. The track was born out of jams at Ralph's house at Putney, and also featured Steve Bonnett on mandolin and Wizz on rhythm guitar.

CHAPTER 8

CLIVE REDISCOVERS THE CORNISH BAGPIPES

– and becomes a shop steward

ON A Youth Training Scheme.

8
Clive rediscovers the Cornish bagpipes – and becomes a shop steward on a Youth Training Scheme

Grahame: 'What happened after you went down to live in Cornwall?'
Clive: 'Nothing.'

he Val Bakers had moved from The Sawmills to a mill house in the Tressider Valley near Land's End. As well as the main house, the grounds contained a caravan and a chalet, which was normally occupied by Stephen Val Baker and his American wife Gina whom he had met in Paris when he was busking there. For the summer of 1975 the chalet was due to be let out as a holiday home and Stephen and Gina were going to spend the time staying with friends in Penzance. As the Val Bakers were going to be away on a cruise of the Greek islands that summer, and knowing that Clive was looking for the opportunity to move down to Cornwall, Martin suggested he become caretaker for the summer; Clive could live in the caravan in return for looking after the house and the family's animals. Clive and Shirley gave up their flat and stayed with Shirley's mum for a while to save as much money as they could before the move. When they arrived in Cornwall, they took on evening jobs as bar staff for the holiday season at the nearby Old Success Inn in Sennen.

John Bidwell had also been in contact with the Val Bakers, to ask if he could join the cruise on their boat Sanu. He was due to finish a Lazy Farmer tour in Germany and intended to take the train down to Athens. Denys initially had his doubts, remembering John from the period he lived at the Sawmills. 'Little John, though already a brilliant musician, had not been notable either for his early rising or his fondness for hard physical work... Jess had grown a little irate to see Demelza do all the hard work while Clive and John spun away the

*Shirley and Clive in Cornwall.
Photo by Derek Brimstone,
courtesy of Shirley Palmer*

hours playing on various musical instruments.' Denys was pleased to find that John had developed a more robust attitude to life since then, going on to prove a useful crew member, and even, after a little help from Jess, able to take his turn in the galley.

Lazy Farmer had recorded an album under their own name for the Songbird label in Germany in January 1975, engineered by Conny Plank, who went on to fame as the producer of Kraftwerk. John declared that the idea behind the band was to avoid the usual clichés imposed by the instruments they used. They had a wide range of instruments to choose from; on the album Wizz played guitar and usually took lead vocal, though John and Jake also sang. John mainly played flute, but also played some guitar, whilst Jake played dulcimer on most tracks, adding hurdy-gurdy on two tracks. Sandy played banjo throughout, with Don also featuring on seven songs. After Lazy Farmer split up following the German tour, Don chose to remain there, though he was later to work with John again in several bands. Wizz: 'If Lazy Farmer could have carried on it would have been great, but the economics of it were too much. I was trying to hold it all together, driving the van and using all my connections to get gigs in Germany. The band was all down to John putting in all that hard work. He did all the arrangements. I'd been listening a lot to Steeleye Span and Martin Carthy and John was doing stuff like Cam Ye O'er Frae France and we were going in that direction. If we'd stayed together we would have a gone a lot more traddy.'

Clive did quite a few gigs in Cornwall once he was settled, Martin

Clive's Cornwall

 1 *The Sawmills*

2 Golant

3 Lostwithiel

 4 *Mylor*

5 *The Lizard*

6 Penzance

7 Newlyn

8 *Mousehole*
(Old Coastguard Hotel)

9 *St Buryan*
(Pipers folk club)

10 *Sennen Cove*

11 St Just

12 *Botallack*
(Count House
folk club)

13 *Gurnard's Head*
(Mermaid folk club)

 14 St Ives

 15 Zennor

16 Cambourne

17 Redruth

18 Rose
(New Folk Cottage club)

19 Zelah

20 Newquay

 21 *Folk Cottage*

22 Mitchell

23 Wadebridge

24 Liskeard

25 Launceston

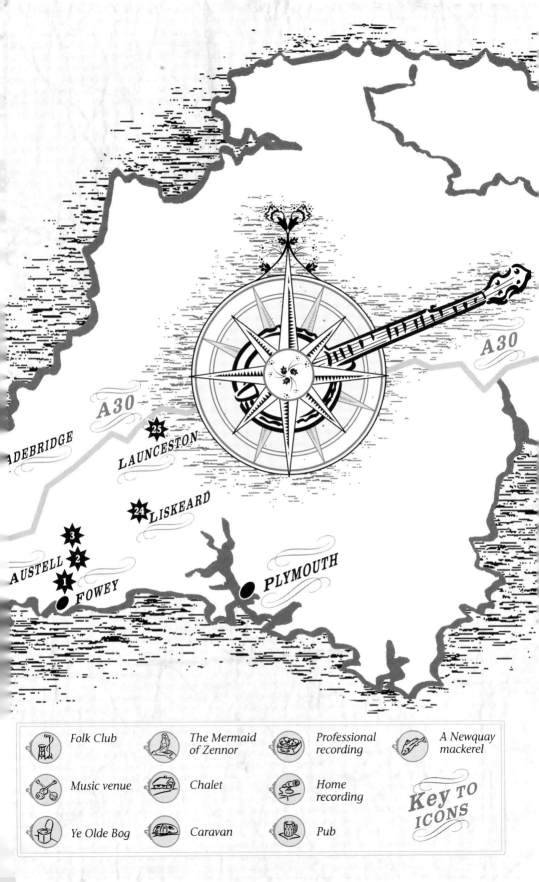

A30

A30

ADEBRIDGE

LAUNCESTON · 25

LISKEARD · 24

AUSTELL · 3 · 2 · 1

FOWEY

PLYMOUTH

Val Baker putting him on at the St. Ives Guildhall in a series of concerts that summer; on the 20th of July he was supported by Keith Hills and Denys Stevens. At the end of the month the bill featured Lazy Farmer, John James, Nigel (Mazlyn) Jones and Chrissy Quayle, all for 75p. On the 14th of August, Clive was supported by Crooks & Nannies, Roger Brooks and Bob Devereux. Crooks & Nannies were basically Tim Wellard and Sandy Spencer, though Mick Bennett and Pete Berryman were also involved. Tim: 'We were a bit stoned one night and Mick came up with the name, and we all thought it was hilarious. We never liked our first name Scarlet Runner, being named after a type of bean! That name was Ralph McTell's idea.' The other story is that Crooks & Nannies were Tim and Sandy's respective occupations at the time! Ralph's brother Bruce took some interest in managing them, though in the end not much came of it, apart from a memorable gig supporting Bert Jansch at The Marquee. They are fondly remembered as a really great band.

Mick: 'At that time I wrote what I consider to be some of my best material. In this period (roughly 1974–76) we were squatting in the Chilean Embassy in Grafton Way, Fitzrovia, but all that's another story. We kept off the dole on principle, and quite often busking in Portobello Road proved more lucrative than gigging.'

Crooks & Nannies busking in Portobello Road. Tim Wellard (guitar – partially obscured), Sandy Spencer, Mick Bennett. Courtesy Mick Bennett.

Bob Devereux was often on the same bill as Clive at this time, though initially they would perform separately. Bob would be MC, but now and then there would be jams with Sandy, Tim, Mick and others, with Bob reading his poetry over the music. By this time Bob was pursuing a living as a painter, and had a stall in the St. Ives Craft Market. Upstairs was a restaurant called The Pudding Bag with a smorgasbord night every Wednesday, for which Bob and Clive were booked to provide the entertainment between courses. They did poems and songs together and solo, and went down so well that they became as much of an attraction as the food, and continued there until 1976. Shirley: 'We lived in the caravan for the summer, and come the autumn the Val Baker family returned home from their boat trip. I've no doubt that, being generous people, they would have let us stay on in the caravan, but we got a flat in Penzance from an old mate of Clive's called Mike Carr, another musician who'd been in and out of lots of bands. We moved into the ground floor flat in Penare Road. His mother lived upstairs. A few years down the line Mike had got a nice girlfriend and decided he would like his little basement flat back, so we moved upstairs. Martin Val Baker was in the attic and we shared a kitchen and bathroom with him for a while, which was a lot of fun.' The year ended in fine style, with Martin promoting a concert at the St Ives Paris Rooms on the 29th of December featuring Crooks & Nannies, Pete Berryman, John Bidwell, Mick Bennett, Roger Brook and Bob Devereux. The next night, the same line-up, with the addition of Clive, played the Penzance Winter Gardens. Martin considers Clive's solo work around this time to be some of the best he ever did, his repertoire including songs such as his own Osiris, Alan Tunbridge's The Grapes Of Life and Tom Lehrer's My Home Town.

Clive made the newspapers twice in December 1977, firstly in the local *Sunday Independent*, under the headline Cornish Bagpipes Are Revived: 'Long before punk came to Cornwall people danced to a different tune; bagpipes. And soon the swirl o' the pipes may echo o'er the

Clive playing the small-pipes at Penare Road.
Photo by Shirley Palmer.

cliffs again if Clive Palmer has his way. Clive, of 15, Penare Road, Penzance is making the first authentic pair of Cornish bagpipes in nearly 500 years. "In medieval times, pipes were popular in every county in Britain," said Clive, who trained as an instrument maker, and shot to fame in the Sixties as a founder member of the Incredible String Band. He said, "Cornwall was especially remote in those days, and people didn't hear much music, only simple pipes and drums. So if a piper started playing at a fair or in a pub, the effect was pretty riveting. Because of this, pickpocketing was a big thing with the pipers. They used to play and keep people occupied, while little boys went through the audience's pockets." Pipes died out in Britain when more sophisticated instruments like the violin and concertina came along. Clive is using old drawings and guesswork to design the pipes, and he hopes they'll sound pretty much like the real thing. His first pair are being made as an experiment and as a favour to a friend.' The friend in question was Mervyn Davey, who played in a local band called Bucca, who sought to try and revive Cornish music.

The second reference was in the *Melody Maker* of 3/12/77 which mentioned that Clive had linked up on a permanent basis with Bob Devereux, 'the poet now settled in Cornwall who was formerly with the band Mask' and 'looks like returning to the folk scene in earnest after a long absence.' The brief article mentioned Clive's Northumbrian pipe building, and announced the duo's first gig would be at the Newlyn Art Gallery, Penzance on December the 20th.

Early in 1978 Bob and Clive went into a studio on the Lizard, and recorded the material that Martin Val Baker then issued on his own Rainyday label as a run of 100 cassettes with the title *Suns & Moons*. After years of working for other people, Martin had started his own printing business. Many years before, the Rainyday name had come to him while on holiday with his girlfriend in Wales, where it rained a great deal. The name Rainyday was used for all his businesses after that: promotions, printing, and later an art gallery.

Queen Of All The Gypsies opens the album in the duo's typical style, Clive playing banjo and singing choruses while Bob recites his lyrics over the music. The song is about ordinary people's fascination with the occult:

The foreman in the factory is into palmistry
and Doctor Rab McKenzie is for phrenology

The song also describes the despair of a 'lonely young musician,' who 'tries to find a friend,' and who finally throws himself from a cliff into the wild Atlantic. Bob says that this was a warning 'not to live by omens.' There are several instrumental solos from Clive on both banjo and Northumbrian pipes, and three of Bob's spoken word pieces. It Used To Be Different has three ageing boarding-house landladies describing how business isn't what it used to be, and comparing the efficiency of various household cleansers, while Turkey is a cautionary tale warning of the dangers of genetic modification. Clive's solo songs with banjo are all very fine, especially his gentle and moving rendition of Bob Dylan's Girl From The North Country. He plays tribute to another of his influences, Pete Seeger, with Sacco's Last Letter. This is an arrangement by Seeger of Nicola Sacco's last letter to his son; Sacco, along with Bartolemeo Vanzetti, was executed in the US in 1927, following six years of appeals, for his part in a murder in 1920. The case caused huge controversy at the time (and since). The song opens with the quietly chilling line: 'If nothing happens, they will electrocute us right after midnight.'

Of the duo tracks remaining, Changes is about a painter trying to paint the sea, while Morris Room is a delightful Edwardian period piece with a young aesthete torn between kissing his girl and spoiling the tableau they have created by sitting together, with only a ludo board between them:

In the Morris Room together, in the lamplight on the sofa,
We made such a charming picture, we should stay this way.

The title track is the album's undoubted highlight; Bob reciting over a slow and haunting air played by Clive on the Northumbrian smallpipes:

This morning when I rose, I saw the sun, shining like a great yellow moon
on a world stiff, stark beneath a winding sheet of snow.
And on the same horizon, the full moon herself, yellow, yellow as the sun.
The strangest thing I ever saw.

Most of the lyrics for this song came from *The Diary Of A Disappointed Man*, by the journalist and naturalist W.M.P. Barbellion.

In the summer Clive and Tim were invited to play a couple of spots at the Osnabrück Folk Festival in Germany, promoted by Willi Schwenken who ran the Autogram record label. Pete Berryman, also

Tim Wellard and Clive. Photo by Shirley Palmer

on the bill, was recording an album at the time for Willi's label for which Tim and Clive played on three tracks, recorded at Schwenken's house. The album was released as *Pete Berryman: And Guitar*. Clive's three tracks were Dordogne Summer, Rose Cottage and So Long Ago. Apart from Dordogne Summer, the album was entirely instrumental. Rose Cottage was inspired by a house Pete had lived in the Helligan woods, and Dordogne Summer is about an American banjo player called Jack Treese, who was a well known character on the French and German folk circuit at the time. Pete had toured France and recorded with Jack in 1977. The lyrics also mentioned Theo Busch, who was a German violinist, and Sandy Spencer. These two had been part of Noah's Roadshow, a German-based band Pete had worked with the same year which also featured Mick Bennett, who explains: 'Pete Berryman and I formed a trio with a great Dutch flautist/guitarist called Ad Van Der Horst which I called Noah Bones and the Skeletones. This was a precursor to Noah's Roadshow although Ad didn't make the transition. Noah's Roadshow was an international collective of all sorts of musicians which toured Holland, Germany and France. We went into the studio but nothing got put onto wax. We even played Shiesaway live on German TV.' The personnel was: Pete Berryman – guitar/backing vocals, Sandy Spencer – cello/vocals, Ronnie di Tomaso – guitar/vocals, Theo Busch – violin/vocals, Mick Bennett – lead vocals/percussion, Jean Claude Assellin – mandolin/guitar, Jean Yves Lacombe – double bass.

Mick and Clive. Photo by Shirley Palmer

Mick and Clive. Photo by Shirley Palmer

Back in Cornwall, Martin Val Baker put on Clive and Bob at the Parish Rooms on the 14th of September as part of the St Ives Festival; two nights later Clive was on at the Guildhall, as part of a one-off reunion of The Stockroom Five. Along with The Celebrated Ratliffe Stout Band, the SF were supporting the popular Scottish folk band The Tannahill Weavers. Joined by Chrissy Quayle on sax, they performed an energetic set including Kissing On The Sly, When The Train Comes Along, Buddy Won't You Roll Down The Line, The Other Side Of Jordan, and Hold The Woodpile Down.

Plans to give the Palmer/Devereux collaboration a wider release came to nothing. Martin: 'After we released *Suns & Moons* as a cassette, I took the tapes to Mooncrest Records in North London in September with the idea that they could release it as an LP. I met the number two man who was very enthusiastic and wanted to do a production job on it as an LP and even release Changes as a single. I returned to Cornwall in a great state of excitement and we were due to go back up to London in November but suddenly the letters stopped and it transpired that the chap had left the company and his successor was no longer interested in the project.'

Around late 1978 or early 1979 Clive took a full-time job with Fisher Controls, an electronic components firm where Shirley already worked in the office. With two full-time wages coming in, they decided to buy a house. However, the house prices in Penzance were still a bit steep, so they moved to No.8 Boswithian Road, Cambourne, paying £13,000.

On the 29th of May, Martin Val Baker promoted a gig at Penzance Arts Centre featuring Bob and Clive joined by Tim Wellard and Dick Reynolds, who played keyboards and guitar. After that gig the quartet took the name of Rhombus. Their repertoire was almost entirely made up of expanded arrangements of the material Bob and Clive had been performing as a duo, though they also did a powerful new song called Hail Now, a chant to the coming of Spring, which was never officially recorded. They also revived several COB numbers, including Wade In The Water, O Bright Eyed One and a completely new version of Soft Touches Of Love set to a new melody, with spoken interjections by Bob. On July the 12th Rhombus supported the Tannahill Weavers at the St Ives Guildhall, headlined at St Austell Arts Centre on the 20th, and completed the month by supporting Robin Williamson's new unit, The Merry Band, at the Guildhall again on the 26th. Both bands were recorded that night for broadcast by Radio Berlin, and Robin certainly enjoyed the evening, telling Ken Hunt in *Swing 51* magazine: 'Clive's new band opened for us in St Ives, which was great. It was the first time I'd heard him play for a long time. It was very, very nice to hear him again.'

*Clive at home, 1979.
Photo by Shirley Palmer*

On 8th August Rhombus played a half hour set at the Polgooth Fair, near St. Austell. On this occasion they opened with a lively Rise When The Rooster Crows in best Stockroom Five style, followed by Morris Room and a poem about summer holidays, read by Bob. Heart Of The Storm was a Tim Wellard song embellished by suitable hurricane noises from Dick's synthesiser and they ended with Changes and

Wade In The Water.

Willi Schwenken got in touch with Clive and asked if he would be interested in doing a solo album for Autogram. Clive was, but didn't want to travel to Germany to do it. Eddie and Dorothy Starkey, who ran the latest version of the Pipers club, put up the money to record ten new tracks in Cornwall to add to the four already issued on *Suns & Moons* that Clive also wanted to use.

Just Me was issued in 1979, mainly in Germany, though some copies found their way to Britain. Willi Schwenken repaid Eddie Starkey the money he had laid out for the recordings, and also gave him a pile of copies of the finished album. Clive played banjo and Northumbrian smallpipes, and was helped out on some tracks by Dick Reynolds on guitar and Niall Timmons on mandolin. Clive, Dick and Niall played several gigs around this time as Clive Palmer & Friends, including one at The Parish Rooms on the 13th of September 1980 as part of the St Ives Festival.

The sleeve of *Just Me* depicted Clive with his banjo and sporting a fine pair of flared jeans under a suit jacket and waistcoat, with a cigarette dangling from his lips in a slightly menacing manner. The photos dated from a shoot done at The Lizard in 1977 around the time *Suns & Moons* was recorded. Several shots on the same contact strip showed milk churns and  farm paraphernalia which somehow ended up on the sleeve too.

The album opens with East Virginia, an American song very much in the Man Of Constant Sorrow mould. Bamiyan is an instrumental, unusually with an overdubbed backing part, also on banjo. It was named after the place Clive had visited in 1966. The famous Buddha statues no longer exist, having been dynamited by the Taliban in March 2001, in what must be one of the most outrageous acts of historical vandalism committed in recent years. The Blackbird and Clive's excellent take on Dylan's Girl From The North Country are the same versions that had appeared on *Suns & Moons*. Cripple Creek is the well-known bluegrass standard, with guitar and mandolin, but played in a slightly more 'old-time' version. Gentle Maiden/ Gunnerton Fellcuddy are a pair of tunes from the North East of England, beautifully played on the Northumbrian smallpipes. The album side ends with State Of Arkansas, one of the 'cowboy blues' songs Clive does so well. It tells the tale of a drifter fallen on hard times who 'never knew what misery was till I hit old Arkansas.' Summer's Night dates from the period at the end of the Stockroom Five (there is a tape of an earlier version, recorded informally in 1969 in a caravan by Clive and John, which features two more verses). It is an evocation of the pleasures of sitting relaxing outside the caravan early in the morning after arriving back from a gig.

In the deepness of a summer's night
I was laughing at the stars so bright
With my hand outstretched towards the moon
In the deepness of a summer's night.

There is a Cornish proverb which states: 'In Summer, remember winter,' and one verse reflects this:

Though in winter rain gets in my shoes
And the cold wind creeps between the sheets
And the dark clouds hide me from the sun.

Ken Hunt reviewed the album enthusiastically, if a little belatedly, in *Swing 51* magazine. '[Clive's] banjo playing is as haunting as ever it was on Niggertown, and at a time when we have become accustomed to banjo virtuosi like Bela Fleck, Bill Keith or Tony Trischka who play in styles which owe much to a dozen or so influences, it is interesting to hear Clive Palmer's style which draws more on his early influences like Uncle Dave Macon and Buell Kazee than later exponents of the banjo. His reading of Earl Scrugg's Foggy Mountain Breakdown is both stirring and personal. The pace and feeling of *Just Me* is not dissimilar to that first Incredible String Band album, that is there is an accent on the string band feeling. According to the accompanying sheet Clive also builds Northumbrian small pipes, a fact I was unaware of, and I like his playing. He is no Alistair Anderson, but he is competent and the three tracks on which he plays this instrument provide tonal balance and relief. *Just Me* is strongly recommended to anyone who has ever liked Clive Palmer in the past.'

In 1980, Bert Jansch released an album called *The Ornament Tree*, which contained the song Three Dreamers, about the flat he had shared with Clive and Robin in West Nicholson Street. It was set to a tune usually associated with The Road To Dundee which Clive had often said was the song Bert always asked him to sing. The verses combine the three characters. Bert: 'With that song I mix up all three figures in the actual verses.' Obviously reminded of the song's origins, on the same album Bert also recorded his own version of The Road To Dundee, using a different tune. Three Dreamers had originally been issued on a version of Bert's 1977 album *A Rare Conundrum*, released only in Denmark. Interestingly the Danish album (*Poormouth*) also contained a song by John Bidwell, Dragonfly, which never appeared anywhere else on a Jansch album. John and Bert had become friends on the 1972 Pentangle tour. John: 'Bert and I used to spend some time together when he lived in Putney. I remember one Sunday afternoon we were having a pick, and we swapped songs – Dragonfly and Fresh As A Sweet Sunday Morning.'

Clive's Cornish bagpipes made the headlines again in the *Camborne & Redruth Packet* in early 1981. Under the telling headline: 'Londoner revives the old Cornish bagpipes,' a '*Packet* reporter' interviewed Clive in great detail about the pipes. 'Clive... admits there is not a big demand for them. Instead he gives them away free to friends and people who take the pipes seriously. It's a labour of love, he said. "It's just something that appeals to me. The cost to do them professionally would be enormous and so the selling price would be out of reach. The labour costs alone would be expensive because each set takes about four months to make." The article went on to tell of how Mervyn Davey asked Clive to make him a set of pipes based on an ancient carving on a church pew. 'With his experience of clarinet making behind him, Clive set to work. The hardest part was drilling in the hole through the long chanter – the part of the pipes that resembles the recorder. He bought some leather and stitched it together to make a bag, sealing it with a special preparation to make it airtight. For the drones, the tentacle-like parts which provide the harmony, he used a special type of cane, only found in Spain, to use as reeds. Since then he has continuously been modifying and developing the pipes. "I'm still learning," he said. "It's one of those things that never comes to an end, you go on developing it all the time. It's a matter of trial and error." To play the bagpipes well takes just as long. As well as having to play the different notes on the chanter, you have to blow into it, or in the case of the Northumbrian pipes, which Clive also plays, you use a bellow, and it is necessary to alternate the pressure of air in the bag.' Clive talked about the need for concentration while playing, and his habit of having the TV or radio on so that he has a distraction to fight against. He also revealed that Shirley could not stand the pipes and he would only play when she was out. 'Unlike the Scottish pipes, the Cornish and Northumbrian pipes are not so loud, and so Clive does not have the neighbours complaining. He plays them in public when he attends the Piper's Folk Club in Penzance, which meets on Sunday evenings in the Turks Head.'

In 1981 both Clive and Shirley were made redundant from Fisher Controls when it was taken over by GEC and Clive started thinking again about his future. Shirley (as Shirley Ward) interviewed Clive for the winter edition of *An Weryn* (The People – Cornwall's Radical Magazine, as it billed itself.) It is an interesting insight into Clive's ambitions at the time, to be an artisan instrument maker, serving local musicians. Shirley remarked that he was known as a 'confirmed group escapologist,' to which Clive replied that in every case it was just to move on to something else and that it was purely coincidental that things had started to happen for the ISB and Famous Jug Band after he had left. He mentioned his travelling: 'I liked Scotland when I was there, in my early twenties. I could do there the things I liked doing at the time. But Cornwall I loved for the peace and quiet and lifestyle. I only left in 1972 because of COB, and came back as soon as I could after giving up full time professional music. I had no desire to do it anymore. That stage of my life was over by 1974. For the last five years in Cornwall I've been playing music on a small scale, supporting local groups and events which I like because there is no pressure on me, no financial complications, no contracts or commitments. I can just go along and play when I feel like it, and not have to play when I'm supposed to. On a practical level I've done seasonal and odd jobs to keep going, and for the past two years have worked in an electronics factory, at shop floor level, but have just been made redundant.' Clive claimed not be overly bothered by his redundancy, pointing out that he had spent his whole life just managing and seeing what will turn up. 'At least you can be poor in a nice place.'

Clive also thought Cornwall provided a good atmosphere for artisans and craftsmen, and that he would like to go in that direction, possibly producing musical instruments using local materials, preferably to be used by local musicians. He looked forward to Cornwall having more autonomy, and greatly approved of the preservation and revival of local culture. 'If people can be made aware of their identity and culture then the acceptance and servility which now exist should eventually disappear. There is a lot going on in Cornwall right now, and the revival has thrown up some good musicians and songwriters. Gwenogan and Bucca are playing Cornish music, and are working hard to collect and preserve Cornish songs and tunes. The interest they have received from many quarters proves that there is potential in the musical traditions of Cornwall, if nothing else. It would be nice to think that one day every village and town in Cornwall would once again have its own piper and indigenous musicians. That would certainly secure my future and make for a very happy existence, making things I want to make in the place that I want to be.'

Shirley quickly got another job with another multi-national, but Clive was unemployed for quite a while. He saw a notice in the Jobcentre looking for someone with expertise in woodwork and it turned out that it was with the Youth Training Scheme, the manager of which was a man who had worked at Fisher Controls. Clive got the job. 'I had a friend who was an old Cornish woodworker, who thought I shouldn't be doing the job as I wasn't a proper tradesman, but he eventually showed me all I needed to know.' Shirley: 'They opened up a new department in Camborne and Clive got a job as a woodwork teacher to all these kids. He was very good at that, he took in old guitars and these kids were suddenly brilliant at woodwork. I was working for a trade union at that time and he became shop steward. He went to the barricades for some of those kids! He was very well known at County Hall, it was "Oh My God! Him again! He's famous isn't he?" What as, a bolshie agitator? "No, wasn't he a famous musician? Didn't you know?" Well actually I did, I'm married to him...'

Clive said at the time: 'The group I run is called the Special Assessment Group, boys and girls, though mainly boys, from 15–18. I take people who have got problems, mentally retarded people, people with social problems or who have been in trouble with the police and I have to turn them into employable people. I work on The Cornwall County Council Youth Training Scheme. I like it. But I have lots of interests besides music. I repair antique watches, I do painting, I make instruments, a bit of engineering, wood turning. I have made instruments for other people, and I suppose I could do with the extra money, but I have a decent full time job, and I can choose what I want to do.'

In May 1983 Shirley, who at the time was Secretary for the West Cornwall District Office of the GMB Union, stood in the local elections to be Labour councillor for

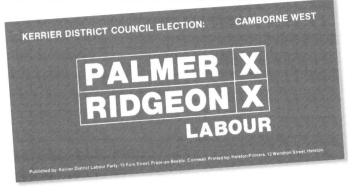

Shirley's campaign leaflet. Courtesy Shirley Palmer

Cambourne West. Her main concerns were local housing and employment and she also proposed that the district should become a Nuclear-Free Zone.

Clive was of course always very supportive of her political ambitions. Shirley: 'He wouldn't have been able to walk round the streets doing door-to door canvassing because of his leg, and he probably wouldn't have been very good at arguing with people, he doesn't suffer fools gladly! But he was always good at driving people to the polling station and things like that.' Clive's father Bill was a true blue Conservative, and Shirley recalls they used to put up pictures of Arthur Scargill to tease him when he came to visit them!

In 1987 Clive formed The Charlie Cool Quartet, featuring himself on clarinet and vocals, Tim Wellard on guitar, John Bickersteth on piano and accordion and Paddy MacDonagh on double bass. Tim had met John when he was working with a cabaret mime artist 'providing sound effects' and Paddy was a well-established local jazz player. They played a pleasant mixture of jazz standards and Jewish Klezmer music, very much in the style of a European Cafe band. The quartet recorded a cassette of their music, which featured standards such as Autumn Leaves, Summertime and Petite Fleur, though the best track was probably Clive's vocal rendition of Pennies From Heaven. Erev Shel Shasha Nim was the tune COB had played as an encore at the Chatham gig fifteen years previously. Another interesting track was Jacques Brel's Ne Me Quitte Pas, which listeners could compare with Clive's A Leaf Must Fall. Two guest vocalists also appeared on the album: Venny Ravenhill, who was Tim's partner at the time, and Gina Val Baker. The band played a few informal gigs at parties as well as several small theatre/Arts-Centre type events.

In a contemporary interview, Clive said: 'I can indulge myself with Charlie Cool and play what I want to play, and it doesn't matter, because we don't have to be commercial. We're not bothered whether anyone books us or not, though it's nice if they do. Tim's doing a little agency thing, he'll ring up and say, "I've been offered a gig, do you fancy doing it?" We don't have to worry about the money. We do it for fun. We do it for the music. I don't think there is a market out there for musicians like us that would sustain us and give us enough to live on. We enjoy our music and do what we like. The people who like it come and see us.'

Shirley and Clive spilt up around this time, as he had begun an affair with Gina Val Baker. After the dust had settled Shirley accepted the situation and admitted that by that stage of their marriage they 'were more like brother and sister than husband and wife.' Shirley was also genuinely fond of Gina and remained so, later saying: 'I didn't as much lose a husband as gain a sister.' Shirley moved out of Cross Street and Gina moved in. However, Gina's husband Stephen, along with his sisters, was much less forgiving, and there was considerable bad feeling directed towards Clive and Gina. Not wishing to offend his brother, Martin Val Baker felt unable to book Clive at any of the gigs he promoted for quite a while. In February 1988, readers of *Folk Roots* were reminded of Clive's existence through an article I wrote on his career to date. Though in retrospect there were a few errors, it did the trick, even to the extent of my receiving a letter from a Russian folk band in Devon, asking if I thought Clive might like to join them. He didn't. The article was illustrated with a current photo of Clive playing his recently-completed lute. The same month, *Record Collector* magazine listed their Top 100 Rare UK LPs, with *Moyshe McStiff* at number 65, valued at £60 in mint condition.

Martin Val Baker took advantage of Clive's temporary rise in profile by releasing a cassette of Clive and Bob Devereux's material, called *The Archive Tapes*. The cover art used photos from the *Just Me* period, with Bob sporting spectacularly flared white trousers and playing a pair of Moroccan clay drums.

Four of the tracks had already been issued on *Suns & Moons*: the title track, Changes, Queen Of All The Gypsies and Morris Room. Bear's Paw was the most intriguing new track, the lyrics being based on a genuine item in the *Larousse Gastronomique*. With Bob adopting a very non-PC mock-Chinese accent and Clive providing suitable banjo accompaniment, we are told how to prepare the great delicacy:

To cook a bear's paw, wrap it in mud. Clean mud. Clean mud.
It must be clean. None of your dirty dirt!

One Cornish critic took great offence at Bear's Paw when he was

THE ARCHIVE TAPES Bob Devereux / Clive Palmer

reviewing the album, going out of his way to condemn it as racist. The anonymous writer in *Folk Roots* who reviewed it at the same time admitted that it wasn't really his scene: 'The Devereux/ Palmer item is a limited edition. I'm not sure if this refers to the number produced or its appeal, because it's certainly an oddity. This is a collection of demos from 77/78, showing that the Sex Pistols' influence was little felt in Cornwall. The formula consists of Devereux declaiming his poems in a strange, nasal tone while Palmer plucks at his banjo in a (usually) ramshackle manner while parroting occasional snatches of the words as if his mind was on something else. On occasion the banjo accelerates or Northumbrian pipes come in but it's hard to see who would get excited about the tape – no doubt someone will.'

In April 1988 Clive was interviewed at length by Martin Gillham for an article entitled Just Who Is Clive Palmer? in *Event South West* magazine. Clive talked frankly about his attitude to fame and the music business: 'The big deal scene has never attracted me at all. Basically I don't compromise, I play music and people can take it or leave it. My problem would always have been that I would have to have changed what I was doing to make it more commercial, and I'm not willing to do that. I think its better. And the funny thing is that I expect in a hundred years' time, if anyone still remembers what happened in the Sixties, I'll probably be remembered more, even though I'm not famous at all. I've never been successful at all, not commercially. I've always thought that you should make an audience work; if they want to work and join in and understand what you are trying to do, then that's great. I want to do something with music. The idea of just doing what the audience wants, to me, seems pointless.'

One surprise in 1989 for Clive watchers was the appearance of a track from *Banjoland* on a double sampler album *Woronzoid*, featuring tracks from the bands on Nick Saloman's Woronzow label. Before he became better known as a label owner and as his alter ego The Bevis Frond, Nick dealt in rare records. He had met Peter Eden as a trader at several record fairs without making the connection with his previous career as a producer. During one of their conversations the name of Clive Palmer and the *Banjoland* tapes came up; knowing of Clive's work from the ISB onwards, Nick expressed an interest in releasing the album on Woronzow. Nick: 'We did a simple deal for me to lease the tapes for a couple of years. I went down to Southend to meet him. He was a Jehovah's Witness and I'd only just got there and sat down when he said he had to go out and knock on people's doors for a while. So I stayed there chatting to his wife for a couple of hours until he came back. He was a nice guy, and I got on well with him.' Nick had not actually heard the tapes at this point, and had been expecting something between the style of the first ISB album and COB. What he got of course, was something entirely different. He liked what he heard, though he did think it was a bit odd and might be a problem to market. The deal was for the tape only, there was no finished artwork, and the tape itself was only just over 30 minutes in length. Nick put the track Coventry Carol on his sampler album, describing it as a 'medieval banjo workout.' In the end he had other albums to work on and the project ended up being left on the back burner for so long that the licensing deal expired. He returned the tapes to Peter Eden.

In 1989, Clive was offered, and accepted, early retirement from his YTS job, as he had been having a lot of back trouble. Gina and he decided to re-locate to France, initially moving to Fontenay in the Deux-Sèvres department, and later to Lorigné, also in Deux-Sèvres.

Around this time, Clive was approached by Archie Fisher about reforming the original line up of the ISB for the Edinburgh Folk Festival. As there was very little money involved and he was just about to move to France, he declined. He believes that Robin made so many conditions that it was obvious he did not really want to do it either.

Clive and Gina returned to Cornwall for a while in the summer of 1992, staying in Newlyn, just round the bay from Penzance. Martin Val Baker booked him as support to the legendary American singer Ramblin' Jack Elliott for two gigs at the Acorn, Penzance, on the 24th and 25th of July. Clive had never met him before, though Jack had lived and played in both London and Paris in the late Fifties. Jack had run across Wizz Jones, who was given some good advice for when he was busking – always keep your money in your boots, that's the last place a mugger will look!

The autumn of 1992 saw the first issue of a new Incredible String Band fanzine, *beGLAD*. The editor was long-time String Band fan Andy Roberts; I contributed a piece about Clive's period with COB and two short reviews of *Suns & Moons* and *The Archive Tapes*. After their first album the ISB had become one of Britain's best-loved bands, initially as a duo, then adding Robin's girlfriend Licorice and afterwards, to restore the balance, Mike's girlfriend Rose Simpson. They got involved in Scientology and played the Woodstock Festival in 1969. Having tried communal living, and found it wanting, they found the ideal solution in renting a whole row of workmen's cottages at The Glen, in the Scottish Borders near Innerleithen, and having one each. Rose left and was replaced by Malcolm Le Maistre, who, though more of a dancer and actor than a musician, added a great deal to the band visually. Licorice left so quietly most people did not even notice, and they added multi-instrumentalist Gerard Dott. Losing Gerard after a short period, the ISB gradually evolved into a fully fledged rock band with acoustic touches. This was exactly what Mike wanted, but Robin became unhappy, leaving the band in 1974 on the eve of their joining a new record company and undertaking a long period of touring which would have taken them to Australia, Europe and the USA. Mike knew how Robin felt but had hoped he would stay long enough to finish the tour dates and perhaps record one last album. 'We knew he had to leave, and it was looking that way, that he would, it was just the way it happened. It put us so much in it, we didn't speak for...' Robin moved to Los Angeles shortly afterwards. Mike remained in Glen Row where he still lives today.

Clive recorded another cassette album at Tim's home studio in St Just around this time, calling it *House Of Images*. It is very much in the same mould as *Just Me*, featuring Clive on vocals, banjo, smallpipes and even keyboards. Tim plays guitar and percussion and Gina plays piano and keyboards. The album opens with Woody Guthrie's Pretty Boy Floyd, going into a slow traditional Scottish song, partly sung in

Gaelic, Fear A Bhata (The Boatman). Soft Dark Eyes is one of Clive's songs, for which Pete Berryman was brought in to add his distinctive acoustic lead guitar. Absent Friends is a smallpipes solo dedicated to Clive's father, who had recently died. Probably the best song on the album is Ewan MacColl's Moving On Song (Go, Move Shift), which is just Clive on banjo with Tim hitting a cymbal on the beat. You hardly notice the percussion at first, but it makes the song. Clive had often talked of how much he admired MacColl's songwriting (his opinion of the man himself was a different matter) and Moving On Song is from one of MacColl's *Radio Ballads*, a series of eight hour-long radio programmes which were broadcast between 1958 and 1964. The programmes mixed recordings of traditional singers, people involved with the subject of the particular ballad, and songs written by Ewan MacColl and Peggy Seeger themselves. The eight programmes covered such subjects as the work of railwaymen, road builders, miners and fishermen, as well as other programmes on the lives of boxers and those affected by polio, and the problems faced by young people. Many of the songs from the *Radio Ballads* went on to become folk-club standards. Moving On Song comes from the last programme, on the Travelling People. The second side of the cassette opens with Swanee Echoes, a charming Edwardian banjo solo composed by Alfred Kirby, played straight from the sheet music accompanied by Gina on piano. Buffalo Skinner's Blues is a traditional American ballad recalling songs such as State Of Arkansas – very personal stories of the less romantic side of life in the American West. Country Lanes is another gentle, rustic-sounding Clive composition, and the album ends with a blues song credited to the American guitarist Leo Kottke, Cold In China.

In the summer of 1993, Clive and Gina revived the Charlie Cool name, applied this time to a new quartet playing bluegrass music. Clive had acquired a new banjo, a Gibson Mastertone, reckoned by many musicians to be *the* model of banjo for playing bluegrass (just as a bluegrass guitarist has to have a Martin D18 and the mandolinist has to have a Gibson F5). Clive dusted off his Earl Scruggs licks, and with Gina on fiddle, Tim Wellard on guitar and Mathew Pullum on bass, Charlie Cool began a residency every Friday night at The Old Coastguard Hotel, Mousehole. They recorded a cassette to sell at the gig, once again at Tim's studio in St Just.

Charlie Cool Goes West is a pleasant set of bluegrass standards, both songs and instrumentals. The most memorable track is Tim's version of Bob Dylan's long narrative song Lily, Rosemary and the Jack Of Hearts, with Salty Dog and Roll On Buddy harking back to the

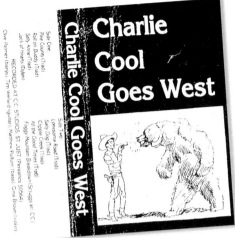

Stockroom Five days in feel. Gina more than holds her own on fiddle too. To be frank, there are probably dozens of British bluegrass bands who could have made an album as good as this, but the music comes across as honest and the musicians all sound as if they are having a lot of fun playing it. It would have been perfect music for a summer's evening in a Cornish pub.

Clive and Gina returned to France again, this time to Brittany, initially living in St-Herbot ('He's the patron saint of cows, you know') then moving just a few kilometres east to Huelgoat. Later still they moved again, to Plourac'h, near Callac, all three addresses being in the Finistère (literally 'The End Of The Earth') department.

Towards the end of 1994, the BBC showed Billy Connolly's World Tour Of Scotland, which featured Billy's rendition of Banjoland as its opening theme. Billy: 'I got it from the COB album. The second I heard it I loved it. Someone sent me the music, but I don't read music, so I got my friend in Scotland, Rob Mears, who's a great banjo player, to put it in tablature for me. I learned it, but I'd nowhere to play it, as I wasn't in a band anymore. I'd play it occasionally, and when I did the World Tour Of Scotland I played it, and the producer loved it and made it the theme. I got lots of write-ups in obscure banjo magazines, the guys who play classical style saying, "Would you believe it! Billy Connolly playing that stuff! Who would have thought?" It was Clive's influence that made me wander in that direction. They're difficult to play, these pieces, and the guys are bit like fly-fishers used to be: "I fish fly, I don't mix with those people who use worms and bits of metal..." Those classical players tended to keep to themselves and wouldn't be found dead in a folk club, or anywhere like it. So it was quite difficult to hear people play like that.'

On the 12th of November 1995, *beGLAD* editor Adrian Whittaker invited Clive to play at The Camden Irish Centre in London. He was supported by co-editor Raymond Greenoaken's band The Half-Remarkable Questionnaires (who covered a selection of Incredible String Band classics) and Malcolm Le Maistre from the ISB itself, performing with his accompanist Pete Baynes. Clive, playing banjo throughout, performed with Gina on fiddle and Tim Wellard on autoharp and guitar. The 90- minute set ranged through Uncle Dave Macon songs from the old Stockroom Five repertoire, and banjo solos like Reverie In F, 'one I learned when I was doing my lessons.' Clive played Elizabeth Cotton's Babe It Ain't No Lie which 'I used to liven up the cinema queues in Paris with.' Wae's Me For Prince Charlie was a Scottish song about the wanderings of Bonny Prince Charlie in the months after the failure of the 1745 Jacobite rebellion, followed by a well-received Niggertown, itself followed by an untitled tune with a distinct Middle Eastern feel, 'memories of music I picked up on my travels all put together.' Dirty Old Town was presented as a tribute to Ewan MacColl who Clive said had been a huge influence on him. 'Mind you, he was a miserable bugger. A great musician, but you couldn't talk to him. Dour...' A Leaf Must Fall was followed by Woody Guthrie's Pretty Boy Floyd, then a song Clive dedicated to 'my long-dead relatives, and if I had it on a desert island it would remind me of all those lovely Christmases just after the war.' He then played Flannagan and Allen's classic Side By Side, followed by a classic of his own, Empty Pocket Blues. Chrissy Quayle joined in on flute and vocals for the final song Wade In The Water, with Uncle Dave Macon's Rise When The Rooster Crows providing the encore. Though the event was poorly attended, the fifty or so who did turn up agreed that the evening was a huge success from a musical point of view, and greatly enhanced Clive's reputation. The night before Clive had shared a gig with Wizz Jones at the 12-Bar Club, in Denmark Street, London.

In 1997, the unthinkable happened. Robin Williamson and Mike Heron played two gigs together. Interviewed in 1996, Mike had hinted things were a little better between them. 'He [Robin] is unbending a bit, there was a project that we were going to do, but it fell through, and he kind of accepted it before I did. So, you never know, the barriers are falling slightly. Perhaps.' The project in question was a request from Donovan to contribute to his Sutras album. Robin and Mike had also been approached by a promoter in Glasgow who wanted them to be part of a proposed African-Scottish cultural festival to be launched by Nelson Mandela. They thought that might be a bit too big for them but expressed interest in playing a smaller event. Eventually they were booked by Roy Harper's manager to appear in the 500-seater Henry Wood Hall in Glasgow on the 27th of September, followed by The Bloomsbury Theatre in London exactly a week later.

The events were most definitely not an ISB reunion. Robin and Mike alternated songs, backed by the guitarist and percussionist from Mike's Incredible Acoustic Band, John Rutherford and Dave Haswell. Sylvie Simmons reviewed the London gig in *Mojo*, humorously saying Mike 'still looks like a small, sad pixie... So, not so much a String Band reunion, then, as a Robin Williamson/Mike Heron one, each essentially performing solo(ish) – in Heron's case solo-plus-band; in Williamson's vocals plus harp/recorder/mandolin/guitar/band – while the other looked tenderly (Heron), or somewhat sternly (Williamson) on. In some ways this was a reunion that showed more why they parted than why they got back together. But, having said that, when they did come together – most notably on Incredibles' songs Everything's Fine and Log Cabin – the cockles of many a hippy's heart were well warmed.'

CHAPTER 9

RENAISSANCE MAN

9
Renaissance Man

'It was great to work with Robin again – we had some good times together...'

ate in 1998, Robin Williamson's then manager Mark Anstey announced in an interview with Simon Jones in *Traditional Music Maker* that Robin was itching to get to work on an album with his old mate Clive Palmer. Simon explained: 'He was the bod who left the ISB after their first album and rather than become famous and sell loads of albums, preferred the life of a strolling beatnik. Well now some thirty-three years on the two have a mind to record again.' Mark added: 'It'll be fun to see what they come up with. Back in the Sixties the music Clive and Robin made was a real mish-mash of music hall, blues, country, jug band and folk. There's one track on an old folk sampler and that's the sole evidence of their early career together. Robin calls what they created "gypsy bluegrass". Clive has re-emerged after a long time away in Brittany. I think the pair of them are keen to get together.'

Robin was even more enthusiastic about the reunion, telling interviewer David Kidman: 'I thought it would be good to see what we could do together again, and I got in touch. He was really keen, too. I always liked the notion of completing circles. Clive's got a wonderful ability to make the most amazing music from very simple elements. He can make a simple chord on the guitar or banjo seem magnificent, and of course he's very good on the Northumbrian pipes too. He used to do such a diversity of things, with the banjo tunes, the rockier things like COB, the Temple Creatures, then the spoken word projects with Bob Devereux, so there's a lot of potential material we could look at... so much scope, and the poetry too.'

Clive and Gina went to Cardiff to stay with Robin in January 1999. He booked them into Lawson Dando's Albany Studios for a week. Former musician and civil servant Lawson had started a small recording studio in Cardiff, initially working part-time until he had had enough work to be able to go fully professional. He had first met Robin about four years earlier when his wife Bina had rung to enquire about using his studio; at this point Robin had completed moving back from Los Angeles to Cardiff. It wasn't until Robin came to have a look at the studio and was sitting there in front of him that Lawson slowly began to realise who he was. It was the start of a rewarding relationship, during which Lawson gained a great deal of valuable experience in recording acoustic instruments. When the sessions were completed, on their way home Clive and Gina dropped in on Henry Bartlett, who was then living in a tiny village called Ibberton, in Dorset, having moved down from London to run an antiques business in Poole. It was the first time they had met since the mid-Seventies.

Rumours of the emergence of *Banjoland* were heard again. It was due to be issued on Rollercoaster Records, who had just put out an acclaimed CD of Davy Graham recorded 'after-hours' at Hull University. Once again, nothing came of the proposal. One re-issue that did make it into the shops, though, was The Famous Jug Band's *Sunshine Possibilities*, which came out on Wooded Hill. Though there were rumours of unissued recordings from the sessions, the only bonus tracks included were God Knows and Rabbit Heels/Chameleon (the song's actual title is Rabbit Hills – by Michael Chapman. It was wrongly labelled on the original *Chameleon* sleeve) from the band's second album. Market Square records had been considering re-issuing the *Chameleon* album itself but decided against it at that point.

Retying the Knot, a half-hour documentary about the Incredible String Band, was shown late on BBC2 in May, having already been broadcast in Scotland. It was reasonably well put together, and featured new interviews with Mike, Robin, Rose Simpson, Malcolm Le Maistre and Joe Boyd. Clive was mentioned of course, and Empty Pocket Blues was played over a picture of him playing guitar while Robin played whistle. The narrator, John Walters, told us that Robin and Clive first got together in 1965, but there were interesting memories of The Incredible Folk Club from Robin and Billy Connolly. We were told: 'Robin returned from Morocco to pick up with the ISB. Clive didn't, preferring more traditional folk to the new psychedelic folk rock Mike and Robin were starting to create.'

The result of the Cardiff sessions was *At The Pure Fountain*, credited to Robin Williamson & Clive Palmer and released on the 21st of June on Robin's Pig's Whisker label. The cover photo cried out for interpretation: the centre point was a print of Bonny Prince Charlie leaving Scotland to go into exile. Arranged around this was a collection of small objects: a medal, a silver chain, charms from a bracelet, a harp brooch, two starfish, three fish (two metal, one bone), a pink plastic pig (which would have made any ISB fan think of their song Big Ted), ten

At The Pure Fountain

cowrie shells, an obsidian knife and a miniature trowel. The same picture, minus the print and some of the objects, appeared on the inside tray. What did it all mean? The rear picture showed Robin and Clive (looking particularly mischievous) seated at a table drinking some transparent spirit, Clive having thrown three dice. Reviewing the album in *beGLAD*, Raymond Greenoaken noticed that the visible dots on the dice added up to 33 – the number of years since the men had last played together. 'Whether or not the objects themselves have specific meanings, they provide an exact metaphor for the contents of the album. The songs and tunes collected here have the feel of objects Robin and Clive have just happened upon and taken a shine to. They're not presented to us as Art; no effort has been made to buff them up. They've just been allowed to glow with their own inner radiance.' The album mainly contained a mixture of the kind of material Robin and Clive used to play: traditional Scottish songs, Clive's banjo solos, music hall and blues, and numbers they simply just liked such as Hank Williams' (I Can't Help It If I'm) Still In Love With You and the Ink Spots' Bless You For Being An Angel, a favourite song of Robin's mother.

The traditional Come A' Ye Tramps And Hawkers opened the album with Robin's rich vocal and tin whistle interludes backed by a banjo part that could hardly have been simpler. Paris was inspired by Clive hearing Gina playing a piano piece one day by the jazz musician Errol Garner called When Paris Cries. Though he had never consciously heard it before, it really evoked memories of the Parisian jazz cellars of the early Sixties. The lyrics were written very quickly based on his memories of that time. He describes walking back to his hotel in the early morning rain and throwing some money to a clochard – one of the die-hard Parisian tramps who would sleep on the grilles in the pavement above Metro stations where warm air was pumped out of the tunnels below. Accordion and sax add to the atmosphere. Robin took For Far Soldier solo, accompanying himself by playing fiddle pizzicato style as if it were a mandolin, and Cam Ye O'er Frae France was done as a throwaway instrumental with fiddle, Clive on mandolin for the first time on record and Gina providing the handclaps.

Clive said at the time that, along with the first ISB album, it was the record he was most proud of. Nick Beale, however, gave the album a lukewarm review in *fRoots* (previously *Folk Roots*). 'There's obviously a fair bit of affectionate nostalgia pervading the exercise. The set has a certain rudimentary quality, including what may well be among the most stilted banjo accompaniments known to science on Tramps And Hawkers and Paris (a city livelier in my experience than this song would suggest). Elsewhere – try For Far Soldier – this avoidance of polish can be a great virtue, letting the voices tell a story with minimal distraction. Williamson's harp and fiddle instrumental of (I Can't Help It If I'm) Still In Love With You, a point or two higher up the sophistication scale, works very well. Bina Williamson's occasional backing vocals have that pitch-independent quality that will only enhance this record's no doubt considerable appeal to the Loyal & Ancient Order of ISB Venerators.'

In *Living Tradition* magazine Hector Christie called it: '... a very strange album, infuriating in bits, and arresting in others with one track so beautiful it would be a sin not to sit down and listen attentively each time it plays.' The track he was referring to was (I Can't Help It If I'm) Still In Love With You, 'rendered in a stunningly heart-stopping way.' Hector rather ashamedly admitted to a snigger at Robin's spoken part on Wae's Me For Prince Charlie, and thought Robin overdid the Scottishness of his vocal on Tramps And Hawkers, 'sounding like someone from the Pasadena amateur dramatic society's version of *Brigadoon*.' He ended by saying the album was 'courageous and fun.'

In August, Clive was interviewed for *Mojo* magazine's Phone Home feature, in which musicians who had not been heard of for a while were invited to let the public know what they have been up to lately. '*Fountain* is the first album I've made that I'm completely happy with. I'm into vignettes now – my concept is to paint a picture with each song. I think Paris is the best song I've ever written – it sums up everything I wanted to say about Paris. It was great to work with Robin again – we had some good times together and he's very mellow these days. I first went on stage at eight. Now I'm 56 and the money I've made out of music is pathetic. I should have been a solicitor. Six years ago I moved to France, mainly for economic reasons. It's very relaxed. I do gigs in a local pub and my partner Gina plays piano. People call me an eccentric and I suppose I am. If the album sells it might pay for a new veranda.'

It was announced that Robin and Clive would undertake a tour together in October. Lawson was delighted to be asked along: 'I was actually mixing another project when Robin was sitting in the control room writing sleeve notes. He mentioned that due to unforeseen problems with the brass album he was no longer interested in touring with the brass five- piece, as was the original plan.' (Robin had recorded a concert with a small brass band at a one-off concert in Halifax in the previous November, issued on Pig's Whisker as *The Old Fangled Tone*.) 'He casually commented, why not get Clive over for a small tour and would I like to join them on keyboards, it would get me out of the studio for a change? I said yes, no problem, not actually thinking it would happen. A week or so later I had a fax from Mark Anstey with all the tour dates. I could only panic as I had not played outside of a studio for about ten years and didn't even have the equipment!' There were nine dates at the end of October, covering the country from Glasgow to Brighton. It was also announced that a mini-CD of tracks that didn't make the album would be on sale at the gigs. Clive recalled they recorded enough material for one and a half albums. The mini-CD never appeared, and Lawson admits to having forgotten about it, though the extra tracks are possibly still hidden away on backup CDs in his studio. The Robin and Clive tour opened at The Old Fruit Market in Glasgow on October the 22nd, attracting a surprisingly small crowd: 200 at most, though some had come from as far away as Germany. Robin and Clive were joined by Robin's wife Bina on vocals and Lawson on keyboards.

At the gig, Clive was amazed to be presented with a banjo. Billy Connolly: 'My daughter Cara rang me, she was in my house in Scotland and said she was going to see Robin and Clive play in Glasgow. I said, "You lucky bugger, I wish I could go," and it came to me about all those rotten banjos that he played. I've got a collection of banjos, maybe about twenty, and I said, "There's a banjo under the billiard table in its case, you'll know it, pull it out. It's got brown velvet lining and it smells like a bible!" This case, I used to close it quickly in case the smell went away! It smelled like a bible in an old bookshop. I said "It's a Vega, and it's got nylon strings, you'll recognise it. Take it with you and give it to Clive. Tell him it's from me as a wee present." So she went, and when she walked in with the banjo Clive thought she was coming to be a performer on the concert. He went up and she introduced herself, "I'm Billy Connolly's daughter, this is for you, from my Dad." And he had a look at it, and she thought it was wonderful, he just fell backwards against the wall, in a relaxed fainty posture. He said "Why?" and, I'll love her forever for this, she said, "Because he loves you!" '

The following night was at Congleton, again attracting an audience of about 150. The set list was still was still in a state of flux, featuring only a few songs from *Pure Fountain*. Clive stopped halfway through Rise When The Rooster Crows, complaining the key was too high for him, and Miss McLeod's Reel was never heard again on the tour either. On the following night at Cecil Sharp House in London, Billy Connolly himself turned up, as did Bert Jansch and Wizz Jones. Billy's banjo was used in the second half of the show, and after a change of strings from nylon to steel, every night for the rest of the tour. Clive has used it live ever since. Billy was heard to tell the person sitting next to him: 'He's never had a decent banjo all the years I've known him!' The tour ended in Brighton on the 31st.

Pig's Whisker's decision to re-issue Clive and Bob Devereux's *Suns & Moons* album on CD was a pleasant surprise. The original track order was changed, to open with Girl From The North Country and end with Sacco's Last Letter which book-ended the album perfectly as they were both played in the same picking style.

Reviewing the re-release for *Rock'n'Reel* magazine, David Kidman was highly impressed. 'Unusual but delightful mixture of songs, tunes and poetry... Sheer magic is the title track, where Bob intones his uncommonly fine poetry over Clive's Northumbrian pipe air, but equally mesmerising are the strange Edwardian-flavoured period piece The Morris Room which rises above superficial recreated nostalgia, and the "mirrored pair" of Changes and Queen Of All The Gypsies, where Clive and Bob take turns in providing sung and spoken sections. The album may be an acquired taste, but ultimately it transcends mere curiosity value.

173

There's a really unique atmosphere about the album, and not just one of amiable eccentricity.'

On the penultimate day of the 20th century Robin and Clive were booked to play in St Mary's Cathedral in Edinburgh. The gig was arranged by Pete Irvine, the man in charge of organising the Edinburgh Hogmanay celebrations, and an ISB fan of old. Mike Heron was asked too and readily agreed. The original plan was for the event to be billed as an evening with Robin, Clive, Mike and friends – intended to evoke the spirit of the sessions at the Crown Bar and the Incredible Folk Club. As on the Robin and Clive tour, they were augmented by Bina and Lawson.

Mike explained the concept of the evening in an interview at the time: 'We did the material that Robin and Clive were playing when I joined way back. It was great for me, a kind of personal nostalgia. It was like when I used to go and see them, skiffle and blues and old English stuff. It was like Clive and Robin at the Crown Bar and me joining in. So we did that. The fans came and it was a disappointment to them because they wanted String Band music, but what they got was the music that influenced us to get going.'

Despite the musicians' wishes, the Incredible String Band name was inevitably used in the publicity, and a great many tickets were sold on the expectation of a full scale reunion. In retrospect it was perhaps naive of the participants to see that this was not going to be the case. There were some very disappointed fans. Jim C. Wilson was one. He wrote an open letter to Robin Williamson (who he seemed to think had masterminded the whole thing) which was published as a review in *The Living Tradition* magazine. 'I am not exaggerating when I say that the music you produced with Mike Heron in the 1960s changed my life. I knew and know every note and nuance of your second album. I could not, therefore, resist going to the Incredible String Band's reunion gig. Something though, went very sadly wrong. I was a fan, no, I was a disciple. How, therefore, did I find myself agreeing with the woman sitting behind me, who said, as the concert ended, "That was shite."?'

Arguably, the concert was not a reunion and never intended to be, though the tickets stated confusingly: 'Robin Williamson, Clive Palmer, Mike Heron and friends.' Below, in larger type, 'The Incredible String Band.' For those who had an idea of what to expect, the event was rather more enjoyable, though the venue had poor acoustics and was very cold. The friends provided added value though: Archie Fisher, Bert Jansch, ('My paper round used to be around that church!') and Billy Connolly, who told the audience:

'These are my heroes, I even got my ears pierced to be like them!'

Billy: 'I think they mentioned it to me at the Cecil Sharp House gig, and I thought it was a lovely idea, and then they asked me if I'd like to come on and do an appearance, and I said, "By Jesus! I would love to!" Really I just wanted to be a part of what they stand for. It was a strange one, but it was very good, they don't ask me to play in churches too often! Robin gave me a lovely introduction, it was nice, and I played a wee bit with Clive backstage and we were talking about Uncle Dave Macon and he was showing me little bits and pieces and tricks. Mike Heron was kind of sad. He sounded great on stage, but backstage he seemed a bit fed up. When I used to know him he was always like a sunflower, exploding with light and hope.'

After the gig, one thing was obvious: there was still a demand for the Incredible String Band.

In June 2000, Channel Four showed Matthew Quinn's documentary on Bert Jansch, *Dreamweaver*, timed to coincide with the release of Colin Harper's biography of Bert and the release of his new album *Crimson Moon*. Many of Bert's friends and colleagues from the early days in Edinburgh and London were interviewed, including Owen Hand, Len Partridge, Dolina McLennan, Roy Harper and Donovan. Matthew also interviewed Robin and Clive and filmed them backstage at one point during their October tour. They appeared in six short scenes, in total sixty seconds at most, talking about Bert's guitar style, The Howff, his singing style and how much he was influenced by the Charles Mingus album *Mingus Ah Um*. A little bizarrely, they were credited as 'Robin Williamson and Clive Palmer, Edinburgh flatmates 1962–63.'

By this time it had been agreed to reform the Incredible String Band. Mike: 'We decided it was quite a good idea to do gigs but we'd better do it properly, so we went to Wales. Clive came over and we settled in Cardiff where Robin lives and Lawson has a studio. We rehearsed for three weeks and worked up people's requests. Fitting Clive in was a bit different. It seemed really natural to have him sing [my song] Air, although he wasn't in the band at the time. So it became like a Best Of the String Band.'

Robin initially had his doubts, saying at the time: 'I don't think it's a good idea to revisit the past. If you go back to a place it can spoil the pleasant memories you had of it. If you had asked me a few years ago if I would ever consider reforming the String Band I would have said no. After all, I've done a lot more since I left. It was Archie Fisher who said to me that I couldn't just let the ISB ride into the sunset.'

The fans' reaction to the news of the reformation varied. Several thought that Clive should not be included as, though a founding member, he had had nothing to do with the ISB as most people knew it. Bina also attracted her share of flak, many feeling she was only in the band because she was married to Robin, and not on merit. Her situation was compared to that of Linda McCartney in Wings. Less fairly, she was criticised for not being Licorice, though at some gigs there were people who had obviously not kept up with things since the early 1970s who assumed she was Licorice! The short tour was scheduled for August 2000.

In the interim, there was another Williamson/Palmer release, *Just Like The Ivy & Other Favourite Songs*. Credited to Williamson, Palmer, Dando and Williamson, it was a recording of many of the songs they had performed on the October tour which had not originally appeared on *At The Pure Fountain*, recorded immediately after the tour had ended. Though not as polished as *Fountain*, *Ivy* was a lovely album, especially Robin's Planxty Irwin/Spanish Is The Loving Tongue, played solo on harp. The jug band songs were highly enjoyable with great interplay between the instruments. The new version of Downtown Dandies had acquired a third part that was not on the version Clive played on *Just Me* and was also taken at a slower pace, slightly to its detriment. At the end of the last track there was a

minute or so of silence followed by a hidden track, a very satisfying version of Paris with Lawson's piano to the fore.

Simon Jones was impressed, giving the collection an enthusiastic review in *fRoots*: 'A wonderfully loose collection of material, displaying a good time diversity capped by moments of pure String Band sound-alike yet touching on blues, trad. British, even vintage musicals and there's more if you dig deep enough. Just about every track is worthy of consideration, from the gloriously down at heel charm of Boston Burglar to the lullaby strain that's Bonny Doon, Williamson's vocal full of cracked, rough charm. Though credited to four, the album's carried by Williamson and Palmer, the former doing his Celtic bard turn and the latter displaying a wider skill than he's formerly been credited with, pipes alongside the more familiar banjo. While not as considered as last year's *At The Pure Fountain*, this offering is much more fun and somehow endearing.'

In July, Clive was also called on to rejoin The Famous Jug Band, which Henry Bartlett finally managed to get back together to record. The ex-members had taken very different paths in the interim. Jill had spent some time in Cornwall after leaving the band: 'Getting well – it took a while, Cornish physicians being just one step up from burning feathers and boiling toad livers in those days!' She started travelling, living in Canada for several years before heading for the sunnier climate of California. Here she got married, had a son, and divorced. By the time she decided to return to England for a year in 1994, she was teaching business computer applications in a college. She met up again with Henry towards the end of her intended stay. They played some music and started working out some songs together before Jill returned. Once she was back in America they communicated via e-mail with Jill singing new songs which they then developed. Pete Berryman had been a busy professional musician since the end of the FJB, undertaking solo tours as well as backing the likes of Julie Felix, (with whom he toured Australia, New Zealand and Fiji!) Bridget St. John and Brenda Wooton, and being a member of various groups including Mormos. Jill was also in the UK and they contacted Pierre Tubbs, their original producer, who offered them the use of his studio. Henry had also meanwhile been in touch with Clive when he stopped by on his way to and from Cardiff. Henry contacted Pete and they met up with him on a flying visit to Cornwall. Henry got them interested in getting together to record, but it was never easy to arrange a point in time where everyone was free to meet. When they finally identified a time they all could get together, Pierre told them there were major road works taking place outside his studio and they could not record there. Henry fortunately found an ex-BBC engineer with his own mobile studio living in the next village and the Ibberton

Village Hall became a recording studio for the two days it took to lay down the basic tracks. Considering the hall was made of corrugated iron, it was fortunate that it did not rain, though a few farm animal noises were accidentally picked up, and had to be removed by the patient Pierre. 'I haven't managed to get rid of the Ibberton dawn chorus (sparrows), but they add a certain authentic charm to what was an uplifting reunion.'

At the recording sessions Clive chatted to Pierre, who had numerous family links in France, about buying a house in Normandy, saying he had a budget of sixty thousand. Naturally assuming Clive meant pounds, Pierre had no trouble in finding several suitable properties. When he got back to Clive, he was confused. He had meant sixty thousand francs, this at a time (before the introduction of the Euro) when the exchange rate was around nine to ten francs to the pound. Suitably chastened, Pierre had another go, and actually managed to find somewhere in Clive's range, but the move to Normandy was never made.

Famous Jug Band outside the Ibberton Village Hall. Clive, Henry, Jill, Pete. Courtesy of Market Square Records.

The revived ISB made its eagerly anticipated debut on the 10th of August on the opening night of Fairport Convention's annual Cropredy Festival. The band enjoyed their set, though having to sleep in his car afterwards did Clive's back little good. A week later they were at The Bloomsbury Theatre in London for two nights; one night was filmed for potential DVD release by Peter Neal, who had made the 1969 ISB documentary, *Be Glad For The Song Has No Ending*.

They were well rehearsed and very much a band with each playing his part. There were plenty of old favourites and some new material from Robin, who was obviously in charge, Mike seemingly content to stay seated behind his keyboard and music stand. Lawson was kept busy and Clive fitted in very well, even on material he had not played on first time round. Bina seemed a lot more confident than she had been on the Robin and Clive tour too. A group version of Queen Of All The Gypsies was a pleasant surprise, and a new song by Clive, Big City Blues, even had Robin playing slide guitar. The faithful fans were delighted with the shows, and began to look forward to how the new ISB might develop.

Some other reviewers were more cautious in their praise, though *The Financial Times* reported: 'It was an endearing occasion, good natured... the signs are that a welcome revival and re-assessment of this seminal band is underway.' *The Times* admitted that some of the songs 'sounded as evocative as ever' but concluded: 'This was a creaky old show.' Adam Sweeting of *The Guardian* was not impressed in the slightest. 'A performance of shambling ineptitude. One thing they had forgotten about was rehearsing, since they made up chunks of the set as they went along, and none too successfully either. Bina, Williamson's wife, had to keep rummaging in her handbag for the band's set list.' Even the fans did not escape his ridicule: 'I wouldn't be surprised if the entire audience has now gone to live on a commune in Wales.'

In *beGLAD*, Raymond Greenoaken was hopeful for the band's future. 'If this were just a one-off series of concerts, there would be nothing much to fret about, but if the ISB are set to be a going concern again, even on a part-time basis, they'll have to make some concessions to contemporary taste. The paradox is that the ISB could so easily be hamstrung by the size and excellence of their own back catalogue. There's enough there to keep several careers afloat without even thinking about turning out any new stuff. But their instincts, I think, are towards a dynamic balance of the old and new, and the three principal songwriters are all well-equipped to take the band forward into the 21st century.'

On the 8th of October the ISB played at The Royal Festival Hall as part of an event called The John Peel Sessions Live and in support to The Delgados, a band from Glasgow who were reported to hold the ISB in high esteem. They played an 11-song set, all material that had been played at the Bloomsbury gigs.

In January 2001 the ISB played a short tour beginning in Cardiff, followed by Milton Keynes and ending at the Old Fruitmarket in Glasgow. The next day they played in Glasgow again, this time at the Royal Concert Hall as part of the Celtic Connections festival, standing in for the ailing Dubliners. In April they travelled to Bergen, where they shared a festival bill with Fairport Convention. A new song by Clive appeared in the band's repertoire: The Land Of No Return. The lyrics were based on Assyrian and Sumerian folklore, the 'land' being

Clive, Gina and Wizz Jones at the Fiction Wine Bar, Battersea,
London 30th October 2000. Photo by Dave Peabody.

The Incredible String Band late 2000. Robin, Bina, Mike, Lawson and Clive.
Pig's Whisker Music.

their underworld, from which there was no return, unless, for love, or by trickery, you could persuade someone else to take your place. Clive: 'Many of their gods were winged, and I've always wondered if that's where the idea of angels came from.'

A welcome 2001 re-release was COB's *Spirit Of Love*, issued on the Beat Goes On label. The original artwork was featured, including the lyrics, though reduced to CD size they were more or less unreadable without a magnifying glass. The Anne Briggs and Wizz Jones records in the series of Lustig-connected CBS albums had already been previously issued on CD by Sony.

In the August issue of FRoots, an advert appeared by a company called Good Ol' Boy Music Ltd, announcing a series of live albums recorded during the first eleven years of the Cambridge Folk Festival. The CDs were to be issued at regular monthly intervals and were to include albums by COB as well as many other artists. Unfortunately the advert never appeared again and no more was heard of the company or its plans.

On the 3rd and 4th of August the ISB played two gigs at The Bloomsbury Theatre before heading west for the Sidmouth Folk Festival on the 6th. The band's appearance at Sidmouth was to prove extremely controversial. Mel McLellan, a self confessed 'fan, old hippy, ISB lyrics imprinted on the psyche etc' thought she knew what to expect: 'I'd read the reviews and letters which spoke of occasional

Pig's Whisker Music Presents

the incredible string band

3rd/4th August 2001

Bloomsbury Theatre

15 Gordon Street, WC1 London

Nearest Tube: Euston / Euston Square
www.ucl.ac.uk/BloomsburyTheatre
Box Office: 020 7388 8822
The Bloomsbury Theatre is owned and founded by University College London

Tickets £16.50   On Sale Now

'Last years concert voted Top 5 London concert of the year'
Time Out Dec 2000

www.incrediblestringband.com

under-rehearsal, lapses of tunefulness and a certain shambolic stagecraft, but there were many speaking in glowing tones.' Mel missed the start of the set and arrived while they were playing Ducks On A Pond, which sounded fine. Then Mike sang Painting Box. 'Mike is off key and the whole thing lurches along rather uncomfortably. There's a palpable air of discomfort in the audience and a few people begin to leave. Robin announces a new song Doorways And Weather. It is obvious there is a problem. Bina is a foot out of tune, and misses cues by half a beat. The band play the Heron classic Air – a song of usually ethereal and delicate atmosphere. It's a caterwaul... Across the hillside of the arena, people are openly laughing and many more are voting with their feet. The applause is lukewarm and there's a steady stream for the exit. At this point I join them. Next day there were queues of people demanding refunds and I overheard snatches of bitter disappointment which lasted throughout the week. Dreams had been shattered and treasured memories thrashed to within an inch of their lives.'

Stephen Robbins, another longstanding ISB fan, did not agree: 'It was a good gig, there were lapses of memory and occasional forgetfulness, but on the whole it was good. It was excellent to hear Strings In The Earth And Air as well as solo Heron stuff like Singing The Dolphin and Don't Kill It Carol. Big City Blues was wonderful and harked back to their older stuff. Considering the audience were so hostile, the band still got an encore, and on the final number Bina took lead vocal as it was sung in Hindi and was from an old Bollywood film. If they had done their set in Hindi or any other language other than English it would have been a huge hit. The mistake was in not telling the soundman that Bina was not the lead vocalist and she was over-miked.' The soundman was unfamiliar with the music and the dynamics of the ISB. Finding her mike was too loud she backed off and the soundman turned it up to compensate. 100

people were supposed to have walked out of the concert, but it was pointed out that 1500 stayed to the end. No money was refunded.

The next day the band played to 650 people at the newly opened Eden Project near St Austell in Cornwall, the first concert to take place there. The Eden Project is in a huge disused quarry with enormous biodomes containing plants from all over the world. A stage had been set up in the arena, a natural amphitheatre with seats near the stage, and a grass slope beyond, with the walls of the quarry behind. *BeGLAD* contributor Jenny Bolders was a member of the Cornish band Carcana, who were booked to support the ISB: 'I really enjoyed the band's show. There was a nice atmosphere at Eden, and the audience seemed to be enjoying themselves. I spoke to Mike Heron after the show and commented on how much nicer the Eden audience had been than at Sidmouth, to which he smiled and replied, "Oh well, they were folkies!" Mark Anstey said that they had been expecting Sidmouth to be the difficult one, which was an interesting comment.' The band took the ferry to Ireland for a gig at the Olympia in Dublin on the 9th August.

The *Bloomsbury 2000* live album, recorded over the two nights at the Bloomsbury Theatre the previous year, was released on the 6th. It is a pleasing souvenir of the two evenings, showing how well the ISB played as a band, though Air is messier than I remember it being on the first night. The CD features Clive's banjo solo from the second night, Goodbye, dedicated to his late father. This had replaced a Clive instrumental called Waltz Gai played at the first show.

On the 13th of August Henry Bartlett died of a heart attack at the age of 58, at his home in Dorset. He was buried ten days later in a quiet woodland site close to the former line of the Somerset & Dorset Railway, which used to run from Bath to Bournemouth. This was a reflection of his interest in both ornithology and railway history. In the early Sixties he had briefly had a job cleaning railway carriages on the southern end of the Somerset & Dorset line at Bournemouth West station. He hated it. The humanist service was conducted by John The Fish and attended by his friends and many of the musicians he had played with over the years. Henry lived in a very rural area, and at the suggestion of one of Henry's and Jenny's two daughters, mourners were guided by posters advertising Henry's Last Gig.

Jenny: 'Henry played a great jug. Many people seemed to blow raspberries and make farty sounds but Henry always aimed to hit notes. The jug was difficult to record well and was often treated as a fun object; however his interest in blues, jug band music, and jazz gave feel for the music and helped him lift jug playing to another level. Being one of the few jug players on the Musician's Union books, he was occasionally called on to do session work for advertisements. An advert for Plumrose Pork Sausages was recorded with a 40-piece orchestra, whose members were fascinated by the jug and gave him a standing ovation after his piece. An advert for Woolworth's had him duetting with Paul Jones on kazoo. Before he died Pierre had sent him an idea for a jug fugue and he and Pete had been working on recording the jug. Henry was a large and generous person who enjoyed every aspect of his life.'

The ISB undertook another short tour in November, beginning on the 8th in Frome, then Manchester, Sheffield, Newcastle and Liverpool. After a short break they played Basingstoke on the 23rd and Bury St. Edmunds the following night.

Clive contributed banjo to two tracks on Wizz Jones' *Lucky The Man* album issued in 2001. The tracks were Roving Cowboy, where Clive added banjo counterpoint to Wizz's guitar and Simeon Jones' (Wizz's son) harmonica. The other track was Wizz's version of Paris, a fair choice given the part he played in the era it celebrated. *beGLAD* said: 'It follows a strikingly different groove to the earlier arrangements. Here it's a twin-banjo affair, with Clive playing ripply fingerstyle under Wizz's brusquer frailing. Much more of a high, lonesome mountain feel than the spiky jazz colouring we're familiar with.'

The ISB opened 2002 with three gigs in January, two at The Point, Cardiff on the 17th and 18th, followed by a gig in the Celtic Connections Festival in Glasgow two nights later.

The Famous Jug Band album *O For Summer* was issued on the 8th of March 2002. With Jill, Clive on banjo, Henry on jug, and Pete Berryman on guitar (plus dobro, bass, mandolin, harmonium and timples) and all four singing, one might reasonably have expected a sound somewhat akin to that of *Sunshine Possibilities*, but it actually leans much more towards the sound of their second album, *Chameleon*. The opening (and title) track is absolutely classic Clive, and indeed classic FJB, with Clive playing banjo as hauntingly as only he can, and Pete adding delicate lead lines on guitar. Henry's jug has never sounded better, and the group harmonies on the chorus are as impressive as ever. Pierre used an interesting piece of technology on Henry's jug, a device called an Antarez Auto Tune, which basically sampled the sound of Henry's jug and brought it exactly into pitch. Much of the material was written by Henry and Jill, separately and together, and is very much in the style of the later FJB material, with jazzy chords and time changes. On a few occasions when her vocals are double-tracked, Jill sounds amazingly like the McGarrigles.

Henry's Baby Please Come Home, sung by the man himself, is a fine piece of tongue-in-cheek Brit-folk-blues ('I'll do anything for you/I'll even sing a happy song!'). Pete's contributions range from a solo instrumental Davy's Signal (which sounds like a reference to Davy Graham, but was in fact inspired by a Cornish legend), through the reverb-soaked Winter Sunshine, which features wonderful harmonica from

Stu Porter, to the penultimate track, Shells, a lovely open-sounding song that perfectly updates the sound of their second album, adding meaty fretless bass and delicate banjo. Clive's song In The Night is in fact a re-titled Country Lanes from *House Of Images*. The last track put a smile on a lot of faces. Danse Des Matelots is a banjo solo which is a worthy successor to Niggertown and Banjoland in the Palmer canon. Though Clive brought his Breton biniou bagpipes to the sessions, and was photographed playing them, they were not used on any of the released tracks. The basic tracks were augmented later in Cornwall, London and California, though arguably a little too much instrumentation was added to a few of the tracks, losing the essence of the FJB sound.

Richard Condon reviewed the album at some length in *The Green Man Review*. 'The songs are not outstandingly strong, especially lyrically, but provide opportunities for the four musicians to display their vocal and instrumental talents.' Richard found Clive's style of writing and singing 'most distinctive,' but admitted he began to find, after repeated listenings, 'the monotonous clanking' of Clive's banjo 'rather irksome.'

'Surprisingly, for a man regarded in the 60s as a virtuoso banjoist, he does not display the musical variety and inventiveness that I mentally associate with his erstwhile companions in the ISB. I am reminded, unfairly perhaps, of the old adage that says a gentleman is someone who knows how to play the banjo, but doesn't.' On a less frivolous note Richard made the valid point that it might have been better for the band to 'revisit some songs from the old days, even to perform some stronger material by other composers, or possibly the odd traditional song in a fresh and distinctive way.'

Nick Beale's review of the album for *fRoots* was, perhaps predictably, lukewarm. 'Jillian Johnson-Sharp (Jill Johnson as was) sings very well throughout and Pete Berryman's guitar skills are undiminished, but the music is by and large soft rock/MOR, the most verve coming on the blues shuffle Baby Please Come Home, while the title track is an apathetic banjo plod from the pen of member Clive Palmer. There just isn't much here to get worked up about.'

Sadly, the album's sales reflected that. Market Square boss Peter Muir confirms that, up to March 2004, it had only sold about 800 copies. 'I found that it sold straight into the ISB fan base but didn't go much beyond it. Critics agreed it was a good record and it should have done better.' With Clive and Jill both being based abroad and Pete having a busy solo career, we can only speculate, had Henry lived, whether the FJB would have gone on to play gigs and enjoyed a renaissance.

On the 19th of July, Billy Connolly was invited to take part in an edition of *Desert Island Discs*, a long running show on BBC Radio 4 on which the guest is asked to nominate their eight favourite records to take with them during an exile to an imaginary desert island. The guest is also allowed to take one luxury item, which by the rules must be both inanimate and of no practical use. Billy chose his banjo as the luxury item, and his choice of records was no great surprise either, including Flatt & Scruggs' Foggy Mountain Breakdown as well as tracks by Hank Williams and Little Richard. What was a surprise though was his choice of the Palmer/Devereux song Morris Room, from *Suns & Moons*. Clive: 'Billy always did like the Bob and Clive stuff.'

In October the ISB began another British tour, starting off in Birmingham on the 18th and ending at the Jazz Cafe in London on the 3rd of November. A recording of their gig at the Newcastle Opera House on the 25th October shows a competent band playing a wide range of material, even reviving Black Jack David in jug band style with prominent kazoo. Big City Blues had been

dropped but they played an excellent version of The Land Of No Return, and the inevitable Empty Pocket Blues. Clive and Robin's smallpipes/fiddle duet was one of the highlights of the second half. Dates were pencilled in for a US tour in April 2003, possibly supported by Donovan, and a gig in Iceland was also planned for May.

In the spring of 2003, Mark Anstey made an announcement to the effect that the tours of 2002 had shown that there was a demand for the ISB to become a full-time touring outfit. Robin, however, was unwilling to commit himself, preferring to continue with his solo gigs and his various projects, and fitting the ISB around those. As this seriously restricted the potential earnings of the others, the bold decision was taken to tour without him. It was later admitted that Robin's insistence on Bina being in the band was a contributory factor too. The remaining line-up of Heron, Palmer and Dando was augmented by the singer and multi-instrumentalist Fluff. In a slightly uneasy compromise, and to acknowledge Williamson's absence, the band name was changed to 'incrediblestringband2003'.

Clive says now: 'My honest opinion of Robin is that he started as a soloist, and he's going to end that way. He's not able to work in a group context. He never wanted to do the [revived] String Band tours, didn't want to go down that road. He did it for various reasons. He did it to see what would happen. He put it down as an extra-mural activity on top of his main thing that he was doing. Mike and I come together on an equal basis, it doesn't affect our solo careers; we don't have solo careers! We have enough of a reputation that people will come and see us. We've done some good things, and it gets better.'

Fluff, who was born in Northampton in 1973 as Clare Smith, was the youngest member of a fairly musical family. 'I owe my musical education to Northamptonshire Music School which took me right through from eight to eighteen, and at the same time some of Northampton's finest folk musicians took me to festivals, asked me to play in ceilidh bands and generally ensured that my education and musical experience was extended well beyond classical.'

After a period at Keele University, where as president of the folk club she booked the likes of Martin Carthy, Dick Gaughan, Vin Garbutt, Gordon Giltrap and Les Barker, Fluff joined a band of roots rockers called Tower Struck Down and spent the next ten years playing with the band. They worked hard and played festivals in the UK (including Glastonbury and Cropredy) and in Europe. When that ended, 'I got a visit from Mark Anstey and [sound man] Tony Pugh to audition me. Tony knew me from Tower days and I think he always rated the band. I played them a couple of things I'd been listening to on the CDs they sent me and that was that. I have so far been given a free hand in arranging, which is great fun for me. I think Clive would prefer me not to play so many countermelodies when I'm working with him, but as that's what I'm about, I find it difficult and restricting to only play the melody. We always manage to find a happy medium though. I've never met Robin. I certainly respect his work but I don't and won't try to be or play like him. As far as I know, only four audience members have ever left a gig when they realised Robin wasn't in the line- up, and actually recently I've had more comments that I don't quite have a voice like Likky's rather than any comparisons with Robin's playing.'

The new line-up decided to play what they thought the audience really wanted to hear: the best songs from the early albums. Most of their material would be Mike Heron songs, with only Maker Of Islands (from 1974), having originally been recorded later than 1969. Apart from Ducks On A Pond, which Clive and Fluff now sang, and

Water Song, played as a duet between Fluff and Lawson, none of Robin's songs were to be featured. Mike was particularly pleased to be able to add his epic A Very Cellular Song to the set. In their prime the Incredibles had always been very prolific, often releasing two albums a year. On tour they tended to play their latest material (not all of which would always later be recorded) with a smattering of older favourites. Despite A Very Cellular Song being one of the original ISB's best-loved tracks, Mike reckoned that they had probably only ever played the complete song live five or six times.

The band debuted in May, with a gig in Chester on the 13th. *beGLAD* reader Alistair McCulloch was very impressed. 'The new line up is excellent, and what's more, it's a band, working together with good arrangements and obviously enjoying themselves much more than was the case during, say, the last tour. I must comment on the difference between the way this band approached the same songs which had also been played by the band on the last tour. This time there was enthusiasm, fun, bounce, oomph!' Chester was followed by another gig in Dublin on the 18th. At the end of the month the new ISB flew to Iceland to play the Islenska Opera, Reykjavik on the 30th.

Following a couple of late August festival gigs at Nantwich and

Canterbury (third on the bill to Robert Plant and Roy Harper), the band set out on a UK tour from 25th September, opening at The Brook Theatre, Chatham. Clive missed both of the festival gigs and the gig at Chatham because of domestic responsibilities.

It was announced that fans would have a chance to take part in the recording of a 'live in the studio' album, due to take place at Peter Gabriel's Real World Studios in Box, Wiltshire, near Bath on 18th of October. For £65 a ticket (including a cold buffet) fans had the opportunity to be part

189

of the sessions. 'This will not be a usual concert performance but will be your chance to see how the band record under studio conditions.' Everyone present was to receive a numbered, limited edition of the resulting CD, which would include their names in the sleevenotes, and possibly an additional track. The ISB had also expanded to include bass guitarist Gavin Dickie, who joined the band for the Glasgow gig on the 5th of October, and stayed for the next three dates, also taking part in the recording at Real World. Gavin was a member of the long-established Border Boogie Band, whose lead guitarist, Frank Usher, was a neighbour of Mike Heron's in Glen Row and had played live and in the studio with Mike on several of his musical projects in the 70s and 80s. In November Gavin was confirmed as a full member of the ISB. At the end of the year the '2003' suffix was quietly dropped.

On 22nd March 2004, the CD recorded at the Real World sessions was released as *Nebulous Nearnesses*. Those present at the recordings received a version with a blue sleeve as opposed to the standard purple one, and an extra track in Heron's Maker Of Islands. For the recording the band had been augmented by Icelandic percussionist Steini Gudmundsson, whom they had met when they played in Reykjavik.

The five-piece band undertook an 11-date tour in April opening at The Queen's Hall in Edinburgh on the 16th and ending in Swindon on the 30th. The repertoire was much as before, with Mike's Sleepers Awake making a welcome addition to the set.

A DVD of the band's performance at the Lowry in Salford on the September 2003 tour was released in May. It is a straight, no-frills film of the band's performance, and highly enjoyable, though the set list is very similar to that on

Nebulous Nearnesses. The DVD pre-dates Gavin joining the band, and Lawson is seen playing bass on a couple of numbers. Mike now stands stage centre, mainly just playing basic rhythm guitar and a bit of piano. It also includes a 25 minute interview with Mike and Clive, recorded before the gig, with the interviewer, Jet Martin, talking them through the origins of all the songs on the set list.

The 15th of September saw Clive, Mike and Mark Anstey in London to get their visas from the American Embassy for their American tour. All concerned were aware that the trip had to be done on a shoestring, and it was decided to tour as a trio of Mike, Lawson and Clive. While they were in London the opportunity was taken to book Clive into the 12-Bar Club in Denmark Street. The gig (shared with Matt Deighton) was intended to promote Clive's forthcoming album *All Roads Lead To Land*, but was something of a failure as a PR exercise. Nonetheless Clive played for nearly an hour and greatly impressed the audience, despite the fact that the majority of them seemed to have no idea who he was...

When the band landed in Newark, New Jersey, one of the first things they saw was a huge poster for the animated film *The Incredibles*. Lawson's physical resemblance to Mr Incredible was noted. Once through immigration they were met by a driver who very soon demonstrated that he had no idea where he was going. 'Good drivers are expensive, unfortunately.' They sacked him, but his replacement was no better. The tour was intense, opening at The Iron Horse, in Northampton, Massachusetts, on the 23rd, then down to Brooklyn and two shows in one night at Joe's Pub in New York, where they were very pleased to outsell Donovan's recent gig there. They headed south through Philadelphia, Virginia, North Carolina, Georgia, and three gigs in Texas. Clive: 'In Austin the lady told us she'd only sold one ticket! We weren't bothered, we just had an early night.'

The 5th of October saw them in Tucson, Arizona, then they travelled into California, including a gig at McCabe's Guitar Shop, Los Angeles, and then headed north into Oregon and Washington, before heading east to Salt Lake City, where the fact that the 'e' had fallen off 'Incredible' on the marquee outside the venue proved to be another bad omen. Once again, only one ticket sold, and another early night. The 16th found them in Denver, then on to Columbia, Montana and through Ohio to Chicago. The audiences were enthusiastic and willing to listen to the music, and Clive was pleasantly surprised to find that his work with COB was not unknown to American audiences either.

Jerry Decicca of The Black Swans (a folk band from Columbus, Ohio) saw the ISB at the Wexner Centre For The Arts, in his home town on the 21st. He had heard the first COB album at a friend's house. 'I walked home with a copy of *Spirit Of Love*, not thinking of Clive Palmer as a living man, but someone who must have already passed through, barely noticed, someone I came across too late to hear in the flesh. After finally picking up the first ISB record, it was Clive's Empty Pocket Blues I liked the most. The turns and humour reminded me of Dave Van Ronk. But it is the first COB album I still listen to over and over. It's chant-y and dreamy, funny and mysterious, emotionally sincere without sounding like some Sixties time capsule, more Appalachian than the American urban-folk stuff at the time. And all that means is that COB was musically rooted in the British Isles, not touching a city corner. They were their own thing. When I finally got to see Clive Palmer play with the ISB after living with just those two COB and that first String Band records for the last five years, I had no idea what to expect. Then he walks on stage, crooked and lean, carrying a banjo that he picks clear and sharp, cawing higher than a hungry hawk, a little like Roscoe Holcomb, rocking in his chair like a creaking splinter. It made me very happy.'

Clive was highly amused at that gig to find that the band had been allocated a personal security guard, a man who had been a military policeman in Vietnam. He attached himself to Clive and followed him everywhere, even when he went out for a cigarette. Gina had come on the tour with Clive and her mother came to see them at that gig. It turned out she had gone to school in Oberlin, Ohio, which was the security guard's home town. After the show Clive said he would go out to meet the audience in case any one wanted him to sign an album or anything. Once again the guard insisted on coming too 'in case you get mobbed!' The tour ended at Oberlin on the 26th of October.

Throughout the tour the ISB had been supported by various acts in the modern folk-based field including Espers, Joanna Newsome ('who sings like Shirley Temple with a harp') and Josephine Foster who was much more to Clive's taste, especially as she had recorded a version of Oh Bright Eyed One. 'Unfortunately she reminded me a bit of Barry Humphries as Dame Edna Everidge, an image I could never quite get out of my mind when I was talking to her!'

'America was amazing [Clive had never visited it before] and the audiences were great.' In real terms, though, the tour made no money and it seemed the band was playing the wrong circuit – pubs and clubs rather than theatres. The travelling was exhausting, 14-hour drives between gigs being not uncommon. The van ended the tour in an even worse state than the band, with various drivers knocking bits off it and bashing the roof in trying to park in a space that was not high enough. Early in the tour they drove into the back of a car which had braked too soon on a slip road and were delayed until Clive walked up to the highway patrol with the band's visas and explained they were a group who had been given permission by the American Embassy to tour here, and they really had to be on their way. The combination of British politeness and American deferral to authority worked and they were allowed to proceed.

On the 4th October Clive's solo album *All Roads Lead To Land* was released on Unique Gravity. The album was originally going to be entitled *Sands Of Time*; some early test copies were made under that title but were rejected, and the opportunity was taken to change the album's name, though Clive preferred the original one. The title is based on a quote from Hamlet: 'The far countries from which no traveller ever returns.' Clive changed it to 'All roads lead to (the) land, from which no traveller ever returns.'

Most of the tracks dated from Cardiff recording sessions in 1999, when Mark Anstey had suggested that Clive should record some solo material while he was in the studio with the idea of releasing a retrospective compilation of his own material. The album was put together by Steve Fellows, who was so impressed by the Cardiff tracks that he suggested putting them out, adding Paris from *Pure Fountain* and the title track of

The Famous Jug Band's *O For Summer*. You Were Meant For Me was a timeless pop song, only the use of the banjo giving it a 1920s feel. Clive: 'It's a pot-pourri from 1920s to 1960s, a feel rather

than a type of music.' There were some delightful tracks: Clive's arrangement of Vaughan Williams' Linden Lea and the Debussy-inspired Dans La Campagne, dedicated to the joys of aimlessly driving around the French countryside. Breizh, the Breton name for Brittany, overdubbed wordless vocals over a bagpipe drone. Big City Blues was familiar from ISB gigs and Gershwin's Embracable You had been learned by ear from an old 78 Clive's parents had.

The album attracted mixed reviews. *Blogcritic*'s Jon Sobel called it 'a creaky solo effort. The songs are mostly forgettable, and the singing is, well, not good. [His vocals] sound weary and emotionally flat. His banjo playing is often dull and non-evocative, unable to carry the weight it's asked to bear.' American reviewer Jennifer Kelly could not agree less; she loved Embracable You. On Paris she thought the banjo sounded 'sadder and wiser'. She concluded: 'It is a wonderful record, clear and direct and heartfelt. Like many older artists at the peak of their powers, Palmer makes complexity seem simple and beautiful.' David Kidman in *fRoots* agreed: 'The handful of instrumental tracks bring a sensitivity that's perhaps not automatically associated with banjo players. Generally what you hear is what you get; an admirably honest, no-frills testament to an ever intriguing musical mind whose undisputed charm draws you in at once and keeps you engaged throughout this CD's 51 minute span.'

Back in Britain the ISB, with Fluff now restored to the line-up (Gavin did not return), set out on a thirteen-date British tour commencing on the 3rd of November in Inverness. On the 6th of November the ISB played the Eastgate Theatre & Arts Centre in Peebles, a venue well known to me in my childhood as the church hall where I used to go every week to the Cub Scouts! The set list that night was almost entirely Heron songs from the ISB era: Everything's Fine Right Now, Ducks On A Pond, Cousin Caterpillar, Maker Of Islands, The Hedgehog Song, Sleepers Awake, Painting Box, Douglas Traherne Harding, You Know What You Could Be, A Very Cellular Song and How Happy I Am, plus Robin's Water Song and Job's Tears. Clive had two songs featured: a group version of Empty Pocket Blues in the first half and a solo Other Side Of Town in the second. Moving south, the tour ended in Wrexham on the 15th.

While the ISB were on tour in the USA, Devendra Banhart had asked Clive to act as support on a 30-date American tour he was due to undertake in November. The dates overlapped with the ISB's British tour, but it was announced that Clive would travel to the USA to support Banhart at two gigs in San Francisco and in Los Angeles on the 19th and 20th of November. Devendra Banhart's management also asked for all the lyrics to the recorded COB repertoire, as there were plans by various members of his musical circle to record an album of COB songs, with Joanna Newsome particularly keen to do a version of Eleven Willows. Ultimately it became obvious that it was not economically viable to fly to America just to do two gigs, and Clive cancelled. The String Band ended an eventful year with a short four-date tour of Spain in mid-December.

The early months of 2005 were awash with rumours. A CD reissue of *Moyshe McStiff* was almost certain. Stranger still, there was talk of an actual COB reunion and even of them touring the USA! In a 2003 interview, Clive had said: 'I'd gladly do a reunion if somebody made a financially feasible proposal. That's the problem with these things. You have to spend ages going through the material, working it all out and it takes time. But I'd be happy to play COB songs at a gig. The main thing is to play what people want to hear. Most of the COB songs are in my head, though, and I could quickly relearn the others.'

Moyshe appeared in April, on Radioactive Records. Radioactive was headed by Richard Morton Jack, a long-term fan of COB. He had interviewed Clive in Oxford while he was on tour with the ISB, and published the results in *The Ptolemaic Terrascope* magazine in 2003. Later he interviewed Ralph McTell, who told him Mick lived in Falmouth, and he tracked him down by ringing all the Bennetts in the local phone book. Richard had a brief article on *Moyshe* published in *Mojo*'s Buried Treasure feature, in which ignored classic albums of the past are re-appraised. Shortly afterwards he got in touch with John Bidwell, and this led to an expanded version of the *Mojo* article appearing in *Record Collector* in March. Richard, Ralph and Mick re-mastered the album in Abbey Road studios, and intended to release it both on CD and on 180g quality vinyl as a limited edition. The album had already been re-issued several times illegally, notably as a CD on the Elegy label in 1995. Most of the bootleg re-issues had also featured Blue Morning/Bones as bonus tracks. After discussion with the band and Ralph, Radioactive decided not to include the single sides on their version of the album. *Mojo* reviewed the re-issue and gave it three stars (Good), commenting that the band name, title and sleeve design were 'almost willing punters to stay away.' The reviewer thought the vocals were either 'sung with a cider-lifting burr (Mick) or a curious plainness, like a distracted geography teacher (Clive).'

The ISB played a short tour in May, Edinburgh, Newcastle, Glasgow and Aberdeen. At the end of the month they flew to Spain for gigs in Barcelona and Palma. At the time they had a Spanish agent who was a great fan and booked them into concerts organised by the Cultural Dept of the local Commune. Clive: 'You can't not go down well in Spain, the concerts are free and the people really enjoy a bit of entertainment.' They visited Spain for single gigs three more times in the next few months.

In August they played at The Green Man Festival in Hay-On-Wye, and two days later at a Music Festival in Innerleithen, in the Scottish Borders, just a couple of miles from where Mike lived in Glen Row. Following the American tour debacle and other financial problems, Mark Anstey had resigned as manager of the ISB, and Mike and Lawson were now running the band's affairs. The purse strings were definitely tighter and Clive was growing increasingly frustrated at Mike's unwillingness to consider new material. The ISB ended the year with a short four-date tour of the UK in November.

Also in November, Richard Morton Jack finally released *Banjoland* on a new label called Sunbeam, set up to re-issue worthy folk rarities. Wizz Jones's 1975 *Lazy Farmer* album was issued at the same time. Richard had got the *Banjoland* tapes from Peter Eden, who was genuinely pleased to have a proper release after so long and so many other attempts. The sleeve design featured some photos of Clive dating from the time he spent in Paris with Wizz Jones and thus approximately eight years out of date, but there were no contemporary shots of him available. The album included four bonus

tracks, taken from tapes belonging to Wizz. Two were from Wizz and Clive's session for the BBC *Country Meets Folk* radio show, and the others were Clive solos which had been informally recorded by Wizz at his house in 1967.

The *Lazy Farmer* album was generally reviewed as a lost classic of sorts while Clive's was seen as a being a little more limited in its appeal, one commentator stating that he wasn't even going to try to listen to an hour of solo banjo. Ken Hunt in *Record Collector* was more enlightened: 'Don't mind Clive Palmer's rough-hewn *Banjoland* grinning in the face of commerciality; it's deserving of the attention of anyone who ever thrilled to the oddnesses on the first Incredible String Band LP. It might be described as a submerged stepping stone linking the Incredibles, The Famous Jug Band and COB.'

CHAPTER 10

FIRE OUR ARROWS STRAIGHT, INTO THE SETTING SUN

10
Fire our arrows straight, into the setting sun

'I was glad to get the ISB reunion over with.'

live and Gina had been considering coming back from Brittany to the UK for some time. There was medical help to consider, Clive not always being able to get what he needed and Gina, being an American citizen, not qualifying for help in France at all. Gina had also just become a grandmother, and wanted to see more of her children. On the evening of the 7th of January 2006, Gina was just about to have a bath and Clive went out to get some wood for the stove. There was a man standing outside the house, obviously very drunk. Clive knew him; he was an Englishman who lived nearby who had worked with Clive on a couple of building projects in the past. Clive was wary of him, and they were not really friends. 'I told him we were just about to go to bed, and he pushed me over. I fell and my glasses came off, so I could just see him as a blur. He had heavy boots on and I thought he was going to kick me. I grabbed my electric chainsaw and switched it on. Unfortunately it cut him under the arm. The police were called and asked if I wanted to make a complaint about him. I didn't but later found out he had made a complaint about me.' The incident was the cause of Clive and Gina's premature return to the UK. They stayed in London with Gina's daughter for a short while, then moved down to Cornwall, initially moving in with Tim Wellard in St. Just.

In February BBC4 showed *Folk Britannia*, a series of programmes about British folk music, which featured contributions from Clive and Mike and Robin and Bina. Clive and Mike were interviewed at The Green Man Festival, Clive talking about how bad the Sixties television show *The White Heather Club* was (featuring an over-jolly Andy Stewart) and discussing drugs. Mike talked about the Incredible String Band playing 'the sort of music we wanted to hear ourselves.' Clive: 'The filming took about a hour, and they never even bought us a cup of coffee!' There was also a brief clip of Mike, Clive and Lawson playing You Get Brighter on stage at the festival (Fluff's recorder was heard, but she wasn't seen). One of the programmes featured archive clips of folk interest from the BBC, including a legendary *Tonight* piece from 1960 about the local authorities clamping down on the beatniks who were invading Newquay. Among the beats was a young Wizz Jones, who chatted about his life to Alan Whicker and played two songs: Hard Times In Newquay Town and an obviously-censored version of Babe It Ain't No Lie in which he pointedly sings about a 'councillor in this town, telling those stories about me.' The original song has the lyric 'telling those lies.'

The BBC4 programmes led to Mike coming down to London on play at the Barbican on the 4th February, on a bill that also included Bert Jansch, Vashti Bunyan and King Creosote. In April he undertook a short solo tour, playing four dates in Spain. The ISB finally came together on the 19th of June, playing at Telford's Warehouse, Chester, though Clive was absent as he was moving house that day, having finally found a place of his own in Cornwall. The following day they were due to play at The Sunrise Festival, an event to celebrate the Summer Solstice at a site in Somerset whose exact location was only to be revealed close to the date, though the organisers were prepared to say the nearest sizeable town was Yeovil. Thinking the whole festival was a little over-ambitious and fearing they would not be paid, Fluff took the decision to pull the band out of the gig. The four-piece eventually made its 2006 debut at a concert in the gardens of a monastery near Bergamo in Northern Italy on July the 10th.

In the summer Tim Wellard released a new album by Clive, *The Land Of No Return*, on his own Acoustic Shadow label. The album had been recorded over a period of a couple of years, both in Cornwall at Tim's home studio and on visits to Brittany. Acoustic Shadow's avowed intention was to promote 'Outlaw music from the Wild West of Cornwall.' As well as the Clive album, Tim had

released albums by his own band The Voices, which also featured John Bickersteth and Sally Mason, and two albums by 'country and eastern' trio The Planters. *The Land Of No Return* contains group versions of Big City Blues and The Land Of No Return and a new Paris, sung by Tim. Since You Went Away is actually You Were Meant For Me, sung by Sally Mason, her fragile vocal giving it a new interpretation. Tim plays dobro on many of the tracks, which is particularly effective on I Miss You, a new Clive song in his 'timeless pop song' style, given a late Forties feel by the accordion and Tim's Hawaiian-style playing. Café Au Lait is a banjo solo, not dissimilar to Banjoland, and underpinned by Uffi Horsley's double bass. Earl's Breakdown, a medium paced bluegrass instrumental with Tim on guitar and dobro, revisits Charlie Cool Goes West territory.

The Incredible String Band would only play one more gig: a folk festival at Moseley, Birmingham on the 2nd of September. There had been rumours of a tour of Japan in October but ultimately everyone involved decided that it was not worth continuing. It was not the emotional occasion it could have been. The band played a short six-song set, all of them Mike Heron songs, joined by Mike's daughter Georgia on Spirit Beautiful. Mike and Georgia also played a five-song set of their own. A Very Cellular Song was an appropriate ending. Clive said shortly afterwards: 'I was glad to get it over with. Mike wished me luck but I didn't see him again. Fluff came over to talk for a while. Lawson and I will be doing some things together in 2007.'

The Times of September the 15th published an interview with Elton John and Bernie Taupin which, perhaps surprisingly, revealed them as Palmer fans. Clive suspects Billy Connolly may have passed *All Roads Lead To Land* their way. Calling it 'one of the most underrated albums of recent years,' Elton and Bernie particularly singled out Baby Sings The Blues and You Were Meant For Me for praise. 'The record has a sonic resemblance to an old timer trapped in his own potting shed with nothing but a banjo and three sizeable tomato plants for sustenance – but this is precisely what lends this album its peculiar appeal... Palmer sounds like a man vainly attempting to prove Johnny Thunders wrong when he wrote, "You can't put your arms round a memory".'

The same month, Ralph McTell released *The Journey*, a box set containing a mixture of released and unissued material as well as some newly recorded songs, including his version of A Leaf Must Fall as a duet with John Renbourn.

In early 2007, Richard Morton Jack released another version of *Moyshe McStiff*, this time with some bonus tracks: *Moyshe McStiff...* expanded. The bonus tracks include the Blue Morning/Bones single along with five others, all of which predate the formation of COB. Falconer's Glove and Summer's Night feature just Clive and John and had been recorded in the caravan at Mitchell in 1969 before Clive went back to London after the Stockroom Five folded. The former is a fiddle/guitar instrumental and Summer's Night features Clive on banjo and vocal with John on open-tuned guitar. Solomon's Song is sung solo by Clive accompanying himself on guitar, and dates from the short-lived Burning Bush period. Child Of The Season was written and sung by John, and had been part of the Temple Creatures repertoire, as had the last of the five, Sweet Spring.

The album attracted much better reviews than the original Radioactive version, Danny Moore in *Rock'n'Reel* calling the album 'a fascinating and ultimately rewarding glimpse into earlier, less commercially fixated days,' amusingly describing Let It Be You as 'skewed acid-folk' and I Told Her as 'Arabic skiffle.'

And that brings the story more or less up-to-date. Clive has now comfortably settled back in Cornwall. He has a couple of album projects in the pipeline and Devendra Banhart is still working on a tribute album of Clive's songs and has been known to perform O Bright Eyed One in concert. Clive recently did a gig at the Tate Gallery in St Ives, which involved him singing unaccompanied Scottish songs alternating with poetry readings. He's been working on learning to play the Scottish Highland bagpipes (on a set bought for £90 on eBay) but hasn't aired them in public yet. As well as rehearsing for local gigs with Tim Wellard's band, he was due to undertake a short tour with Lawson Dando in May 2007 of theatres and arts centres in the South West, though these gigs were cancelled. He has played with Mick Bennett and John Bidwell again (though John now lives mainly in Thailand) and they have worked on some songs together. An album of new COB material is not out of the question, though no-one thinks they will play live again.

Clive recorded another album's worth of material with Tim Wellard in the summer of 2007. It features Clive, Tim, Sally and John

Bickersteth, along with Nick McLeod on drums and Neil McPhail on guitar and bass. The recordings revisit all the stages of Clive's career, with a wonderful piano/banjo romp through Niggertown, Mike Heron's Chinese White, and two COB songs, Evening Air and Spirit of Love, the former sung by Sally. Land Of No Return and Big City Blues are done in new band versions and there is a fine version of Ernest Tubb's country weepy Have You Ever Been Lonely which suits Clive a treat.

Ramon Jove of Quadrant Records is releasing another album shortly, also to be called *The Land Of No Return*. The CD will include tracks from both Tim's version of *Land Of No Return* and some of the newer recordings with Neil and Nick.

Sally, John, Clive, Tim, Neil and Nick. Photo courtesy of Tim Wellard

Clive: 'I've come to the conclusion that I'm just going to look forward to seeing what happens. I never envisaged being a "serious musician". I don't really like show-business, I just don't have the ambition to be successful. I've got bored with touring; I want to do little gigs I can drive to myself. I just want to play with friends and have a relaxed, easy time. See what comes along – like fishing, I suppose!'

Discography,
Sources & Acknowledgements
Bibliography

Discography

When Clive only plays on a few tracks of someone else's album, only the relevant tracks are listed. All entries are in LP form except where otherwise shown.

Various Artists: *Edinburgh Folk Festival Vol. 1* Decca 4546 (1963) Clive Palmer and Robin Williamson
  Jazz Bo's Holiday (trad. arr. Williamson/Palmer).

The Incredible String Band: *The Incredible String Band* Elektra EUK 254 (1966)
  Maybe Someday (Heron); October Song (Williamson); When The Music Starts To Play (Heron); Schaeffer's Jig (trad.); Womankind (Williamson); The Tree (Heron); Whistle Tune (trad. arr. Williamson); Dandelion Blues (Williamson); How Happy I Am (Heron); Empty Pocket Blues (Palmer); Smoke  Shovelling Song (Williamson); Can't Keep Me Here (Heron); Good As Gone (Williamson); Footsteps Of The Heron (Heron); Niggertown (trad. arr. Palmer); Everything's Fine Right Now (Heron).

Hamish Imlach: *The Two Sides Of Hamish Imlach* XTRA 1069 (1968)
  Jean Harlow; Clapped Out Motor; I Got Fooled; Bourgeois Blues; Horny Bull; Happiest Day; The McGregors; Anthony Riley; Deep Elum Blues; D-Day Dodgers; History Of Football; The Priest and the Minister.

The Famous Jug Band: *The Only Friend I Own/A Leaf Must Fall*
Liberty LBF 15224 (05/1969) (single)

(Berryman)/(Palmer)

The Famous Jug Band*: Sunshine Possibilities*
Liberty LBS 83263 (07/1969)

Can't Stop Thinking About It (Tunbridge);
Nickolson Sq. (Palmer); He Never Came
Back (trad. arr. FJB); A Leaf Must Fall
(Palmer); Shaky Train Blues (Berryman); The
Only Friend I Own (Berryman); Black Is The
Colour (trad. arr. FJB); Saro Jane (?); Train
On The Island (trad. arr. FJB); The Main
Thing (Berryman); Sunshine Possibilities (Berryman).

Ralph McTell: *My Side Of Your Window* Transatlantic TRA 209 (1969)
Blues In More Than 12 Bars (McTell).

C.O.B.: *Spirit of Love* CBS 69010 (11/1971)

Spirit of Love; Music Of The Ages; Soft
Touches Of Love; Banjo Land; Wade In The
Water; Scranky Black Farmer; Evening Air;
Serpent' Kiss; Sweet Slavery; When He
Came Home.

All credited Palmer/Bidwell/Bennett except
Banjo Land and Scranky Black Farmer (trad.
arr. Palmer/Bidwell/Bennett).

C.O.B.: *A Folk Sampler* CBS 3049 (1971)
(6-track 7" 33 1/3 maxi single-promo only)
Sweet Slavery; Music Of The Ages.

C.O.B.: *Blue Morning/Bones* Polydor 2058-
260 (14/07/72) (single)
(Palmer/Bidwell/Bennett)

C.O.B.: *Moyshe McStiff and the Tartan Lancers of the Sacred Heart* Polydor Folk Mill 2383 161 (10/1972)

Sheba's Return/The Lion Of Judah; Let It Be You; Solomon's Song; Eleven Willow; I Told Her; Oh Bright-Eyed One; Chain Of Love; Pretty Kerry; Martha And Mary; Heart Dancer.

All credited Palmer/Bidwell/Bennett.

All (Palmer/Bidwell/Bennett)

Bob Devereux & Clive Palmer: *Suns & Moons*
Rainyday (1978) (cassette)

Queen Of All The Gypsies; Blackbird (trad.); It Used To Be Different; Morris Room; Man Behind The Mask; Sacco's Last Letter (Seeger); Girl From The North Country (Dylan); Suns And Moons; D Tune (Palmer); Turkey; House Carpenter (trad.).

Music: Palmer/Lyrics: Devereux except as stated.

Pete Berryman: *And Guitar* Autogram FLLP 5909 (1978)
Dordogne Summer; Rose Cottage; So Long Ago.

(all Berryman)

Clive Palmer: *Just Me* Autogram ALLP 258 (1979)

East Virginia (trad.); Bamiyan (Palmer); The Blackbird (trad.); Girl From The North Country (Dylan); Cripple Creek (trad.); Gentle Maiden/Gunnerton Fellcuddy (trad.); State Of Arkansas (trad.); House Carpenter (trad.);

Downtown Dandies (Palmer); Summer's Night (Palmer); The Wandering Minstrel (trad.); Foggy Mountain Breakdown (Scruggs); Jack In The Box (trad.); Melody In D (Palmer).

Charlie Cool Quartet: *Charlie Cool Quartet* DDS011 (1987) (cassette)
2/3 Petite Fleur; Yiddish Tune; Autumn Leaves; Erev Shel Shasha Nim; Motl The Operator; Pennies From Heaven; Mame Is Geganen; Ne Me Quitte Pas; Summertime; Yiddish Tune II; Indian Summer.

(No credits given)

Bob Devereux & Clive Palmer: *The Archive Tapes* Rainyday (1989) (cassette)
Please Understand Me; Flowers; Changes; Yew & Beech; Taffy; Fairground; Bear's Paw; Higgledy Piggledy; Suns And Moons; The Queen Of All The Gypsies; Morris Room; Mr Origami; Seal Island.

All lyrics by Devereux. Music to Yew & Beech and Taffy are trad. Flowers and Mr Origami are set to Edwardian banjo tunes from Clive's collection, all other music by Clive.

Various Artists: *Woronzoid Woronzow* WOO10 (1989) (Double sampler LP)
Coventry Carol (trad. arr. Palmer).

Clive Palmer: *House Of Images* 1992 (cassette)
Pretty Boy Floyd (Guthrie); Fear A Bhata (trad.); Soft Dark Eyes (Palmer); Absent Friends (Palmer); Moving-on Song (MacColl); Swanee Echoes (Alfred Kirby); Buffalo Skinners Blues (trad.); Country Lanes (Palmer); Cold In China (Leo Kottke).

Charlie Cool: *Charlie Cool Goes West* 1993 (cassette)
Pike County (trad.); Roll On Buddy (trad.);
Sally Anne (trad.); Lily, Rosemary And The
Jack Of Hearts (Dylan); Lonesome Road
(trad.); Salty Dog (trad.); Cripple Creek
(trad.); All The Good Times (trad.); Foggy
Mountain Breakdown (Scruggs).

Robin Williamson & Clive Palmer: *At The
Pure Fountain* Pig's Whisker Music
PWMD5017 (21/06/99) (CD)
Come All Ye Tramps and Hawkers; Pretty
Fair Maid; Paris; (music based on a theme
by Errol Garner, arranged Palmer/
Williamson, lyrics Palmer); For Far Soldier;
(I Can't Help It If) I'm Still In Love With
You (Williams); Relax Your Mind; Cam Ye

O'er Frae France; Rise When The Rooster Crows; A La Belle Etoile;
Bless You (For Being An Angel) (Lane/Baker); Sally Ann; Green
Grow The Laurels; The Show Must Go On; Wae's Me For Prince
Charlie; Salty Dog; The Night Of The Ragman's Ball.

All trad. arr. Williamson/Palmer except as shown.

Clive Palmer & Bob Devereux: *Suns &
Moons* Pig's Whisker Music PWMD5020
(1999) (CD)
Re-issue of 1978 album, but with revised
order, starting with Girl From The North
Country (opening track on original B-side)
and ending with Sacco's Last Letter.

Williamson, Palmer, Dando, Williamson:
Just Like The Ivy & Other Favourite Songs
Pig's Whisker Music PWMD5021 (2000) (CD)
You've Been A Friend To Me (Carter); Going
Across The Sea; Planxty Irwin/Spanish Is
The Loving Tongue (O'Carolan/trad.);
Boston Burglar; Downtown Dandies; Blind
Fiddler; Just Like The Ivy (Casting/Mills);

Bonny Cragside/Neil Gow's Wife; The Storm Is On The Ocean;
Empty Pocket Blues (Palmer); Salty Dog; Bonny Doon (Burns);
Rambling Boy (trad./new words Williamson); Side By Side (Woods);
plus "hidden track": Paris (Garner/Palmer).

All trad. arr. Williamson/Palmer/Dando except where shown.

Incredible String Band: *Bloomsbury 2000*
Pig's Whisker Music PWMD5024 (06/08/01)
(CD)

Air (Heron); Ducks On A Pond
(Williamson); Maker Of Islands (Heron);
The Storm Is On The Ocean (trad.); Big
City Blues (Palmer); Waltz Of The New
Moon (Williamson); Goodbye (Palmer);
You Know What You Could Be (Heron);
October Song (Williamson).

The Famous Jug Band: *O For Summer* Market
Square MSMCD110 (08/03/2002) (CD)

O For Summer (Palmer); The Waiting Game
(Johnson-Sharp/ Bartlett); Hole In The
Ground (Berryman); Around Again (Save
Me) (Johnson-Sharp/Bartlett); Baby Please
Come Home (Bartlett); Time And
Momentum (Johnson-Sharp/Bartlett);
Winter Sunshine (Berryman); Where Have
You Been So Long (Berryman); In The Night (Palmer); Davy's Signal
(Berryman); Gone With The Light (Johnson-Sharp); Sitting Alone
(Bartlett); Heartstop (Johnson-Sharp/Bartlett); Out of The Blue
(Johnson-Sharp/Bartlett); Shells (Berryman); Danse Des Matelots
(trad. arr. Palmer).

Incredible String Band: *Nebulous Nearnesses*
Amoeba Recordings AR002 (22/03/04) (CD)

You Know What You Could Be; Cousin
Caterpillar; Everything's Fine Right Now;
Chinese White; Ducks On A Pond
(Williamson); How Happy I Am; The Water
Song (Williamson); Banjo Tune (Palmer);
Log Cabin Home In The Sky; Painting Box;
Empty Pocket Blues (Palmer); The

Hedgehog's Song; A Very Cellular Song,

All songs by Mike Heron except where shown.

Incredible String Band: *Live At The Lowry* Secret Films SECDVD123 (06/04) (DVD)

Everything's Fine Right Now; Ducks On A Pond (Williamson); Log Cabin Home In The Sky; Maker Of Islands; Banjo Tune (Palmer); Painting Box; Empty Pocket Blues (Palmer); You Know What You Could Be; Cousin Caterpillar; This Moment; How Happy I Am; The Hedgehog's Song; The Water Song (Williamson); Chinese White; Douglas Traherne Harding; Medley of Fiddle And Pipe Tunes: Cuckolds Awry/Because He Was A Bonny Lad; Worlds They Rise And Fall; A Very Cellular Song; Black Jack Davy.

All songs by Mike Heron except where shown.

Clive Palmer: *All Roads Lead To Land* Unique Gravity UGCD5413 (04/10/04) (CD)

O For Summer (Palmer); You Were Meant For Me (Palmer); Lament For Shelley (Palmer); Sands Of Time (Palmer); Breizh (trad. Breton arr. Palmer); Broken Dreams (Palmer); Paris (music based on a theme by Errol Garner/words Palmer); Linden Lea (words Barnes/ tune Vaughan Williams arr. Palmer); Dans La Campagne (Palmer); Big City Blues (Palmer); Baby Sings The Blues (Palmer); Embracable You (Gershwin arr. Palmer).

Clive Palmer: *Banjoland* Sunbeam SBRCD5004 (11/05) (CD)

Banjoland; Boy In The Gallery; Christmas Carol; Winter's Tale; Danse Arlequin; Ma-Koush-La; Irish Fantasy; Stories Of Jesus; Variations; Smiling Through; Sea Breeze; I hear You Calling Me; Coventry Carol; Swanoa Tunnel; Come All You Fair And Tender Ladies; Country Blues; Old Maid's Song.

All credited "traditional, arr. Palmer".

Clive Palmer: *The Land Of No Return*
Acoustic Shadow (2006) (CD)
  Eastern Lament (intro); Paris; Cafe Au Lait (trad. arr. Palmer); I Miss You; Earl's Breakdown (Scruggs); Big City Blues; Since You Went Away; Danville Girl (trad); The Land Of No Return; Side By Side (Flanagan & Allen); Eastern Lament (outro).

All Clive Palmer except where shown.

C.O.B.: *Moyshe McStiff... expanded* Sunbeam SBRCD5029 (2006) (CD)
  Sheba's Return/The Lion Of Judah; Let It Be You; Solomon's Song; Eleven Willow; I Told Her; Oh Bright-Eyed One; Chain Of Love; Pretty Kerry; Martha And Mary; Heart Dancer; Falconer's Glove; Summer's Night; Solomon's Song (version 2); Child Of The Season; Sweet Spring; Blue Morning; Bones.

All credited to Palmer/ Bidwell/Bennett.

Incredible String Band: *Everything's Fine*
Secret Records CRIDE 74 (05/07) (CD)
  Everything's Fine Right Now; Ducks On A Pond (Williamson); Log Cabin Home In The Sky; Maker Of Islands; Banjo Tune (Palmer); Painting Box; Empty Pocket Blues (Palmer); You Know What You Could Be; Cousin Caterpillar; This Moment; How Happy I Am; The Hedgehog's Song; The Water Song (Williamson); Chinese White; Douglas Traherne Harding; Medley of Fiddle And Pipe Tunes: Cuckolds Awry/Because He Was A Bonny Lad; Worlds They Rise And Fall; A Very Cellular Song; Black Jack Davy.

All songs by Mike Heron except where shown.
These are the same recordings as on *Live At The Lowry*

Clive Palmer *The Land of No Return* Quadrant Q00010CG
  For more information contact Quadrant Records: www.quadrantcorner.com

Sources & acknowledgements

I have often been asked what first got me interested in Clive's music and I can only think it must have been the review of *Just Me* by Ken Hunt in his magazine *Swing 51*, around early 1981. *Swing 51* carried long interviews with maverick roots musicians such as David Lindley, David Grisman and Peter Rowan, and introduced me to music I love to this day. I shall quote the first paragraph of Ken's review in full, as indicative of what was known of Clive at the time.

'Clive Palmer has earned the reputation of being something of an enigma. He was one of the founding fathers of the Incredible String Band but departed with their first LP barely in the can amidst a flurry of rumours; he was said to have gone to India, Afghanistan or to gaol according to hearsay. Then he popped up as a member of The Famous Jug Band in time for *Sunshine Possibilities* but had disappeared as soon as he had been "identified". Clive's Original Band (COB) had a spate of recordings in the early Seventies while on CBS or Polydor, but otherwise there were only fleeting glimpses of him as a member of the Stockroom Five/Barrelhouse Five, Temple Creatures or Rhombus – this aspect of his career remains unchronicled and remains shrouded by mystery for rarely did he go out of his way to play outside Cornwall.'

I was intrigued! At that time I collected and dealt in albums of the genre that is now called 'wyrd folk' or 'acid-folk', and was in touch with collectors in Germany and Italy. Then *Sunshine Possibilities* and *Spirit Of Love* could still be had for around £3 in second hand record shops, but I have never owned a vinyl copy of *Moyshe McStiff* and indeed have only ever seen about three copies. Many years earlier a friend in Edinburgh who had seen COB on the Pentangle tour and actually bought their album, offered to lend it to me thinking it was the sort of thing I would like. I took one look at the sleeve and passed! I soon collected most of the albums (or tapes of them) that Clive appeared on. I was also making my first steps into amateur music journalism. I think the first time I wrote about Clive was for a newsletter put out by a group of folk musicians in Kent. Somehow I had got in touch with Martin Val Baker (I don't remember how) who helped me a lot and sent me tapes of the Stockroom Five, The Temple Creatures, Rhombus and Clive's solo material.

In February 1988 an article I had written on Clive's career to date was published in *Folk Roots*. In 1992 I was contacted by Andy Roberts who was starting a fanzine devoted to the Incredible String Band, called *beGLAD*. I wrote an article about Clive's COB years for the first issue and went on to be a regular contributor up until the magazine's demise in 2002, after 20 issues. Andy Roberts later resigned as editor, and from Issue 8, *beGLAD* was edited alternately by Adrian Whittaker and Raymond Greenoaken. In 2003 Adrian put together a compendium of articles and writing from *beGLAD* in book form, published by Helter Skelter. At the launch party at the 12-Bar Club in London (attended by Malcolm Le Maistre and The Archbishop of Canterbury!) he suggested I should write a biography of Clive. Clive was approached and proved willing, provided everything in the book was true (no tittle-tattle!).

One of my first interviews was with Wizz and Sandy Jones. I shall always remember Wizz saying that if you interviewed enough people the book would write itself. It has not been that easy. Memories vary a lot. For example, all three members of COB, as well as Ralph McTell, who produced them, initially remembered the Blue Morning/Bones single as having been recorded and released after the *Moyshe McStiff* album, which was not the case. I proved this by digging out a photocopy of a promo copy of the single's label showing the release date, and a contemporary article in *Disc* magazine.

I originally considered calling the book *In The Deepness Of A Summer's Night*, after a song by Clive dating from the period between the Stockroom Five and the Temple Creatures. The lyrics summed up the whole Cornish period for me, a time when Clive, John and Mick were living in caravans and would practise all day and play all night and when Cornwall was the best place in Britain to spend your summer holidays and folk music was the hippest thing to listen to. I once mentioned to Henry Bartlett that an older brother of a friend of mine in Scotland had gone to Cornwall on holiday at this time and come back transformed. I told Henry he had made Cornwall sound like Paradise. 'It was!' he replied.

I can only end by hoping that I have done justice to the music, and the people who made it.

Grahame Hood, January 2008

Without whom etc...

Firstly, thanks to Adrian Whittaker, who gave me the encouragement to both start and finish the project, which would otherwise have been one of the many things I would later seriously regret never having done.

Special thanks also to Stephen Robbins, the sage of Carmarthen, my very long term pen pal and later e-mail buddy who has been incredibly generous with music and facts, and served as a sounding board for my often very strange ideas. Ian Ferguson also deserves more thanks than he probably realises; his accurate dates for the opening of Clive's Incredible Folk Club and the LSD trial helped me to finally make chronological sense of the events of the latter half of 1966. Thanks to Clive himself of course, especially for the many phone conversations we had in the last year or so, which were always interesting and often very amusing. Shirley Palmer was incredibly generous too, allowing me to make free with her scrapbooks and photographs, and giving valuable insight into some of the least documented periods of Clive's life. Richard Morton Jack was also very generous, selflessly sharing information with me and sending me any new artefacts he came across. Thanks very much also to Sean Body and Graeme Milton at Helter Skelter Publishing, to Caroline Walker for the layout and to Mychael Gerstenberger for the cover and all the graphics.

All of the following contributed something, a quote, a cutting, encouragement; in person, by phone, by letter or e-mail:

Mark Anstey; Dave Arthur; the late Henry Bartlett; Jenny Bartlett; Mick Bennett; Pete Berryman; John Bickersteth; John Bidwell; Steve Bonnett; Joe Boyd; Derek Brimstone; Gina Brown; Gavin and Ronnie Browne; Nick Burdett; Billy Connolly; Tony Corden; Lawson Dando; Jerry Decicca; Stephen Delft; Bob Devereux; Peter Eden; Martin Gillham; Raymond Greenoaken; the late Geoff Harden; Colin Harper; Mike Heron; Colin Hill; Jean Howe (née Palmer); Doug Hudson; Bert Jansch; Jill Johnson-Sharp; John The Fish; Sandy Jones; Wizz Jones; Dave Kenningham; Bruce May; Gillie McPherson; Peter Muir; Chris Newman; Sean O'Rourke; Chrissy Quayle; Doug Parry (John Alvey Turner); Dave Peabody; Andy Roberts; Nick Saloman; Andy Scappaticcio; Ronnie Simpson; Mike Swann; Pierre Tubbs; Demelza Val Baker; Genevieve Val Baker; Martin Val Baker; Jake Walton; Tim Wellard; Clive Whichelow; Robin Williamson; and the staff at Bromley library.

One night when I was sixteen I came home from school to find a copy of the Incredible String Band's *5,000 Spirits Or The Layers Of The Onion* on the kitchen table. A gentleman called Paul Bassett who lived a few doors away had given it to my mother saying, 'Grahame might like this.' How right he was. I hope it's not too late to thank him too. Lastly, thanks also to my dear wife Marion, and yes, I have finished it!

Bibliography

Joe Boyd: *White Bicycles – Making Music In The Sixties* – Serpent's Tail 2005

Norman Buchan & Peter Hall: *The Scottish Folksinger* – Collins 1973

Colin Harper: *Dazzling Stranger – Bert Jansch And The British Folk Blues Revival* – Bloomsbury 2000

Hamish Imlach & Ewan McVicar: *Cod Liver Oil and The Orange Juice* – Mainstream Publishing 1992

Incredible String Band Songbook – Music Sales Corporation 1969

Ralph McTell: *Summer Lightning* – Amber Waves 2002

Barry Miles: *In The Sixties* – Jonathan Cape 2002

Horst Pohl: *The Folk Record Source Book (Second Edition)* – Self-Published 1987

Sheila Rowbotham: *Promise Of A Dream – Remembering The Sixties* – Allen Lane/The Penguin Press 2000

Denys Val Baker: *Life Up The Creek* – John Baker 1971

Denys Val Baker: *A Long Way To Land's End* – Kimber 1977

Adrian Whittaker (Editor); *beGLAD – An Incredible String Band Compendium* – Helter Skelter 2003

Robin Williamson: *English, Welsh, Scottish & Irish Fiddle Tunes* – Oak 1976

Lewis Winstock: *Songs & Music Of The Redcoats 1642–1902* – Leo Cooper 1970

Magazines

Various issues of *beGLAD*; *Disc & Music Echo*; *Folk & Country/Folk Review*; *Folk Roots/fRoots*; *Melody Maker*; *Mojo*; *Rock'n'Reel*; *Sounds*.

Appendix
A note on pre-decimal currency in Britain

Britain adopted decimal currency on the 15th of November 1971; there were now one hundred new pence to the pound. Before that the pound had been split into twenty shillings, which in turn contained twelve pennies each, making a total of 240 pennies to the pound. There were originally coins for ¼ penny (a farthing), a ½ penny, one penny, threepence, sixpence (commonly known as a tanner), one shilling (known as a bob), two shillings (two bob, or a florin) and two and sixpence, known as a half crown. This was the largest coin in general use, though along with the farthing it had been phased out by 1971. Any larger denominations, ten shillings, one pound, five pounds and above, were in paper note form. Some professions still billed their customers using the archaic guineas, which were worth twenty-one shillings, and this pricing was sometimes still used in shops, often for luxury items.

Prices could be written as L.s.d (pounds shillings and pence, though inevitably there were some hippy jokes on the subject) e.g. £1 19 11 (One pound nineteen shillings and eleven pence) or as 39/11.

The British Retail Price Index compares the purchasing price of the pound from year to year. In 1953 the pound was worth 19.80 times what it was in 2006. Clive's half-crown banjo lesson would cost the equivalent of £2.48. In 1966 the figure was 13.24, making entrance to The Incredible Folk Club a very reasonable £3.31. However the first album at 35/6 would have cost the equivalent of £23.50! By 1971 the figure was 9.5, meaning that COB were paid an amount equivalent to £273 for their gig at Chatham, though a copy of *Spirit Of Love* at £2.30 would still be the equivalent of £21.85, showing how relatively expensive records were compared with today.

Recent Highlights and Bestsellers from Helter Skelter Publishing

Be Glad: An Incredible String Band Compendium
edited by Adrian Whittaker

Paperback ISBN 978-1-900924-64-1
448pp 234 x 156mm b/w illustrated throughout
~~£16.99~~ online price £10.99

Cited as 'an inspiration and a sign' by Led Zeppelin's Robert Plant, admired by artists as diverse as KLF, Billy Connolly, Paul McCartney, the Delgados and the Pet Shop Boys' Neil Tennant, the Incredible String Band have always exerted an influence that far outstripped their record sales. From their Edinburgh folk club beginnings to pioneering an eclectic, 'world music' approach on Sixties albums such as *5000 Spirits Or The Layers Of The Onion* and *The Hangman's Beautiful Daughter*, taking in enthusiastic experiments with theatre, film and lifestyles along the way, to a final incarnation as a six-piece folk-rock group, theirs has been a fascinating career. In the first major book about the Incredible String Band, writers from award-winning magazine *Be Glad* present the fruits of a decade of research. Featuring interviews with Mike Heron, Robin Williamson and all the ISB key players, as well as a wealth of background information, reminiscence, critical evaluations and arcane trivia, this is a book that will delight any reader with more than a passing interest in the ISB.

'Pick of 2003' – *Observer Music Magazine*

'Something of a luminous rabbit from the top hat of mystery…the book…fascinates and delights like a lingering glimpse through the keyhole of the door in October Song' – Colin Harper, *Mojo*

'Chock full of insider knowledge and liberally strewn with photographs and assorted ephemera…it's hard to put it down…File under Essential Reading' – *BBC Radio 2 Folk website*

'Full of insights that will cast light on [the ISB's] creative process' – *Record Collector*

'Delightfully illuminating' – *Classic Rock*

Let's Spend The Night Together
by Pamela Des Barres

Hardback ISBN 978-1-905139-17-0
256pp 234 x 156mm 16pp b/w photos
~~£17.99~~ online price £11.99

Legendary groupie author of *I'm With The Band*, tells the full history of the groupie – girls who take their love of rock stars to the ultimate level. Beginning with the contention that Marie Magdelene was the first groupie, she charts the growth of literary 'muses' on to the rise of early rock pioneers like Cynthia Plastercaster, on to the phenomenon of 'models' marrying rock royalty, and on to the young groupies of today. Des Barres documents what it has meant to be a groupie and interviews many modern practitioners about what they do and why they do it. The first in-depth study of rock 'n' roll's ultimate fans.

The Pink Floyd Odyssey: A Saucerful Of Secrets
(Post Live8 – Fully Updated)
by Nicholas Schaffner

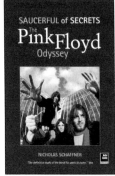

Paperback ISBN 978-1-905139-09-5
352pp 198 X 129mm 8pp b/w photos
UK £10.99 online price £6.99

From the psychedelic explorations of the Syd Barrett-era to 70s superstardom with *Dark Side Of The Moon*, and on to the triumph of *The Wall*, before internecine strife tore the group apart, Schaffner's definitive history also covers the improbable return of Pink Floyd without Roger Waters, and the hugely successful *Momentary Lapse Of Reason* album and tour. This revised edition contains a full update that covers in depth Pink Floyd's reunion performance at 2005's Live8 concert.

'Very nearly classic.' *Q******

'Pink Floyd rarely let fans get past its walls; Schaffner has come from behind those walls with a worthwhile study.' *Rolling Stone*

Here Come The Nice: A Small Faces Songbook
edited by Paul Weller and John Hellier

Paperback ISBN 978-1-905139-12-5
128pp 229 x 305mm b/w illustrated throughout
UK £17.99 US $24.95 online price £10.99

New collection of Small Faces songs selected and introduced by Paul Weller, with additional text by John Hellier and many rare photos. Features guitar-vocal arrangements of 'All or Nothing', 'Itchycoo Park', 'Here Come The Nice' and 12 other Small Faces classics.

'Weller and Hellier deliver something more than "just" a collection of sheet music and lyrics.' *Scootering Magazine*

'There's plenty on offer here, even for the non-musician.' *PlayMusic* magazine

'Makes for both an enjoyable read and a practical guide to performing the band's music.' *Rockpile* magazine

I'm With The Band: Confessions Of A Groupie
by Pamela Des Barres

Paperback ISBN 978-1-900924-61-0
320pp 198 X 129mm 16pp b/w photos
UK ~~£9.99~~ online price £6.99

Return to print for the ultimate story of sex, drugs and rock 'n' roll - the definitive groupie memoir from the ultimate groupie. From the day she peeked at Paul McCartney through the windows of a Bel Air mansion, Pamela was hooked. Graduating high school, she headed for the sunset strip and rock and roll. Over the next ten years, she dallied with Mick Jagger, turned down a date with Elvis Presley, had affairs with Keith Moon, Noel Redding and Jim Morrison, and travelled with Led Zeppelin as Jimmy Page's girlfriend – he had 'dark chilling powers' and kept whips in his suitcase. She hung out with Cynthia Plastercaster, formed the all-girl group the GTOs, and was best friends with Robert Plant, Gram Parsons, Ray Davies and Frank Zappa.

'Ah, those were the days, and this is still one of the most likeable and sparky first-hand accounts.' ****Q

'Pamela's mixture of hippy enlightenment and teenage lust is terrific.' *The Guardian*

'I couldn't have done it better myself. I will always love you and, again, a thousand apologies for the premature ejaculation.' *Robert Plant*

'A kiss-and-tell that doesn't make you want to go and wash your hands.' *Music Week*

Al Stewart: The True Life Adventures Of A Folk Rock Troubadour
by Neville Judd

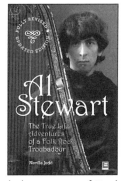

Paperback ISBN 978-1-900924-76-4
384pp 234 X 156mm b/w illustrated throughout
UK ~~£14.99~~ US $19.95 online price £9.99

Fully revised, expanded and updated paperback edition of the definitive biography of Al Stewart, the Scottish cult folk hero behind chart hit 'Year of The Cat' who enjoyed Top Ten success in the US. Leaning on extended interviews with Stewart – and many other 60s folk stars – this is a vivid insider's account of the pivotal coffee house scene which built the careers of Paul Simon – with whom Al shared a flat in 1965 – and many others, as well as a wry memoir of a 60s folk star's trials and tribulations through subsequent decades.

'The whole thing is a thoroughly absorbing read. Decidedly definitive.' *Record Collector*

www.helterskelterpublishing.com
Helter Skelter Publishing
18a Radbourne Rd, London SW12 0DZ
Tel: 020 8673 6320